Insiders' Guide® to the

NASCAR® Tracks

Help Us Keep This Guide Up to Date

Every effort has been made by the authors and editors to make this guide as accurate and useful as possible. However, many things can change after a guide is published—establishments close, phone numbers change, facilities come under new management, etc.

We would love to hear from you concerning your experiences with this guide and how you feel it could be improved and kept up to date. While we may not be able to respond to all comments and suggestions, we'll take them to heart and we'll also make certain to share them with the authors. Please send your comments and suggestions to the following address:

The Globe Pequot Press
Reader Response/Editorial Department
P.O. Box 480
Guilford, CT 06437

Or you may e-mail us at:

editorial@GlobePequot.com

Thanks for your input, and happy travels!

Insiders' Guide® to the
NASCAR® Tracks

The Unofficial, Opinionated, Fan's Guide to the Nextel Cup Circuit

Don Coble and Lee Buchanan

INSIDERS'GUIDE®

GUILFORD, CONNECTICUT
AN IMPRINT OF THE GLOBE PEQUOT PRESS

The prices and rates listed in this guidebook were confirmed at press time. We recommend, however, that you call establishments to obtain current information before traveling.

INSIDERS'GUIDE®

Photo credits: pp. 2, 21, 29, 38, 47, 57, 65, 79, 88, 98, 100, 111, 121, 122, 131, 139, 150, 161, 173, 183, 198, 211, 221, 232, 248, and 261 courtesy of Thomas Silva; pp. 15, 49, 60, 113, 152, and 162 courtesy of Dan Olver; pp. 17, 71, 75, and 143 courtesy of Kelly Howser; pp. 24, 32, and 39 courtesy of Russell Olver Jr.; p. 103 courtesy of Marilyn White; ticket stubs courtesy of Kelly Howser, Dan Olver, and Russell Olver Jr.; all other photos courtesy of Don Coble.

Maps by Stefanie Ward © The Globe Pequot Press

ISSN 1547–8769
ISBN 0–7627–2723–3

Manufactured in the United States of America
First Edition/First Printing

To Pam, who makes every day a wonderful adventure.

—D.C.

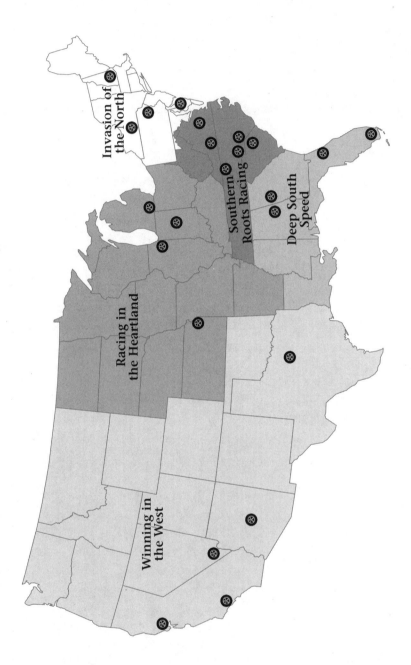

Invasion of
the North

Southern
Roots Racing

Deep South
Speed

Racing in
the Heartland

Winning in
the West

Contents

Acknowledgments

Much like the construction of a speeding stock car, it's too easy to over-look all the important people who make a project like this possible. There are countless mechanics back at the shop, far away from the public's eye, who take a pile of iron and cut and twist it into a 3,400-pound race car. There are engine builders and chassis specialists who then have the tedious responsibility of fine-tuning the car to make it even faster, often at one-hundredth of a second at a time. This book has its share of its own "mechanics back at the shop" who turned a pile of ideas into one constant theme for this book: What are the best things every racetrack on the circuit has to offer? It starts with my father who made me proud to be a racing reporter, even twenty-five years ago when it wasn't a popular assignment. Special thanks go to Pam, Tammy, Donald, and Courtney, for putting up with my demanding schedule and reading over my shoulder; Walter Jones and John Winters, who weren't afraid to keep pushing; and to the millions of racing fans who make it all worthwhile. Have fun!

—Don Coble

Introduction

My heroes drive race cars, but it wasn't always like that. I grew up less than an hour from the Daytona International Speedway, and I probably drove past it 300 times on the way to the beach without giving it a second thought. I was a stick-and-ball sports junkie, like everyone else I knew. The notion of grown men driving in circles all afternoon seemed to make as much sense as a Braille keyboard on a drive-up ATM machine. What was the point?

The point is this: Racing doesn't have to make sense. It is entertainment that slaps every one of your senses with excitement and awe. Why else would we do it? It's ear-shattering and eye-burning. It's the mordant smell of molten tires and searing brakes. It's a six-pack of beer, a bucket of day-old fried chicken, and stale popcorn. It's the intoxicating smell of burning octane. It's the worst traffic of the year, with tickets that cost one month's rent. It's a day in the sun that's like a road crew working off community service time.

And we love it.

Since the beginning of time, man has been mesmerized by racing. It probably started with cavemen on foot, the loser becoming dinner for a saber-toothed tiger. It evolved into the great chariot races, then to the horse-and-wagon races across the Plains. Modern-day racers, my heroes, use 3,400-pound cars with 800-horsepower engines, and they seem to do it with the same win-or-else attitude of their racing brethren before them. It's a dock fight with fire suits and crash helmets, 200 mph gridlock traffic, and three-alarm fender benders—all at the same time. And when it's over, there's only one winner. Everyone else loses.

My first race was somebody else's idea. An editor sent me to Daytona in 1978 to watch the Firecracker 400. It was the hottest, loudest, most uncomfortable day of my life—and when it was over, I couldn't wait to do it again. Back then, racing wasn't chic. It was somewhere between junior high football and local tennis on the ladder of social importance in most sports departments. Now it's a plum assignment, with many of the same people who cover pro football, basketball, and baseball asking for space to park their computers at the weekly 500-miler. The only sport hotter in television ratings is football, and, with an attendance of more than 115,000 a race, no other sport averages more fans. Not football. Not basketball. Not baseball. Not hockey. Racing is like a potato chip: You can't do just one.

With popularity, however, comes expense. Every racing weekend is like a Super Bowl or a Final Four. Hotels are packed, restaurants have long lines, and roads are clogged. It takes a lot of planning and a little know-how to make the most of your time. More than twenty-five years of traveling with these thrill-seeking vagabonds has taught me that the true measure of a racing weekend is the entire experience—both at and away from the racetrack. That's what this book is all about.

New tracks have sprouted in NASCAR like kudzu on a Georgia hillside; old tracks have gone through radical makeovers to keep up with a more modern, more demanding clientele. Rickety wooden bleachers have been replaced with shiny aluminum. Placards on telephone poles and barber-shop walls have been replaced by million-dollar radio ads. And billion-dollar network television contracts keep the entire sport under the white-hot spotlight and in your living room every day of the week. But the way you get ready for a racing weekend hasn't changed since the sport's first official lap in 1948. Knowing what to do, how to do it, and when to do it can mean the difference between a memorable experience and an exercise in futility.

There's an adage in racing: If you're caught up, you're already behind. The same goes for being a fan. You have to think ahead if you want to get everything out of your racing weekend. Race teams start booking their hotel rooms a year in advance, and you should do the same. Speedways traditionally put their tickets on sale eight or nine months in advance. If you need to buy tickets nine months in advance to get the best seats, it makes sense to make a hotel reservation that far in advance to get the best room. By the time you read this, all of my reservations for the entire season will have been made.

It took a lot of wrong turns and bad roast beef sandwiches to learn what not to do during a race weekend. At the same time, I occasionally stumbled across some real gems. Hidden amid the carnival-like atmosphere of racing's Big Show are some places that are every bit as interesting as a three-wide pass for the lead at Talladega. Take a ride down Las Vegas Boulevard at midnight and watch the water fountains at the Bellagio. Play a round of golf at Southern Pines. Absorb the beauty of a sunset in the misty hills of the Napa Valley. Bodysurf at Daytona Beach. Watch the leaves change color in New Hampshire. Eat a steak at the Fort Worth Stockyards. Join in the rattlesnake roundup in Arizona. And when you're done with that, there's always a race.

What prompted this book are the continual questions from friends and fans about the best races to attend, the best way to get there, the best places to stay, and the best places to eat. What those same friends and fans don't know is that my answer is never the same. One day I believe either one of the night races at Richmond is the highlight of the season. Then I remember the night race at Bristol—or Talladega and Atlanta and their wont for lead changes and dramatic finishes. Chicagoland and Kansas, the newest speedways on the circuit, are diamonds in the rough that will get better with time, and the fabled Darlington Speedway remains as cantankerous and unrelenting as it was on opening day in 1950.

One size does not fit all when it comes to rating the overall experience for each speedway. For this guide we rated each raceway in three categories: Racing, Amenities, and Area Appeal. **Racing,** as you might expect, looks at the quality of the competition. **Amenities** deals with the comforts each speedway has to offer. And **Area Appeal** covers what you can find in the local communities.

We used a five-star rating system for each category with five being the best, and one being the worst. A five-star rating means it's something that shouldn't be missed, like a photo finish at the Atlanta Motor Speedway, or the enormity of the Bristol Motor Speedway, or the bright lights of Las Vegas. A one-star rating is something that you might want to avoid.

You be the judge.

It's easier if you know what you like. Every racetrack has something special to offer. Find the amenities that interest you in the pages that follow, and then make a game plan. A few telephone calls to a few of the major hotel chains around each speedway will help you find the magical boundary between the area of high prices and the rest of the world. You'll find that's generally an hour away. A little drive isn't a bad sacrifice for the opportunity to save more than $200 a night for a hotel room. For example, three nights at hotels close to Bristol, Daytona, Michigan, Talladega, and Sonoma can cost as much as $1,000 for the weekend— but a few minutes farther down the road can bring the bill down to $300. To put that in perspective, one night's savings is enough to buy two seats at the finish line at Martinsville, with enough left over for a sack full of their famous chili dogs or a nice down payment for a single tower seat at the Daytona 500.

I also know this: The best way to enjoy a day at the races is to share it with friends and family. Plan to get there in the morning, before traffic gets heavy. Circle the cars, break out the portable tables and lawn chairs, turn up the radio, and make it a day. No hamburger or hot dog you'll ever eat in your life will taste as good.

I've learned a lot of lessons in more than twenty-five years of watching grown men driving in circles all afternoon. Different venues and the element of a thousand moving automobile parts keep the sport from ever getting too predictable. Every lap brings our favorite driver a little closer to, or a little farther away from, a victory. And if he doesn't win, he's got as good a chance as anyone else at the next race. One week it's a flat short track; the next, a twisting road course; and the next, a high-banked superspeedway. It's like finding things to do at and away from the track during a racing weekend getaway: There's a little something for everyone.

And if you're lucky like I am, you get to spend more than a quarter of a century sorting the good from the bad. Not a bad gig for a stick-and-ball sports junkie. Not a bad gig at all.

—Don Coble

Life in the Fast Lane:

a NASCAR

Primer

From moonshine runners tearing down Appalachian back roads to high-tech, high-dollar teams racing for millions at gleaming new motorsports palaces in places like Dallas, Southern California, Kansas City, and Chicago, the National Association for Stock Car Racing (NASCAR) is a uniquely American rags-to-riches success story. While other big-league motorsports series have seen declining attendance and television ratings, NASCAR continues to soar, packing grandstands at tracks every weekend and pulling in millions more on television.

There's good reason for that phenomenal growth, and it's not just the high-speed thrills and spills. These drivers are like folks you know, driving cars that look like the ones you see every day. It's really the personalities that make the sport so compelling, providing drama on and off the track. NASCAR is like a huge dysfunctional family, with all the feuds and alliances you'd expect.

Each weekend, hundreds of thousands of fans pack up their coolers and cameras, their sunscreen and scanner radios, and head for the high-banked tracks that stretch from California to Delaware. Sure, they can watch the races in the comfort of their living rooms, but hard-core race fans know there's nothing like the visceral thrill of live thunder.

The roots of NASCAR racing run deepest in the South, where for decades the sport was associated with the working class, and correctly so. If you frequented the local short track, you'd find that fistfights were as common as corn dogs. You can still get corn dogs at Hickory (North Carolina) Speedway, but you're not as likely to see one driver chasing another with a tire iron.

NASCAR's rough and rowdy days are long gone. And while purists might miss grassroots racing, today's typical race fan has it made. The racing complexes, particularly the newer ones, are first rate. At Dover you can watch the action from your sumptuous suite in a first-class hotel towering over the track. At Atlanta, Texas, or Charlotte, you can sip champagne in a members-only suite dinner club and watch everyone on the other side of the tinted glass brave the noise and elements.

NASCAR racing has come of age in recent years, and the change is obvious to long-term observers. Professional types have discovered the rush of racing, and you'll find them sitting down next to Bubba for a day at the races. There are about as many BMWs and Mercedes Benzes in the racetrack parking lots as there are Ford and Chevy pickups. You find as many doctors, lawyers, and accountants wearing Dale Earnhardt T-shirts as there are bricklayers, mechanics, and refrigerator repairmen.

Yes, the bare-knuckle brawls of the 1950s may be gone—except for an occasional outburst by Jimmy Spencer—but there's still plenty of color left. And you can find it most every weekend at some twenty-three tracks across the country. So let's go racing!

The Tracks: NASCAR Nation

At the heart of NASCAR racing are the personalities that make up the sport—the forty-plus unique combinations of talent, brains, and guts that make race teams. Just as central to the sport, though, are the twenty-three racetracks that are the playing fields for these compelling characters.

These places have distinct personalities, too. No two are alike, despite the recent popularity of 1.5-mile quad-ovals patterned after Charlotte and Atlanta and the recent creation of Chicagoland and Kansas. In no other sport does the venue play such a vital role in an event.

The diversity of the tracks on the NASCAR schedule gives the sport much of its appeal. In the span of a single week, the race teams might go from the 80 mph "beatin' and bangin'" at Martinsville to the white-knuckle 200 mph three-wide, ten-deep packs of traffic at Talladega, Alabama.

The track diversity also contributes mightily to the challenge of winning the series points championship, which demands consistent performances at a dizzying mix of racetracks.

One driver's favorite track is another's nightmare. Then it all changes a week later.

Take forty-three race teams, put forty-three unique lead-footed drivers behind the wheel, then turn them loose for thirty-six weekends at twenty-three different speedways—that thrilling blend has made NASCAR the country's hottest sport.

A Little Track History

The first NASCAR race—the series was originally called Grand National, then the Winston Cup, and now the Nextel Cup—rolled off in 1948 on the beach course at Daytona Beach, Florida. For years the series stuck to its Southern roots, thrilling crowds at new tracks in North Carolina, South Carolina, Virginia, Tennessee, Alabama, and Florida. Then as other parts of the country began developing a taste for Southern stock car racing, tracks began to spring up across the nation—from New York to Phoenix, from Chicago to California, from New Hampshire to San Francisco. There are now twenty-three racetracks that play host to

NASCAR Nextel Cup events, and each offers a distinct take on America's fastest-growing sport.

The twenty-three tracks that currently make up the Cup tour fall loosely into four categories: superspeedways, intermediate tracks, short tracks, and road courses. Each type of track serves up its own brand of racing. Want the thrill of sheer speed and inherent danger found at the 200 mph superspeedways? Pack the sunscreen and head south for a long Fourth of July weekend at Daytona Beach. Want to vacation in the mountains and watch the sparks fly at a Saturday night short-track slugfest? Bring a sweater and head for the hills around Bristol, Tennessee. You prefer wine and cheese in a picnic basket? Get ready to spread a blanket outside Turn 7 at Infineon Raceway in Sonoma, California.

The Short Tracks

The so-called short tracks—raceways of less than a mile—are the smallest on the circuit, but there's no shortage of excitement at Richmond, Martinsville, and Bristol. Martinsville and Bristol are the two surviving half-mile tracks that still host big-league stock car racing. These tracks represent NASCAR's roots, and for many hard-core fans the shows they put on are still racing at its best.

Intermediate Tracks

Most of the NASCAR tracks fall into this loose classification, ranging from the 1.0-mile ovals at Dover, Rockingham, Phoenix, and New Hampshire to the 2.5-mile speedways at Indianapolis and Pocono. These are fast racetracks, where the only limitation for an 800-horsepower vehicle is a driver's nerve.

Superspeedways

The only two superspeedways on the circuit—Daytona (2.5 miles) and Talladega (2.66 miles)—are known as the "plate tracks" in NASCAR parlance, named for the carburetor restrictor plates used here to cut horsepower by reducing the flow of air into the engine. After speeds passed the 210 mph barrier in 1987 and Bobby Allison's car became airborne at Talladega and nearly cartwheeled into the grandstands, NASCAR decided to slow things down. The result: underpowered cars running in huge packs at a mere 190 mph, just inches apart. Drivers hate it; most fans find it thrilling.

Road Courses

The circuit's two road courses, Watkins Glen in Upstate New York and Infineon Raceway in California, are something of an oddity in NASCAR. The vast major-

The

Points Race

Every driver approaches each race with a single-minded determination to win. But in the back of their mind, the big prize waits at the end of the season: the NASCAR Nextel Cup championship.

Cup champions have to be fast, consistent, and versatile enough to run strong at intermediate tracks, superspeedways, and short tracks and at least hold their own at the road courses.

NASCAR's point system rewards consistency above all else. That's why you'll see crews working feverishly to patch up wrecked cars and get them back on the track to complete as many laps as possible. NASCAR rules allow teams to replace and repair pretty much anything on a car during a race, short of a complete engine change.

Aside from the fame that comes with being Cup champ, there's big money involved. For 2003 the payout among the top twenty drivers in the standings was $17 million, with at least $4.25 million going to the champ.

ity of Cup drivers, especially the veterans, grew up racing on short ovals, where turning left is all that matters. Racing at these places is a different game, requiring drivers to shift gears and negotiate right-hand turns. Some drivers and fans may not like them, but the road courses provide a unique test of driving ability. Only the most talented drivers run up front on these courses.

Too Many Tracks, Too Little Time

As NASCAR has broadened its appeal and extended its reach beyond its Southern roots, the sport's organizers have had to make some tough choices. The thirty-six-race schedule has to be one of the most demanding in all of sports. Except for a three-month break from the season-ending race in November through SpeedWeeks at Daytona in February, the teams are on the road almost nonstop.

As new tracks join the schedule in major markets such as Chicago, Kansas City, and Las Vegas, some of the older, small-market Southern tracks are in jeopardy of losing out. One victim was North Wilkesboro, North Carolina, home of stock car legend Junior Johnson. That storied half-mile track was dropped from the NASCAR Nextel Cup schedule in 1997 to make room for a second race at New Hampshire and a single race at the new Texas Motor Speedway.

The North Carolina Speedway lost its fall race in 2004 to make room for some shuffling that included the Darlington Raceway and California Speedway. Darlington sent its Labor Day weekend Southern 500 date to California, then it got North Carolina's mid-November slot.

Traditionalists know more changes are inevitable, especially as the sport tries to keep pace with the ever-increasing demands of television.

Such tough choices are a price of growth, but purists will lament the loss of racing tradition at these legendary tracks. A word of advice to new NASCAR fans: See a race at these endangered tracks before it's too late. Who knows, your support may help keep them on the schedule.

Not Just the NASCAR Nextel Cup

This book focuses on the tracks that host Nextel Cup races, but there's far more to stock car racing. Some of the best racing in the country happens in other NASCAR divisions or in other leagues. For example, the best race at Daytona in 2003 didn't even involve cars. It was the Craftsman Truck series that produced one of the most exciting finishes anywhere during Daytona's SpeedWeeks with Rick Crawford winning a daring three-wide pass in the final 100 yards.

The NASCAR Busch Series is considered a sort of minor league for the Nextel Cup—a proving ground for young talent and a circuit for teams without the financial backing to move up to the major league. The Busch Series also is one of the most competitive racing series anywhere, with drivers often putting on a better show than their Nextel Cup counterparts.

When you're planning a trip to attend a NASCAR Nextel Cup event, be sure to check the other races running at the track that weekend. These "companion" events, most often Busch Series races, are usually run the day before the Nextel Cup race.

In addition to the Busch and Craftsman Truck races, the ARCA, Hooters Pro Cup, and ASA Series also serve up first-rate stock car racing thrills at tracks across the country.

It's a Team Sport

In the old days of NASCAR, many race "teams" were one-man operations, with pioneers like Junior Johnson building the car, hauling it to the track, changing into a driver's suit that consisted of a T-shirt and comfortable shoes, and then hitting the track. The sport's come a long way, and today owner-drivers and single-car teams are a rare breed.

Multicar teams, such as Hendrick Motorsports, Roush Racing, Richard Childress Racing, Chip Ganassi Racing, and Dale Earnhardt Inc., now dominate NASCAR. As you watch a race, it's helpful to know who's who as far as teams go. For example, Dale Earnhardt Jr. and Michael Waltrip, who both drive for DEI, are known for working together on the track to help each other get to the front of the pack at the superspeedways—and to keep rivals behind them.

The Pits

The drivers may get all the glory out on the track, but races are often won in the pits. Most tracks sell separate tickets to the pits so that fans can check out the action on the other side of the track. A pit pass will let you roam pit lane before the race begins. Outside of a staged event, this is your best opportunity to get autographs and meet drivers in their workplace.

Support Your Local Track

Think you need a primer on racing before spending a week at Daytona? Check out the local racing action. No matter where you are in the country, chances are there's a short track putting on a show every week.

From the NASCAR-sanctioned tracks in the South to the dirt-slinging sprint cars in the Midwest, weekly racing series are alive and well. They're a great way to get your racing feet wet before you move up to the big time—and they provide terrific racing action in their own right.

While NASCAR Nextel Cup has moved away from the short tracks that started it all decades ago, local heroes are still doing battle every Friday and Saturday night at a "bull ring" near you.

You'll usually have to sign an insurance waiver to get a pit pass, and most tracks don't allow children in the pits—and for good reason: The garage area is a work zone, with race teams hustling around with all sorts of equipment. You need to pay attention here, for your own safety, and be respectful of the people working around you.

Being There

For longtime NASCAR fans, today's exhaustive live television coverage is a dream come true. But television only tickles the imagination. Seeing a race in person spawns the true passion. It's true in most sports: Attending an event provides a more immediate and visceral satisfaction, even if you can't see the replays and close-ups. In racing, though, the difference between being in the Turn 4 grandstands and sitting on your sofa is about the same as reading about a concert and *being* there.

First, there's the sound. During a four-hour event you may want to use earplugs—or, better yet, radio headphones tuned into the race—but you should let yourself experience the full thunder of forty-three stock cars in all their glory. There's just nothing else like it.

After two or three "quiet" hours in the grandstands, watching whatever gala events the track puts on, drivers finally fire up their cars after the call: "Gentlemen, start your engines." The crowd, too, begins to get fired up in anticipation, as the throaty rumble of forty-three cars destroys the silence. When the full field rumbles by in front of your seat during the first pace lap, the electricity coursing through the grandstands is palpable. And when the flagman turns the drivers loose with a wave of the green flag, the bone-thudding roar is unforgettable. You'll never watch a race on TV the same way again.

Television also robs racing of its speed. You just don't get the sense of speed, no matter how wide the television screen or how loud the home theater sound system. On TV a three-wide, ten-row pack of cars screaming around Talladega at 190 mph can look a lot like rush hour on the interstate at 65 mph. But when you experience it for yourself, a few yards from the track, it becomes a heart-pounding mix of speed, power, and fury. You'll never forget it.

There's also the sense of community and color you can get only by being there in person. Race fans are a friendly lot. While the guy wearing the Rusty Wallace colors may profess to hate Jeff Gordon and all his fans, he's probably not dangerous. The stands are full of such characters—yet another reason to see it for yourself.

Race Week

For the teams and racing families that devote their lives to this circuit, an event is made up of far more than three hours of intense action on Sunday. Teams typically arrive at the track on Thursday for practice, followed by qualifying on Friday and final practice on Saturday. Usually there's at least one companion event, often a highly competitive race from either the Busch or ARCA Series. If you can spend the weekend, go for it. You'll be able to monitor the progress of teams as they aim to fine-tune their cars for the big show on Sunday.

Also, nonrace days are often the best times to meet your favorite drivers. Many of the top stars spend Saturday afternoon signing autographs at their souvenir trailers. NASCAR deserves a lot of credit for making its stars accessible to the fans, and that's clearly one of the reasons the sport is so popular. Many tracks stage events in the days leading up to a race that also give fans a chance to meet drivers.

Allow yourself plenty of time to get to the track. You'll be joined by more than 120,000 other fans, all using the same roads. Even if you're staying in a nearby hotel, you should probably plan to leave by 8:00 or 9:00 in the morning to make a 1:00 P.M. race.

Make It a Vacation

Just as the NASCAR Nextel Cup tracks reflect a dizzying diversity of styles—from the mammoth superspeedway at Talladega to the friendly confines of little Martinsville—the areas that host these events also offer wildly different experiences.

Sure, a quick-hit race weekend can be a blast. Drive or fly in on Saturday, watch a Busch race as a prelude to the Nextel Cup show on Sunday, then head for home after the checkered flag falls. You'll have a great time, but that weekend schedule can be a grind, especially with a long drive home facing you at the end.

Our solution: Make it a vacation. Every one of these tracks has terrific tourist or recreational destinations within striking distance, and we're not just talking about Las Vegas here. Tiny Darlington, South Carolina, may not be a garden spot, but Myrtle Beach is only 80 miles away. A Civil War buff? A week in Richmond, Virginia, is a treasure.

The racing vacation is also a sure-fire way to make your race experience a family affair. Can't get the wife interested in the race? (Don't worry, she'll come around. Women make up half of NASCAR's fan base.) Maybe a Fourth of July weekend at Daytona Beach will change her mind. Even if it doesn't, she and the kids can lounge by the pool while you hoot for your favorite driver.

Today there's one really great reason to turn a race trip into a full-blown vacation: your pocketbook. Ticket prices and the costs for the attendant necessities—hotels, restaurants, and gas—have all risen dramatically in recent years. If you want tickets to some of NASCAR's hottest tracks, be prepared to pay far more than face value—$200 and up—unless you're willing to buy season tickets and get on a waiting list. But don't worry: Most tracks don't push the all-or-nothing ticket package. We'll give you plenty of alternative choices.

And then there's the weather. There are few things as disappointing as planning a race weekend for a year and then having rain wash it all away. These cars don't run on wet tracks, so weather can play havoc with scheduling. Sunday races that are rained out are usually run on Monday, weather permitting.

If you have the luxury of turning a race into a weeklong vacation, consider stretching your stay through that Monday. It sure beats having to sell those tickets for a fraction of what you paid just because you have to be back at work on Monday morning.

Around and Around: The Art of Race Watching

It's easy for race rookies to get lost in everything that happens after the adrenaline rush wears off from the first couple laps. A common complaint is that they can't figure out who's running where.

At many tracks the lead cars will begin overtaking the slowest cars pretty quickly, maybe 50 laps into a 400-lap event. This can cause confusion for new fans, because the leader of the race may have a pack of cars in front of him, and the car behind him may not be the second-place runner. Check the scoring pylon, usually located in the infield. It will list the running order for at least the top five cars, by car number. Those are the cars you should keep track of most of the time. Find each one on the track, then continually cycle through them to see how they're running in relation to one another—and who's gaining on whom.

Listen Up

If you really want to know what's going on, buy a radio headset and tune into the broadcast from the Motor Racing Network (MRN), the Performance Racing Network (PRN), or Indianapolis Racing Network. The headsets are inexpensive—about $20 at most tracks and about half that much at one of the discount superstores—and the broadcast really brings the race alive. An event that might seem boring is often full of drama and strategy—if you know what's going on behind the scenes. You'll know who's fast and who's not, whether the leader is pulling away or the second-place guy is chasing him down. A radio headset is required equipment for watching a race live. Never go to the track without one.

Snooping with Scanners

Radio scanners have become all the rage among veteran fans. These devices allow listeners to monitor radio communications between crew chiefs, spotters, and drivers. Scanners are an excellent way to get the scoop on what's happening with your favorite team during the race. You'll

The Best of *nascar*

What are the best races to attend on the NASCAR Nextel Cup Series? Where are the best restaurants on the circuit? Which speedway offers the best food? What races offer the best bargains? Here are some of our suggestions:

Must-See Races

Night race at Bristol Motor Speedway

Either race at Richmond International Raceway

Spring race at Atlanta Motor Speedway

Fall race at Darlington Raceway

Fall race at Talladega Superspeedway

The Nextel All-Star Challenge at Lowe's Motor Speedway

Must-Eat Restaurants

The Chart House, Daytona Beach, Florida (Daytona International Speedway)

Rosa's, Ontario, California (California Speedway)

The Tobacco Company, Richmond, Virginia (Richmond International Raceway)

Rio Carnival World Buffet, Las Vegas, Nevada (Las Vegas Motor Speedway)

Sambo's Tavern, Leipsic, Delaware (Dover International Speedway)

Edelweiss Restaurant, Blakeslee, Pennsylvania (Pocono Raceway)

Must-Try Speedway Food

Chili dogs at Martinsville Speedway

Smoked turkey legs at Atlanta Motor Speedway

Pulled pork at Bristol Motor Speedway

Brisket sandwich at Texas Motor Speedway

Smoked sausage at Lowe's Motor Speedway

Corn dogs at Indianapolis Motor Speedway

Can-Do Races on a Budget

Either race at Martinsville Speedway

Season finale at Homestead–Miami Speedway

Either race at Pocono Raceway

Either race at Atlanta Motor Speedway

Fall race at North Carolina Speedway

Either race at Michigan International Speedway

hear drivers complain about handling problems—and about the tactics of their competitors. Specific frequency information is required. These babies can be expensive, but you can rent them at some tracks. Warning: The language can get colorful in the heat of action.

Pick a Favorite

You don't have to pick a favorite driver right away, but you'll need one to really get involved in the sport. NASCAR racing is as much about personalities as it is speed, and there's someone for everyone. Want ornery old school? Try Tony Stewart on for size. Looking for Mr. Right? Jeff Gordon's your man. Prefer the underdog? Check out Johnny Benson or Ken Schrader. Oh, and NASCAR fans love to pull *against* drivers, too. Here's a suggestion: Pull for one of the Bodines. There are as many as three of the New York brothers in any given race, and they are the butt of a lot of good-natured jokes in the sport, as well some not-so-good-natured criticism for their alleged tendency to be smack in the middle of a lot of wrecks. They need some fans.

Required Equipment

Without proper preparation and equipment, a day at the track can be grueling. Remember, you're going to be there for six or even eight hours. Pack light. Seats are small, and space is tight. Before you lock the front door, run through this list of race-day essentials:

- Radio headset, essential equipment for a true understanding of what's going on
- Earplugs, required unless you're wearing a radio headset
- Sunscreen
- Rain ponchos—no umbrellas allowed
- Aspirin or other headache remedy
- Seat cushion, especially for concrete grandstands
- Binoculars, a must for the big tracks

A note about coolers and backpacks: With tighter security, most tracks don't permit coolers, and it's a source of controversy among fans. Soft-sided coolers no bigger than 14 inches across or deep currently seem to be allowed at every racetrack. Many tracks only allow clear plastic bags for food, radios, binoculars, hats, and sunglasses. Check track regulations before you go.

Glossary of Racing Lingo

If you're a racing rookie, get ready to learn a new language. Race talk can be confusing, so you should become familiar with some of the terminology used by commentators. You will be tested at the track.

A word about turn terminology: What looks like a single curve at a track is actually divided, for reference, into two parts—the entrance, or first half of the turn, and the exit, or second half. On an oval track, the turn after the start/finish line is referred to as Turn 1 and Turn 2. The turn at the other end of the speedway is called Turn 3 and Turn 4.

Aerodynamics: How the air moves over and around a car at race speed. This has become a critical performance factor.

Apex: The middle of a turn.

Apron: The flat part of the speedway below the given racing surface.

Banking: The angle, measured in degrees, of a turn or straightaway. The most steeply banked track in NASCAR is Bristol, at 36 degrees.

Back marker: A car that usually runs in the back of the pack.

Camber: The amount a tire is tilted up and down.

DNF: Did not finish.

Dialed in: Describes a car that has been mechanically adjusted for maximum performance at a particular track. Example: "Bob's team really has that car dialed in."

Dirty air: Turbulence created by the lead pack of cars.

Downforce: An aerodynamic effect that describes the amount of force pushing the car down onto the track, providing improved traction and tire grip.

Draft: A car moving at high speed creates a vacuum effect behind it. Another car following closely gains speed by traveling in the tunnel of calm air. Two cars running nose-to-tail usually are faster than one car since two cars can divide the wind resistance.

Field: All forty-three cars in a starting lineup.

Handling: The driving characteristics, or balance, of a car.

Happy hour: The final practice session, usually held the day before the race, after qualifying. Oddly enough, the session is generally only forty-five minutes, not an hour.

Infield: The area inside the track containing the pits, garage area, and parking for car haulers and RVs.

Loose: A condition in which the car loses grip in the rear tires while cornering, making the back end want to come around.

Marbles: The higher groove that collects debris and small pieces of worn tires. A car that ventures into the marbles usually crashes.

Pole: The fastest qualifier and number-one starter who lines up on the inside of the front row for the start of the race.

Push: The opposite of loose. A condition in which the front tires lose grip in the corners, making the car difficult to turn; also known as "tight."

Provisional: A driver who didn't qualify fast enough to make the field may still make the race based on past Cup championships or car owner points.

Restrictor plate: A plate that fits between the carburetor and the intake manifold. Holes bored into the plate restrict airflow to the engine, reducing horsepower and speed. Used only at Daytona and Talladega.

Roof flap: Hinged flaps on the top of the car designed to deploy when the car is spinning backward, catching air and preventing the car from becoming airborne.

From
On-line to Track

His computer name was dalejr3, and he was good at racing games.

T. J. Majors considered dalejr3 his toughest competition in on-line racing games. What he didn't know was that dalejr3 had a bit of an advantage. If the two raced against each other at the Talladega Superspeedway, dalejr3 could draw on real-life experience. But to Majors dalejr3—Dale Earnhardt Jr.—was nothing more than a formidable on-line opponent. The two spent hours playing racing games without ever seeing each other or knowing each other's real name.

Earnhardt Jr. enjoyed the fact that he was racing against hundreds of other computer geeks and none of them knew, or cared, that he was the son of a seven-time NASCAR champion. They weren't impressed by his family's fame or fortune. As dalejr3 he was good competition for the best computer wizards and nothing more.

"People never believed it was me anyway, so I gave up trying to convince them," Earnhardt Jr. says. "I try to keep a low profile."

No matter how many people were signed into Total Entertainment Network, an interactive Web site, the racing games always seemed to come down to two people: Earnhardt Jr. and Majors.

"I was doing a lot of on-line racing with people from all over the place," Earnhardt Jr. says. "Some knew who I was, but this was back in my Busch days, so I wasn't really as well known as now. T. J. and I were always the two guys battling to win, and we kind of became friends that way. He didn't really know or care who I was. He shared some of his setups for the games with me, and we became buddies."

By the time Earnhardt Jr. became the

NASCAR Busch Series champion in 1998, the two had become e-mail pen pals. Majors eventually discovered the identity of dalejr3, but he remained more impressed with Earnhardt Jr.'s computer skills than his celebrity status. "I was really good at (computer games); he was really good at it," Majors said. "That's all I knew about him."

Earnhardt Jr. was so impressed with Majors' computer racing setups—his attention to shocks and springs—that he was convinced they would work in a real car as well. He talked Majors into leaving New York for a life of sweeping shop floors and learning the business from the ground up.

It's not easy—a part-time job at MB2 Motorsports doing odd jobs, another part-time job working at Earnhardt Jr.'s Late Model shop; and racing on weekends. "He's making me learn the business the way he did," Majors says.

Majors has been driving for Earnhardt Jr. since 2000. He started in three-quarter-scale stock cars, moved up to limited Late Models, and now races Late Models and Dash Series. "I had never driven a race car before I met Dale Jr.—except on the computer," Majors says.

Although both now have new commitments that rob them of most of their free time, they still find time to turn on, log on, and play. Despite being the most dominant figure of the NASCAR Nextel Cup Series, Earnhardt now has four computers in his house and a high-speed connection for each in case his friends want to play, too. He checks his e-mail every day and surfs the Net. And every once in a while, he plays games all night.

"I borrowed money from my sister Kelley to buy a computer when I was still in high school," Earnhardt Jr. says. "I learned a lot about that computer and got to the point where I could change just about any of its components. I was always adding new stuff to make it faster and better for games."

Earnhardt Jr. is so involved in his computer games that he hired a man to build a special steering wheel so that his racing would be more realistic.

Majors said the biggest difference for him was when his mother bought him a computer and then added a steering wheel and gas pedal to make it easier for him to play racing games. "Once I got the steering wheel and gas pedal for my computer, all I wanted to do was race," he says.

The same goes for dalejr3.

Scuffed tires: Tires that have been run a few laps.

Spotters: Team members positioned in a designated area high above the track. They're in radio communication with the drivers, warning them of wrecks and providing information about the position of other cars.

Sticker tires: Brand-new tires with the Goodyear stickers still on them.

Tight: See "Push."

Links to the Racing Community

NASCAR racing is hotly competitive, and the feuds and debates aren't limited to the tracks. Race fans take their sport very seriously, as evidenced by the spirited—and often offensive—discussions that sizzle every day online. There are also plenty of racing news sites, where you'll find stories, analysis, opinion columns, and other racing info. The discussion groups are where the real action takes place, though. Be warned: These folks can be brutal.

Here are some of the best:

NASCAR.com	www.NASCAR.com	NASCAR's official site
That's Racin'	www.thatsracin.com	news, opinions, lively forum
Jayski's	www.jayskithatsracin.com	the inside source
SpeedFX	www.speedfx.com	NASCAR and other series
Augusta Chronicle	www.augustachronicle. com/sports	daily coverage of NASCAR
Usenet	rec.autos.sport.NASCAR	hot, unmoderated discussions
Usenet	rec.autos.sport.NASCAR. moderated	moderated version

Southern Roots Racing

T his is NASCAR country, and these are the tracks where it all began, where legendary former moonshine runners like Junior Johnson and Curtis Turner moved up from the bullring dirt tracks across the Carolinas and into Prime Time. Each of these tracks is steeped in history, and each is unique—from the egg-shaped treachery of Darlington to the slambang fury of Bristol.

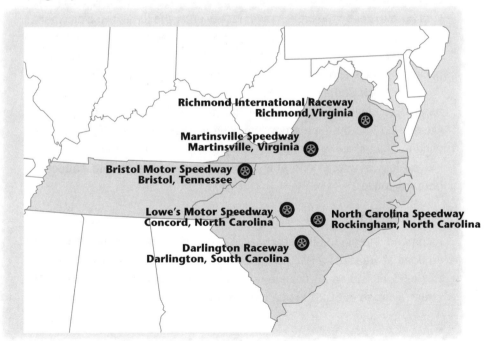

Richmond International Raceway:
Night Fever

They've been racing at the Virginia State Fairgrounds since 1948, when moonshine runners and action-hungry World War II vets came to run on the rough half-mile dirt track. Today, after a complete redesign in 1988, Richmond is the scene of some of the most exciting racing on the circuit, and the facility is among the finest in NASCAR.

Steeped in NASCAR history, Richmond also points to the sport's future. Both 400-lap Nextel Cup races are run under the lights, and its 0.75-mile layout—unique on the circuit—produces some of the best racing of the season.

Terrific racing, a historic area, and a vibrant city: A Richmond race trip should be near the top of any wish list.

Let's Go Racing

The track is wide, with a choice of racing grooves making it a favorite for both drivers and fans. Cars can pass to the outside here, which makes for some of the most competitive door-to-door action of the season.

Speeds can be deceiving in racing. Average lap speeds here in the 120 mph range may not seem all that impressive, but the cars carry tremendous speed into the corners at this track, and that's what matters to drivers. Drivers have to get on the brakes hard as they enter the turns. Grinding crashes are common at Richmond, especially when cars have a problem getting into the corners, such as blowing a right front tire. But it's not the wrecks that pack the grandstands at Richmond; it's the side-by-side racing action.

The track surface has been unpredictable in recent years, with the asphalt coming apart a bit in the low groove. Those bits of asphalt are washed up into the high groove, making it treacherously slick. When that occurs, this place becomes a one-groove racetrack, and that usually means lots of wrecks and angry drivers as everyone tries to protect the bottom groove.

How to Get There

Richmond International Speedway is located on the Virginia State Fairgrounds at Strawberry Hill, near the intersection of Interstates 95 and 64. Exit I–95 at Laburnum Avenue, and follow the signs to the raceway. The street address is 602 East Laburnum Avenue.

RICHMOND INTERNATIONAL RACEWAY

TURN 3

TURN 2

Pit Road

TURN 4

TURN 1

START/FINISH

Our Ratings	Racing: 🏁 🏁 🏁 🏁 🏁 Amenities: 🏁 🏁 🏁 🏁 Area Appeal: 🏁 🏁 🏁 🏁
Track Facts	0.75-mile oval Seating capacity: 105,000 P.O. Box 9257 Richmond, VA 23227 (804) 345–7223 www.rir.com
Annual Events	Two 400-lap Nextel Cup Series, May and September Companion events: Busch Series, May and September; NASCAR Craftsman Truck Series, September
Weather	Average High (F): May 77.5 September 80.0 Average Low (F): May 54.7 September 60.0
Top Gun	Richard Petty, 13 wins
Qualifying Record	Ward Burton, 127.389 mph

Best Seats in the House

Buy seats in the highest rows you can afford—Row 20 or higher—or you'll be disappointed to find your views of the other side of the track partially obstructed by the team haulers. Otherwise, you can't go wrong here—there's plenty of hot action all around the speedway.

Richmond Memories

Two drivers have ruled Richmond. On the old half-mile, it was The King, **Richard Petty,** who once won seven straight races here. After the track was rebuilt in 1988, **Rusty Wallace** became the man to beat, with six wins.

In 1986 third-generation driver **Kyle Petty,** driving for the legendary Wood Brothers of Virginia, won here for his first career Winston Cup victory.

David Pearson took the checkered flag here in 1969, the fiftieth victory of his career. Pearson would go on to win fifty-five more races. His 105 victories are second only to Richard Petty.

Joe Nemechek on Richmond

"Richmond is an action-packed track," says Joe Nemechek. "In the past it's been very good for racing, depending on what they do with the sealers there. The sealer is the stuff they put down on the asphalt to protect it from the elements. Normally we end up having two grooves and you get a lot of side-by-side racing. There's racing all over the track, both ends. There's a lot of passing down the front straightaway. It's a great track for the fans because you see awesome racing anywhere you sit."

Richmond combines terrific action and some roll-the-dice strategic decisions. "I've won a Busch Series race and have been very competitive in Nextel Cup [including a victory here in May 2003]. When the tires were a little bit softer, it was really a lot of tire management. There was a lot of strategy involved—how you use tires and how you'd end up pitting. Normally there are a lot of cautions, but lately we've had a lot of green-flag pit stops that kind of throw a monkeywrench into everything."

Make It a Vacation

Whether your interest lies in Colonial America, the American Revolution, or the Civil War, the Richmond area is a history buff's dream. Add a historic, vibrant downtown, with world-class entertainment parks an easy drive away, and you have the recipe for a first-rate vacation—centered on some of the most exciting racing anywhere.

For starters, discover your country on the eve of the American Revolution at **Colonial Williamsburg,** about 50 miles from Richmond. This living reenactment offers a unique opportunity to relive American history. Call (800) 447–8679, or visit www.colonialwilliamsburg.org.

The **James River Plantations,** located between Richmond and Williamsburg, serve up another taste of Virginia history. Here, along scenic Virginia Highway 5 in Charles City County, you'll see how Virginia aristocracy lived before the War Between the States, as it's called in these parts. Several of the plantations now operate as bed-and-breakfasts: **Edgewood Plantation** (4800 John Tyler Highway, Charles City; 804–829–2962); **Piney Grove at Southall's Plantation** (16920 Southall Plantation Lane, Charles City; 804–829–2480); and **North Bend Plantation** (12200 Weyanoke Road, Charles City; 804–829–5176).

The region was also the scene of some of the bloodiest battles of the Civil War. Nearby **battlefields** include **Richmond, Petersburg,** and **Fredericksburg.**

When the kids get tired of the history lessons, load up the car for **Busch Gardens** in Williamsburg, where you'll find dozens of thrilling rides and attractions, along with plenty of entertainment. Call (800) 343–7946, or visit www.4adventure.com. There's more action for thrill-seekers at Paramount's **Kings Dominion,** the entertainment park just north of Richmond in Doswell. Call (804) 876–5561, or visit www.kingsdominion.com.

Richmond's oldest church, **St. John's Episcopal Church** (2401 East Broad Street, Richmond; 804–648–5015) was the scene in 1775 of Patrick Henry's "Give me liberty or give me death" speech. Paid tours are available.

Where to Eat

There are several fast-food joints near the speedway, but if you're willing to drive into Richmond, you'll find a host of excellent restaurants. If you can eat out only once, try **The Tobacco Company,** a Richmond institution, in the historic Shockoe Slip area of downtown (1201 East Cary Street, Richmond; 804–782–9555). If terrific Virginia barbecue is more to your liking, you're in for a treat at **Alexander's** (1126 Westbriar Drive, Richmond; 804–740–3135). **King's Barbecue** (3221 West Washington Street, Petersburg; 804–732–5861) in nearby Petersburg is worth the drive down the Jefferson Davis Highway. If price is not an issue, make reservations at **La Petite France** (2108 Maywill Street, Richmond; 804–353–8729) or **LeMaire** (101 West Franklin Street, Richmond; 804–788–8000). La Petite France is a five-star restaurant that specializes in seafood; LeMaire turns Southern cooking into a culinary event.

Where to Stay

There's an abundance of hotels in Richmond. If you want to spring for the finest lodging in the city—indeed one of the grand hotels in the country—check into **The Jefferson** (101 West Franklin Street, Richmond; 804–788–8000). If you're lucky—or rich—enough to get a glimpse inside the presidential suite, be sure to tickle the ivories of the baby grand piano the way Elvis, Frank Sinatra, and Neil Diamond have done.

Want to be downtown but can't afford The Jefferson? The **Richmond Marriot** (500 East Broad Street, Richmond; 804–643–3400) is more moderately priced and conveniently located near the trendy bars and restaurants at **Shockoe Slip**. Nearby is the **Crowne Plaza** (555 East Canal Street, Richmond; 804–788–0900), also moderately priced and boasting rooms with a view of the James River. A good bargain bet is the **Sleep Inn** (2321 Willis Road, Richmond; 804–275–8800). Our favorite: the **Virginia Cliffe Inn** (2900 Mountain Road, Glen Allen; 804–266–7344), which sits on six beautiful garden acres in Glen Allen, 12 miles north of Richmond. The inn fronts historic Mountain Road, the path Thomas Jefferson traveled on his trips to Richmond and Williamsburg. Reserve one of the four guest rooms, all with private bath and TV, or book the Clifton Cottage and have a party for forty of your closest NASCAR friends.

Richmond Area Restaurants

Alexander's Barbecue
1126 Westbriar Drive
Richmond, VA
(804) 740–3135

Awful Arthur's Oyster Bar
101 North Eighteenth
    Street
Richmond, VA
(804) 643–1700

Blue Marlin Seafood
    Kitchen
7502 West Broad Street
Richmond, VA
(804) 672–3838

Brookside Seafood
5221 Brook Road
Richmond, VA
(804) 262–5716

Crab Louie's Seafood
    Tavern
Sycamore Square Shop-
    ping Center
Richmond, VA
(804) 275–2722

El Rio Grande
1324 West Cary
Richmond, VA
(804) 278–9244

Franco's Ristorante and
    Cafe
9031 West Broad Street
Richmond, VA
(804) 270–9124

Graywolf Grill
1601 Willow Lawn Drive
Richmond, VA
(804) 673–4110

Havana 59
7367 Seventeenth Street
Richmond, VA
(804) 649–2822

Italian Kitchen West
8115 West Broad Street
Richmond, VA
(804) 270–6350

Japan House
4702 Forest Hill Avenue
Richmond, VA
(804) 230–4599

Julian's
2617 West Broad Street
Richmond, VA
(804) 359–0605

Kabuto Japanese House
    of Steaks
8052 West Broad Street
Richmond, VA
(804) 747–9573

King's Barbecue
3221 West Washington
    Street
Petersburg, VA
(804) 732–5861

La Petite France
2108 Maywill Street
Richmond, VA
(804) 353–8729

LeMaire
101 West Franklin Street
Richmond, VA
(804) 788–8000

Outback Steakhouse
7917 West Broad Street
Richmond, VA
(804) 527–0583

Pasta Luna
8902 West Broad Street
Richmond, VA
(804) 762–9029

River City Diner
1712 East Main
Richmond, VA
(804) 644–9418

Ruth's Chris Steakhouse
11500 West Hugenot Road
Richmond, VA
(804) 378–0600

Skilligalee Restaurant
5416 Glenside Drive
Richmond, VA
(804) 672–6200

Third Street Diner
Third and Main Streets
Richmond, VA
(804) 788–4750

The Tobacco Company
1201 East Cary Street
Richmond, VA
(804) 782–9555

Richmond Area Lodging

Best Western Kings
    Quarters
16102 Theme Park Way
Doswell, VA
(804) 876–3321

Comfort Inn
3200 West Broad Street
Richmond, VA
(804) 359–4061

Commonwealth Park
    Suites
901 Bank Street
Richmond, VA
(804) 343–7300

Courtyard by Marriott
6400 West Broad Street
Richmond, VA
(804) 282–1881

Crowne Plaza
555 East Canal Street
Richmond, VA
(804) 788–0900

Edgewood Plantation
4800 John Tyler Highway
Charles City, VA
(804) 829–2962

Embassy Suites
2925 Emerywood Parkway
Richmond, VA
(804) 672–8585

Guesthouse International
8901 Brook Road
Glen Allen, VA
(804) 553–8395

Hilton Airport
5501 Eubank Road
Sandston, VA
(804) 226–6400

Holiday Inn Airport
5203 Williamsburg Road
Sandston, VA
(804) 222–6450

Holiday Inn Central
3207 North Boulevard
Richmond, VA
(804) 359–9441

Holiday Inn Express
7441 Bell Creek Road
Mechanicsville, VA
(804) 559–0022

The Jefferson
101 West Franklin Street
Richmond, VA
(804) 788–8000

La Quinta
6910 Midlothian Pike
Richmond, VA
(804) 745–7100

Massad House Hotel
11 North Fourth Street
Richmond, VA
(804) 648–2893

North Bend Plantation
12200 Weyanoke Road
Charles City, VA
(804) 829–5176

Omni
100 South Twelfth Street
Richmond, VA
(804) 344–7000

Piney Grove at Southall's
   Plantation
16920 Southall Plantation
   Lane
Charles City, VA
(804) 829–2480

Quality Inn and Suites
5701 Chamberlayne Road
Richmond, VA
(804) 266–7616

Quality Inn West End
8008 West Broad Street
Richmond, VA
(804) 346–0000

Richmond Hotel and Con-
   ference Center
6531 West Broad Street
Richmond, VA
(804) 285–9951

Richmond Marriott
500 East Broad Street
Richmond, VA
(804) 643–3400

Sheraton West
6624 West Broad Street
Richmond, VA
(804) 285–2000

Sleep Inn
2321 Willis Road
Richmond, VA
(804) 275–8800

The Virginia Cliffe Inn
2900 Mountain Road
Glen Allen, VA
(804) 266–7344

Wyndham Garden Hotel
4700 South Laburnum
   Avenue
Richmond, VA
(804) 226–4300

Richmond Area Camping

Amelia Family
   Campgrounds
9720 Military Road
Amelia, VA
(804) 561–3011

Americamps
396 Air Park Road
Ashland, VA
(804) 798–5298

KOA Bowling Green
U.S. Highway 360
Bowling Green, VA
(804) 633–7592

Williamsburg KOA Resorts
4000 Newman Road
Williamsburg, VA
(757) 565–2907

Martinsville Speedway:
Contact Sport

Martinsville is the only original track remaining from NASCAR's first full season in 1949, and it's still a little jewel on the circuit. Newcomers to the sport may wonder why today's high-tech, multi-million-dollar race teams still slug it out on this tiny, paper clip–shaped short track, but the old-timers understand: This is how it all began. No other track on today's season calendar offers the slam-bang, fender-crunching action you can see here. Forget speed. Forget size. Martinsville's brand of racing is a throwback to the Saturday-night short-track shootouts that were once the backbone of the sport. If you want to really understand American stock car racing, come to Martinsville.

Let's Go Racing

Martinsville is the oldest and shortest track on the circuit, but the racing is as intense here as anywhere else NASCAR runs. And it gets physical—often the only way to pass is to bump the guy in front of you out of the way. Fenders get crumpled and tempers run hot. It's rare for a car to finish 500 laps here unscathed.

Unlike many of the faster tracks—heck, they're *all* faster than Martinsville—the richest teams with the top sponsorships don't always win here. Here the driver and a savvy chassis man can overcome millions of dollars in funding.

The banking here is only 12 degrees in the turns, and the straightaways are flat. The quick line through the corners is right at the bottom—and no driver willingly gives up the low groove. Watch for cars that are able to run low; those are the ones headed toward the front.

Because passing is so difficult, pit stops are of supreme importance. A crack team that can shave the competition by a half second can pass four or five cars in the pits. Pit road is extremely tight here. Be sure to bring binoculars for an up-close view of the action in the pits—it's often as exciting as the on-track bump and grind.

Brakes are a key to winning Martinsville, and drivers use brakes harder here than at any other track. The track has been described as two quarter-mile drag strips connected by hairpin turns. Savvy racers—usually the more experienced ones—know to conserve their brakes until late in the race, when they need to turn their quickest laps. Keep brakes in mind

MARTINSVILLE SPEEDWAY

START/FINISH

Pit Road

TURN 1

TURN 2

TURN 4

TURN 3

Our Ratings	Racing: 🏁 🏁 🏁 🏁
	Amenities: 🏁 🏁 🏁
	Area Appeal: 🏁 🏁

Track Facts

0.526-mile oval
Seating capacity: 91,000
P.O. Box 3311
Martinsville, VA 24112
(276) 956–3151
www.martinsvillespeedway.com

Annual Events

Two 500-lap Nextel Cup Series races, April and October
Companion event: Craftsman Truck Series, April

Weather

Average High (F):	April 68.9	October 70.0
Average Low (F):	April 39.4	October 40.2

Top Gun

Richard Petty, 15 wins

Qualifying Record

Tony Stewart, 95.371 mph

when you're watching that young gun pull away from the rest of the field. You just might see veterans passing him by when he loses brakes later on.

Remember, the best racing isn't necessarily at the front—or even for position. It's easy to fall behind the leader by a lap or more here because of an unscheduled pit stop or an ill-handling car. The top crews will usually fine-tune the car's handling during the race, so that guy who went two laps down earlier just might be faster than the leader—and be pressing hard to get back in the lead lap.

How to Get There

The speedway is located 2 miles south of Martinsville on U.S. Highway 220 South Business. From Piedmont Triad International Airport in Greensboro, North Carolina, take North Carolina Highway 68 north from airport exit and then US 220 north. The speedway is about 45 miles from the airport.

Ricky Craven on Martinsville

"Martinsville is a great track to watch a race at," says Ricky Craven, the New England native who came south to go racing and won his first Nextel Cup race here. "I enjoy going on top of the hauler during the different practices when I'm not in the car and just watching the cars here. This is real racing, where you need to work for every position on the track. As a fan, just look at any corner on the racetrack and you will always see great racing.

"Since they ground the concrete surface last year, the real fast line appears to be about a lane and a half up, but you can be on the very inside or even the outside and still be fast. When watching the race, pay attention to the different lines that various drivers take around the track. My favorite line at Martinsville is the inside, but depending on the track conditions you may see me move up the track in order to go faster."

Craven's favorite Martinsville memory? That's easy: "Banging doors with Dale Jarrett with a few laps to go in October 2001. That was my first Cup win, and I will always remember the great feeling and the great race we put on for the fans."

Best Seats in the House

Seats higher in the grandstands will give you a panoramic view of this little beauty of a racetrack, but there's truly not a bad seat in the house. It's often chilly here on race day, so you might appreciate the warmth and comfort of Martinsville's two forty-eight–seat enclosed suites. If you don't mind the elements—and you like the sound of crunching metal—consider tickets in the middle of the two sets of turns. Don't have a ticket? The speedway holds several sections of the backstretch grandstand for unreserved seating for families with children. Tickets go on sale the morning of the race.

Martinsville Memories

Fonty Flock won the first race held at Martinsville under the NASCAR banner on July 4, 1948, outracing **Pee Wee Martin, Buck Baker, Bill Blair,** and his brother, **Tim Flock.** NASCAR founder **Bill France** finished eighth.

According to the late **Clay Earles,** the speedway's founder, the most memorable finish here came in the 1981 Dogwood Classic in a race in NASCAR's "modified" division. Modified legend **Richie Evans** and **Geoffrey Bodine** came off the fourth turn side by side headed for the checkered flag. The two cars slammed together, with Evans's car climbing up the outside wall "so high you could read the number on the top of his car from the infield." Missing his right-front wheel, Evans somehow kept his foot on the gas and won the race. Three years later, Bodine won his first Nextel Cup race, right here at Martinsville.

Make It a Vacation

Here's a great chance to enjoy the peaceful splendor of Virginia's Blue Ridge Mountains—and then revel in the thunderous short-track action at the speedway. Spend a few days around a race weekend to explore the scenic mountains via the **Blue Ridge Parkway.** You might get lucky in October and catch the autumn leaves in all their glory. Lodges, cabins, and bed-and-breakfasts are numerous. Here are a couple of suggestions: **Rocky Knob Cabins,** Meadows of Dan, Virginia (540–593–3503); **Doe Run Lodge,** Milepost 189, Blue Ridge Parkway, Fancy Gap, Virginia (800–325–6189); and **Primland Resort,** Ararat, Virginia (276–251–8012).

There are very few hotel rooms around Martinsville, so your best option is staying over in Greensboro or Winston-Salem, North Carolina. It's an easy drive, and the area amenities are a lot more inviting.

Away from the Track

Need a break from the sound and fury of the racetrack? Here are some family-friendly getaways within striking distance of Martinsville Speedway.

Take a look back in time at the **Wood Brothers Racing Museum** (21 Performance Drive, Stuart, Virginia; 276–694–2121), just thirty minutes from Martinsville Speedway, just off Virginia Highway 58 in the industrial park. The museum is open weekdays and the Saturdays of the Martinsville races. There's no admission fee, and there's a gift shop. Brief guided visits to the Wood Brothers Racing shop area are also available.

Take a look even further back in time at the **Virginia Museum of Natural History** (1001 Douglas Avenue, Martinsville, Virginia; 276–666–8600). The museum offers exhibits, programs, and field trips on a variety of topics including dinosaurs, mammals, bugs, fossils, and minerals.

The **Virginia Museum of Transportation** (303 Norfolk Avenue, Roanoke, Virginia; 540–342–5670) offers the chance to visit a restored rail yard with a wealth of vintage rail cars and engines; there's an auto museum, too.

Where to Eat

Don't settle for the usual fast-food fare. Here are a few local spots that should hit the spot. Barbecue is a local specialty. Two of Martinsville's best are **Pigs-R-Us** (1014 Liberty Street; 276–632–1161) and the **Dixie Pig** (US 220 North Business; 276–632–9082). If you're staying in the area a few days, spend an afternoon at the **Chateau Morrisette** (287 Winery Road Southwest; 540–593–2865) winery, about 40 miles from Martinsville in lovely Meadows of Dan, Virginia. Sample the local vintage and have lunch or dinner at the terrific gourmet restaurant. Oh, and at the track itself, make sure to sample the famous baloney sandwiches. (Sorry, race fans just don't say "bologna.")

The **Amsterdam Room** at the **Dutch Inn** (US 220 North Business, Collinsville; 276–647–3721) is recognized as *the* dining tradition of Martinsville's foothills valley. The moderately priced menu is extensive, but if you don't find something that appeals, there's always the lavish buffet and the popular make-your-own-sundae bar. The **Flying Dutchman Lounge** overlooks the Dutch Inn's lobby, where happy hour with daily specials is four hours long.

Another terrific restaurant-lounge combo can be found at the **Best Western** (1755 Virginia Avenue, Martinsville; 276–632–5611). **Marigold's** offers everything from traditional home-cooked Southern cuisine to Nouvelle style. If you don't see what you want on the menu, ask: If they have the ingredients, they'll make it for you. The **Brass Rail Lounge** is a great place to kick back and meet racing friends, and you don't have to move when it's time for dinner: Marigold's full menu is available in the lounge during restaurant hours.

Buffets are popular in these parts. If you like Golden Corral, you'll like **Ryan's Family Steakhouse** (361 East Commonwealth Boulevard, Martinsville; 276–634–5335), a similar chain that's a tad fancier but still a good value for the family. Treat yourself to the Mega Bar Buffet, or have grilled steak, chicken, or seafood made just for you. Save room for dessert from the Bakery Bar, included with any meal.

Where to Stay

Martinsville and sister city Collinsville have a lot of lodging to offer for small mountain towns, but there's also plenty of lodging in Stuart and Danville, Virginia, each about 30 miles away, and in Greensboro, North Carolina, 40 miles or so south. A great choice on the Collinsville side of US 220 is the **Dutch Inn** (US 220 Business, Collinsville; 276–647–3721). It has a full-service dining room and lounge, well-appointed guest rooms, and, get this, *free* Internet access. Look for the big windmill out front. Another good choice among hotels used to catering to race fans is the **Jameson Inn** (378 Commonwealth Boulevard, Martinsville; 276–638–0478). Complimentary breakfast here includes made-to-order Belgian waffles, and the inn is pet friendly.

In Stuart you'll find the **Chocolate Moose Bed & Breakfast** (117 East Blue Ridge Street, Stuart; 276–694–3745), which is owned and operated by a naturopathic physician and a massage therapist. Staying here lends new meaning to unwinding after the race. They only have two rooms, though, so call well in advance to avoid disappointment. Also in the B&B category is **Dutchies View Bed and Breakfast** (10448 Woolwine Highway, Woolwine; 276–930–3701), known for its "gezelligheid," a special Dutch custom that loosely translates to "homey service" for guests in any of the six rooms, all with private bath. On Friday night catch the live bluegrass music at the General Store in Floyd, just 12 miles away.

Martinsville Area Restaurants

Aloha Wok Chinese
Restaurant
3424 Virginia Avenue
Collinsville, VA
(276) 647–1443

Applebee's
281 Commonwealth
Boulevard
Martinsville, VA
(276) 638–2377

Captain Tom's Seafood
US 220 South
Martinsville, VA
(276) 666–0326

Clarence's Steak House
US 220 South
Ridgeway, VA
(276) 956–3400

Country Cookin'
Liberty Fair Mall
Martinsville, VA
(276) 666–0768

D&A Cafe
1221 Memorial Boulevard
Martinsville, VA
(276) 632–1820

Dixie Pig Barbecue
Restaurant
US 220 North Business
Martinsville, VA
(276) 632–9082

Dutch Inn
US 220 North Business
Collinsville, VA
(276) 647–3721

El Ranchito
3069 Virginia Avenue
Collinsville, VA
(276) 647–4330

Hong Kong Restaurant
Patrick Henry Mall
Martinsville, VA
(276) 632–6429

Jan's Dutch Boy Drive-In
502 North Virginia Avenue
Collinsville, VA
(276) 647–8873

Mackie's Restaurant
US 220 North Business
Collinsville, VA
(276) 647–3138

Marigold's
US 220 North Business
Martinsville, VA
(276) 632–5611

Michael's Steak and More
US 220 North Business
Collinsville, VA
(276) 647–3720

Mi Ranchito
1212 South Memorial
   Boulevard
Martinsville, VA
(276) 632–6363

Pigs-R-Us
1014 Liberty Street
Martinsville, VA
(276) 632–1161

Ryan's Family Steakhouse
361 East Commonwealth
   Boulevard
Martinsville, VA
(276) 634–5335

Texas Steakhouse and
   Saloon
283 Commonwealth
   Boulevard
Martinsville, VA
(276) 632–7133

Third Bay Cafe
1163 Spruce Street
Martinsville, VA
(276) 666–8414

Time Out
2280 Virginia Avenue
Collinsville, VA
(276) 647–6364

The Williamsburg Cafeteria
603 South Memorial
   Boulevard
Martinsville, VA
(276) 638–3314

Martinsville Area Lodging

Best Lodge
US 220 Business
Martinsville, VA
(276) 647–3941

Blue Ridge Motel
US 58
Meadows of Dan, VA
(276) 952–2244

Carolina Inn
421 Vine Street
Eden, NC
(336) 623–2997

Chocolate Moose Bed &
   Breakfast
117 East Blue Ridge Street
Stuart, VA
(276) 694–3745

Comfort Inn
2203 Barnes Street
Reidsville, NC
(336) 634–0111

Days Inn
US 220 Business
Ridgeway, VA
(276) 638–3914

Days Inn
115 West Kings Highway
Eden, NC
(336) 623–1500

Days Inn
2205 Barnes Street
Reidsville, NC
(336) 342–2800

Doe Run Lodge
Milepost 189
Blue Ridge Parkway
Fancy Gap, VA
(800) 325–6189

Dutch Inn Hotel
US 220 Business
Collinsville, VA
(276) 647–3721

Dutchies View Bed &
   Breakfast
10448 Woolwine Highway
Woolwine, VA
(276) 930–3701

Hampton Inn
50 Hampton Drive
Collinsville, VA
(276) 647–4700

Hampton Inn
724 South Van Buren
   Road
Eden, NC
(336) 627–1111

Holiday Inn Express
101 Express Drive
Reidsville, NC
(336) 361–4000

Holiday Inn Express
US 220 North Business
Martinsville, VA
(276) 666–6835

Jameson Inn
378 Commonwealth
   Boulevard
Martinsville, VA
(276) 638–0478

Jameson Inn
716 Linden Drive
Eden, NC
(336) 627–0472

King's Court
US 220 South
Ridgeway, VA
(276) 956–3101

Knights Inn
US 220 North Business
Collinsville, VA
(276) 647–3716

Mar-Gre Motel
213 South Van Buren
   Road
Eden, NC
(336) 623–9161

Mountain Rose Inn
1787 Charity Highway
Woolwine, VA
(276) 930–1057

Old Spring Farm
7629 Charity Highway
Woolwine, VA
(276) 930–3404

Primland Resort
4621 Busted Rock Road
Meadows of Dan, VA
(276) 251–8012

Ramada Inn
2100 Barnes Street
Reidsville, NC
(336) 342–0341

Rocky Knob Cabins
Milepost 174
Meadows of Dan, VA
(540) 593–3503

Super 8 Motel
US 220 North Business
Martinsville, VA
(276) 666–8888

Virginian Motel
105 Blue Ridge Street
Stuart, VA
(276) 694–4244

Martinsville Area Camping

Fairy Stone State Park
State Road 346
Martinsville, VA
(276) 930–2424

Speedway Campground
Martinsville Speedway
Martinsville, VA
(276) 956–3151

Bristol Motor Speedway:
Thunder Valley

Bristol Motor Speedway, carved out of the rugged Appalachian Mountains of East Tennessee, is home to the wildest, most frenetic white-knuckle racing anywhere. It's only a half mile around, but Bristol has the highest banking of any NASCAR track, producing fast, close-quarters racing, furious action, grinding crashes—and lots of angry drivers.

Even before they fire up the engines, the atmosphere and scenery here are unforgettable. With towering grandstands seating more than 150,000—and more on the way, always—the place looks more like the Rose Bowl than a half-mile racetrack.

Nextel Cup races run 500 laps here, about 267 miles. Events are held in March and August. Any race at Bristol is a thrill, but the night race in August is flat-out electrifying. Put this one at the top of your list.

Let's Go Racing

It's no mystery why Bristol is the toughest ticket in all of NASCAR: Bristol means lightning-fast speeds and nonstop action. If you see only one race in your life, make it the August night race at Bristol. They call it Thunder Valley, and it's like no other show in racing.

The fast speeds and small track aren't a good mix if you want to see a lot of passing. There's a lot of action here but not much side-by-side racing. In fact, more passes are made here by using a bump-and-run. The overall experience, however, makes it easy to forget about the lack of lead changes.

Racing speeds can be deceiving. Bristol's the shortest track on the NASCAR circuit, but it's probably the fastest in relation to its size. Its 36-degree banking—highest on the circuit—makes Bristol something like racing in a bowl, with cars hurtling around the track at incredible speeds. G-forces are a real factor in the corners, wearing down less-fit drivers over a three- or four-hour race. Unlike at many other tracks, drivers have no chance to relax here. They're constantly in heavy traffic, rocketing around the concrete surface, just inches from the closest bumper.

Radio headsets, tuned into the race broadcast, are virtually required equipment here. With forty-three cars crammed onto this half-mile roller coaster, the lead cars quickly overtake the slowest cars. It can be a challenge to keep track of the top five or ten cars when they're mixed in with slower, lapped cars. The broadcast will keep you tuned in to who's running where.

BRISTOL MOTOR SPEEDWAY

Our Ratings

Racing: 🏁 🏁 🏁

Amenities: 🏁 🏁 🏁 🏁 🏁

Area Appeal: 🏁 🏁 🏁

Track Facts

0.533-mile oval

Seating capacity: 164,000

151 Speedway Boulevard

P.O. Box 3966

Bristol, TN 37625

(423) 764–1161

www.bristolmotorspeedway.com

Annual Events

Two NASCAR Nextel Cup events, March and August

Companion events: Busch Series, March and August;

NASCAR Craftsman Truck Series, August

Weather

Average High (F):	March 55.5	August 84.0
Average Low (F):	March 35.2	August 63.0

Top Gun

Darrell Waltrip, 12 wins

Qualifying Record

Ryan Newman, 128.709 mph

Wherever you look you'll find hot racing action. Bristol is essentially a one-groove racetrack—instead of choosing to drive higher or lower around the oval, every driver needs to drive the same line through the corners and down the short straightaway for maximum speed. The preferred line through the corners here is right at the bottom, so passing the car in front often gets physical. Sometimes the only way to pass is to bump the guy in front of you, knock him up the racetrack, and drive underneath. It's called the bump-and-run, and it's turned more than a few racing friends into bitter enemies.

How to Get There

The track is located on Volunteer Parkway, Tennessee Highway 11E, on the south side of Bristol, Tennessee. From the south: Exit Interstate 81 at Interstate 181 to TN 11E; or take Tennessee exit 69, and follow Tennessee Highway 37 to TN 11E north. From the north: Exit I–81 at Virginia exit 3 and take VA 11E south; or take Virginia exit 17 and follow Virginia Highway 75 south to Tennessee Highway 44 south to U.S. Highway 421 north to Tennessee Highway 394 south (the Bristol Beltway).

Best Seats in the House

Because the grandstands tower above the track, there's truly not a bad seat at Bristol. Try to avoid the first few rows near the track, where it's grittier and noisier and the view of some parts of the track can be obscured. Otherwise, any seat's a good seat, from which every inch of the action is in plain view. All the seats have backs, and the concession areas have been drastically improved.

Doing Deluxe

If you want to watch the down-and-dirty racing from air-conditioned or heated comfort, spring for one of the one hundred skyboxes. Luxury suites are fully enclosed and include theater-style seating, air-conditioning, bar and food stations, as well as closed circuit television.

Kevin Harvick
on Bristol

Kevin Harvick loves Bristol, and it shows in the way this young gun runs the high banks at this place. Whether he's running Nextel Cup or Busch, look for Harvick up front here. He knows why it's one of the sport's top venues.

"The best thing about Bristol is that you can see everything that happens, from anywhere around the racetrack," Harvick says. "And believe me a lot happens when you put forty-three cars on a half-mile, high-banked oval. Just be careful. If you get up to go get something to eat or drink, make it quick. Things tend to change very quickly at Bristol, and you might miss something."

That doesn't mean his strongest memories at Bristol are good ones. His biggest disappointment: "leading my first Winston Cup race with twenty laps to go when I got a flat tire and had to come down onto pit road early."

Like many other drivers, Harvick likes to attend some of the activities in town leading up to the race. "Enjoy the other events that surround the race weekend," he says. "There's always plenty to do, like the Racefest and souvenir row. Make it a full weekend—stay close or camp, and watch the other races like the Busch and Craftsman Truck Series. Culminate it with the Cup race on the last night."

Bristol Memories

Sparks fly, literally and figuratively, at every Bristol race. One feud, though, stands out from the smoking rubble: the late **Dale Earnhardt** versus former Winston Cup champion **Terry Labonte.**

In the 1995 night race, Labonte was leading late in the wreck-filled race, with Earnhardt's black No. 3 in hot pursuit. Earnhardt the Intimidator caught Labonte on the last lap, bumping the leader sideways in Turn Four. Earnhardt slammed Labonte again as the cars roared toward the finish line. Labonte's car spun around and slid in a shower of sparks across the line for the win, with Earnhardt finishing second.

Four years later, another hot August night in Bristol found Earnhardt and Labonte tangling again for the win. Labonte passed Earnhardt for the lead on Lap 439, but as the cars slowed for a yellow flag on Lap 490, another car tapped Labonte and spun him out. Labonte was forced to pit for repairs, giving the lead back to Earnhardt. Labonte came back out in fifth place when the race restarted, with just five laps to go. Labonte, who had put on four fresh tires, knifed his way through the lead pack, roaring past Earnhardt at the white flag. One lap to go. Earnhardt drove deep into Turn 2, hitting Labonte and sending his Chevy slamming into the wall. Earnhardt slipped through and raced back around to take the checkered flag.

"I didn't mean to wreck him," Earnhardt said afterward. "I was just trying to rattle his cage."

Make It a Vacation

The scenic beauty of the Tennessee and Virginia mountains is a great excuse to turn a weekend of racing into a week's vacation. Our choice: Just across the state line, 16 miles away in Abingdon, Virginia, is the **Martha Washington Inn** (276–628–3161; www.marthawashingtoninn.com), a lovely and historic hotel that's sure to provide a charming respite from the rigors of racing. If you prefer a more modern resort with all the amenities—and a terrific golf course—try the **Marriott MeadowView Conference and Convention Center** (423–378–0100) in nearby Kingsport, Tennessee. If you're an outdoors enthusiast, the mountains offer splendid camping, hiking, or trout fishing. Or consider spending a few days in the mountain resort town of **Blowing Rock,** North Carolina (75 miles), or the lovely city of **Asheville,** North Carolina (87 miles). In Asheville stay at the famous **Grove Park Inn**

(800–438–5800; www.groveparkinn.com), or contact the excellent local bed-and-breakfast association (877–262–6867; www.ashevillebba.com).

Away from the Track

Need a break from the sound and fury of the racetrack? Here are some family-friendly getaways within striking distance of Bristol Motor Speedway.

The **Barter Theatre** (133 West Main Street; 276–628–3991; www. bartertheatre.com) in Abingdon, Virginia, got its name from its food-for-admission barter system during the Great Depression. Acting alumni include Gregory Peck, Patricia Neal, and Ned Beatty.

Feeling presidential? Located 14 miles from I–81 is the **Andrew Johnson National Historical Site** (101 North College Street, Greenville, Tennessee; 423–639–3711; www.nps.gov/anjo/), home of the nation's seventeenth president, who served from 1865 to 1869 and worked his way from tailor to the White House.

Bristol is recognized by the Country Music Association as the birthplace of country music, and rightly so. The first commercially and nationally successful country music stars, Jimmie Rodgers and the Carter Family, made their first recordings in Bristol. A museum operated by the **Birthplace of Country Music Alliance** (500 Gate City Highway; 276–645–0035; www.birthplace ofcountrymusic.org), recently relocated to the Bristol Mall, tells the story of the famous 1927 Bristol Sessions, the recordings that started the commercial country music business. The museum is located at exit 1 off I–81.

Used by Native Americans as an attack and escape route, **Bristol Caverns** (1157 Bristol Caverns Parkway; 423–878–2011) feature many unusual formations created more than 400 million years ago. A tour of the caverns includes a walk along the banks of an underground river; guided tours start every twenty minutes. The caverns are located 8 miles from I–81. For more stalactite fun, **Appalachian Caverns** (420 Cave Hill Road; 423–323–2337) in nearby Blountville, Tennessee, offer almost a mile of walkways.

Where to Eat

The finest restaurant in these hills is the elegant **Troutdale Dining Room** (412 Sixth Street, Bristol; 423–968–9099), where the house specialties are swimming in a 600-gallon tank for your viewing pleasure. There's additional fine dining at **Peerless Restaurant** in Johnson City, Tennessee (2531 North Roan Street; 423–282–2351). For the flat-out best barbecue in the area, take the family to **Ridgewood Barbeque** (900 Old Elizabethton Highway, Bluff City, Tennessee; 423–538–7543).

Where to Stay

Like race tickets hotel rooms can be tough to find in Bristol. If you want a room in town for a race weekend, you'll need to make reservations at least a year in advance—and be prepared to pay $200 or more a night with a three-night minimum for an in-town room. The speedway office has a **Hotel Hotline** (276–466–5411; www.racehotels.com). **Guest Housing Inc.** is a brokerage that provides home rentals and guest rooms within local homes. Call (423) 652–0292.

Our suggestion is to look about an hour away from the speedway in scenic Asheville, North Carolina, or Pigeon Forge, Tennessee. There are plenty of rooms there, and you're just outside the boundary of inflated race weekend prices.

Bristol Area Restaurants

Applebee's
1661 East Stone Drive
Kingsport, TN
(423) 246–6373

Applebee's
425 Volunteer Parkway
Bristol, TN
(423) 968–1855

Chaco's Southwest Grill
1237 Volunteer Parkway
Bristol, TN
(423) 764–1000

Chops
3005 Linden Drive
Bristol, VA
(276) 466–4900

Damon's
5 Clear Creek Road
Bristol, VA
(276) 669–5250

Firehouse Restaurant
627 West Walnut Street
Johnson City, TN
(423) 929–7377

Fuddruckers
2519 Knob Creek Road
Johnson City, TN
(423) 915–1004

Logan's Roadhouse
3112 Browns Mill Road
Johnson City, TN
(423) 915–1122

Logan's Roadhouse
3174 Linden Drive
Bristol, VA
(276) 669–2886

Makato's Japanese
    Steakhouse
3021 East Oakland
    Avenue
Johnson City, TN
(423) 282–4441

O'Charley's
112 Broyles Drive
Johnson City, TN
(423) 854–9110

O'Charley's
3173 Linden Drive
Bristol, VA
(276) 642–0113

Olive Garden
1903 North Roan Street
Johnson City, TN
(423) 929–0137

Outback Steakhouse
3101 Browns Mill Road
Johnson City, TN
(423) 283–9222

Peerless Restaurant
2531 North Roan Street
Johnson City, TN
(423) 282–2351

Perkins Restaurant
102 Bristol East Road
Bristol, VA
(276) 669–7737

Ridgewood Barbeque
900 Old Elizabethton
   Highway
Bluff City, TN
(423) 538–7543

Ruby Tuesday's
3171 Linden Drive
Bristol, VA
(276) 669–6280

Simply Delicious
2600 Volunteer Parkway
Bristol, TN
(423) 764–3354

Skoby's Restaurant
1001 Konnarock Road
Kingsport, TN
(423) 245–5754

Tony Roma's
1905 North Roan Street
Johnson City, TN
(423) 929–7878

Troutdale Dining Room
412 Sixth Street
Bristol, TN
(423) 968–9099

The Vineyards
603 Gate City Highway
Bristol, VA
(276) 466–4244

Bristol Area Lodging

Best Western-Medical
   Center
111 Holiday Drive
Bristol, TN
(423) 968–1101

Century Square
291 Bethel Drive
Bristol, TN
(423) 968–7084

Comfort Inn
2368 Lee Highway
Bristol, VA
(276) 466–3881

Comfort Suites
3118 Brownsmill Road
Johnson City, TN
(423) 610–0010

Days Inn
536 Volunteer Highway
Bristol, TN
(423) 968–2171

Days Inn
3281 West State Street
Bristol, TN
(423) 968–9119

Econo Lodge
912 Commonwealth
   Avenue
Bristol, VA
(276) 466–2112

Holiday Inn
101 West Springbrook
   Drive
Johnson City, TN
(423) 282–4611

Holiday Inn
3005 Linden Drive
Bristol, VA
(276) 466–4100

Holiday Inn Express
4234 Fort Henry Drive
Kingsport, TN
(423) 239–3400

Howard Johnson Plaza
   Hotel
2406 North Roan Street
Johnson City, TN
(423) 282–2161

La Quinta Inn
1014 Old Airport Road
Bristol, VA
(276) 669–9353

Marriott Meadowview
   Conference Resort and
   Convention Center
1001 Meadowview
   Parkway
Kingsport, TN
(423) 378–0100

Martha Washington Inn
150 West Main Street
Abingdon, VA
(276) 628–3161

Microtel Inn
131 Bristol East Road
Bristol, VA
(276) 669–8164

Motel 6
21561 Clear Creek Road
Bristol, VA
(276) 466–0755

Ramada Inn
2005 LaMasa Drive
Kingsport, TN
(423) 245–0271

Ramada Limited
2606 North Roan Street
Johnson City, TN
(423) 282–4011

Red Carpet Inn
15589 Lee Highway
Bristol, VA
(276) 669–1151

Red Roof Inn
210 Broyles Drive
Johnson City, TN
(423) 282–3040

Regency Inn
975 Volunteer Parkway
Bristol, TN
(423) 968–9474

Super 8
2139 Lee Highway
Bristol, VA
(276) 466–8800

Bristol Area Camping

All American Campground
Bristol Motor Speedway
Bristol, TN
(423) 764–9454

Bristol Campground and
    Event Parking
Tennessee Highway 394
    at Sportsway Drive
Bristol, TN
(423) 341–3022

Century Square
291 Bethel Drive
Bristol, TN
(423) 341–5746

Cochran's Lakeview
    Campground
821 Painter Creek Road
Bristol, TN
(423) 878–8045

Dockside Family
    Campground
725 Painter Creek Road
Bristol, TN
(423) 878–2155

Lake Front Family
    Campground
350 Jones Road
Bristol, TN
(423) 878–6730

Observation Knob Park
337 Knob Park Road
Bristol, TN
(423) 878–1881

Race Camping
155 Essex Drive
Bristol, TN
(800) 541–9169

Shadrack Campground
2537 Volunteer Parkway
Johnson City, TN
(423) 652–0120

Sugar Hollow Park
Lee Highway at I–81
Bristol, VA
(276) 645–7275

Thunder Valley
    Campground
2623 Volunteer Parkway
Johnson City, TN
(423) 652–2267

Twin City Campground
2512 Volunteer Parkway
Johnson City, TN
(423) 968–7083

Lowe's Motor Speedway, still known simply as "Charlotte" among fans and the race teams, is one of the shining stars among NASCAR tracks. It's a first-rate facility, from the luxury condos looming over Turn 1 to the camper-friendly RV areas in the infield. A 1.5-mile quad-oval, the track has become a blueprint for several other similarly configured tracks in Las Vegas, Atlanta, and Texas.

NASCAR may be headquartered in Daytona Beach, Florida, but it is Charlotte, North Carolina, that has become the de facto home of Nextel Cup racing. Most of the drivers live in the area—many have grand homes at nearby Lake Norman—and the majority of the race teams have their headquarters and shops in the area. That means plenty of friends and family in the stands at Charlotte, making these events even more important to the drivers and teams. Everyone wants to win at Charlotte.

Thanks to track president H. A. "Humpy" Wheeler, a weekend or a week at Lowe's Motor Speedway means more than a few hours of racing. Wheeler is one of the sport's real characters—a no-holds-barred showman who always adds a dose of entertainment to the proceedings. Let's face it: Sitting in the sun-drenched stands for three hours waiting for the green flag can be tedious. Not at Charlotte, where you might see a school bus jump rows of cars, a guy with a jetpack taking off in the infield, or a flyover of stealth bombers. The only thing certain: An event at Charlotte won't be boring.

NASCAR's
All-Star Night

May is 600 month in North Carolina. If you're dreaming of a racing vacation make plans for a week at Lowe's Motor Speedway in the spring. The Coca-Cola 600 is the climax of a week's worth of racing at the track kicking off with the all-star race the week before the 600. The Nextel All-Star Challenge is a non-points race, a short dash for cash that can produce some of the most exciting racing of the season.

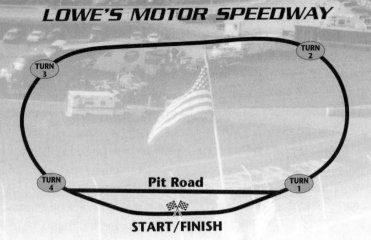

LOWE'S MOTOR SPEEDWAY

TURN 2

TURN 3

TURN 4

Pit Road

TURN 1

🏁 🏁

START/FINISH

Our Ratings	Racing: 🏁 🏁 🏁 🏁 Amenities: 🏁 🏁 🏁 🏁 🏁 Area Appeal: 🏁 🏁 🏁 🏁 🏁
Track Facts	1.5-mile quad-oval Seating capacity: 167,000 5555 Concord Parkway South Concord, NC 28027 (800) 455–3200 www.lowesmotorspeedway.com
Annual Events	Two Nextel Cup Series events, May and October Companion events: Busch Series, May and October; NASCAR Craftsman Truck Series and ARCA Re/Max Series, May
Weather	Average High (F): May 78.3 October 72.0 Average Low (F): May 56.3 October 50.5
Top Gun	Dale Earnhardt, 8 wins
Qualifying Record	Ryan Newman, 186.657 mph

Let's Go Racing

What's a quad-oval, you ask? It's the so-called double-dogleg that gives this track much of its fan appeal—and provides headaches for the drivers. While the 2,000-foot backstretch is straight, the frontstretch is anything but. The two slight turns on the frontstretch require racers to steer in a wide arc, whistling within a couple feet of the concrete barrier. It also provides aggressive drivers an excellent—if risky—passing opportunity.

The pack tends to get strung out at Charlotte, especially during long green-flag runs. Remember, the best race on the track might not be up front. Find the leader, then work your way back through the pack to find the tightest battles for position. Also, watch the leader occasionally to see if he's threatening to put cars a lap down. A lap is very difficult to make up here, so drivers will fight hard to keep the leader behind them.

Both Nextel Cup races here are run at night, under the lights. The 600 in May actually begins in late afternoon, when the track is still hot. Since track temperature is a key factor in setting up a race car, the transition from day to night presents a special challenge to the teams turning the wrenches on these cars. The cars that are fastest during the day might be at the back of the pack after the sun sets.

Joe Nemechek
on Charlotte

"This is a good racetrack for racing side-by-side," says Joe Nemechek. "The low groove works, the high groove works, and there are lots of bumps down in Turns 3 and 4. That can make it exciting. You have to have a very good handling race car to end up going fast here."

Nemechek has won here in the Busch Series and has been a contender in several Nextel Cup races. "It's a tough racetrack. You've got to have a good motor, but the biggest thing is having a car that handles well. You'll start in the daytime and go into the night, so you really have to build a lot of adjustability into your car to go with the track as it changes."

How to Get There

Charlotte is easily accessible via Interstates 77 and 85. From town take I–85 north; from Greensboro take I–85 south. Get off at Speedway Boulevard (exit 49), which will take you to the parking lot. From South Carolina

take I–77 north to I–85 north to Speedway Boulevard. From the Lake Norman area, take I–77 south to Speedway Boulevard East.

If you're flying, Charlotte Douglas International Airport is a major hub for US Airways.

Best Seats in the House

Turn 4 is the action spot at this 1.5-mile track, with a bump complicating things for drivers trying to get their cars straightened out or lined up to make a move for position as they rocket down the frontstretch. A seat in Turn 1 affords a great view of cars negotiating the tricky double-dogleg—nearly brushing the wall coming off Turn 4, then almost clipping the infield grass as they cross under the flag stand. Like at most other tracks, the higher the seats the better the view at Lowe's Motor Speedway. Aim for Row 20 or higher.

Charlotte Memories

In 1978 country music star **Marty Robbins,** a devoted driver for many years, slammed into the concrete wall at 160 mph as he tried to avoid stalled and wrecked cars in front. Robbins was seriously hurt but continued to race for years.

Dale Earnhardt's famed **"Pass in the Grass:"** With a lap to go in the 1991 Winston all-star race, the late Earnhardt straightened out the dogleg by running through the infield grass to get alongside leader **Bill Elliott.** He pulled it off to win the race and add to the Earnhardt legend. That race also featured a battle between Earnhardt and **Geoffrey Bodine.** All three drivers were warned by NASCAR to knock off their roughness, and eventually NASCAR had to call Earnhardt and Bodine to its Daytona Beach offices for a formal warning—a meeting that was portrayed in the movie *Days of Thunder.*

In spring 1993 the Intimidator endured three penalties, including one for rough driving when Earnhardt spun a car on purpose to bring out a caution and keep from going a lap down. NASCAR officials assessed a one-lap penalty. The irate Earnhardt then roared through the field, got the lap back, charged to the front again and won the race, beating rookie **Jeff Gordon.**

Shawna Robinson won here in the Charlotte/Daytona Dash Series in 1988, making her the first woman to win a NASCAR touring series event.

Make It a Vacation

Charlotte is one of the shining capitals of the South, and the surrounding area offers more than enough attractions and diversions.

We recommend spending a week visiting all the race shops in the area. Just minutes from the track is **Hendrick Motorsports** (4400 Papa Joe Hendrick Boulevard, Charlotte; 704–455–3400), the race shop for four-time Winston Cup champion Jeff Gordon and two-time champ Terry Labonte. To the north is **Roush Racing** (122 Knob Hill Road, Mooresville; 704–664–3800), the shop for Mark Martin, Greg Biffle, Kurt Busch, Jeff Burton and Matt Kenseth. Mooresville is also home to **Dale Earnhardt Inc.** (1675 Coddle Creek Road, Mooresville; 704–662–8000), the base for Dale Earnhardt Jr. and Michael Waltrip. The complex doubles as a memorial to the seven-time Winston Cup champion, who died in February 2001 in a last-lap crash during the Daytona 500.

Other race shops include **Joe Gibbs Racing** (13415 Reese Boulevard West, Huntersville; 704–944–5000), with shops for 2002 champion Tony Stewart and 2000 champion Bobby Labonte. **Evernham Motorsports** (160 Munday Road, Statesville; 704–924–9404) is the base for 1988 champion Bill Elliott and Jeremy Mayfield. And no pilgrimage to the racing mecca would be complete without a stop at **Petty Enterprises** (311 Branson Mill Road, Randleman; 336–498–1443). Located about an hour north of Charlotte, it's home to NASCAR's royal family. The museum there not only has most of Richard Petty's 200 trophies for winning NASCAR races and his seven NASCAR championship trophies but also has many of his old familiar red-and-blue racers and other memorabilia collected during the past fifty years.

Away from the Track

Need a break from the sound and fury of the racetrack? Here are some family-friendly getaways within striking distance of Lowe's Motor Speedway.

Try **Discovery Place** (301 North Tryon Street, Charlotte; 704–372–6261). A trip to this hands-on science museum in downtown (they call it Uptown) Charlotte will provide a welcome respite for the kids. **Paramount's Carowinds,** located about fifteen minutes south of Uptown at I–77 exit 90 (800–888–4386), is a super amusement park that has something for everyone, including roller coasters and other thrill rides, a water park, and a variety of entertainment.

Just up the road is the **North Carolina Auto Racing Hall of Fame** (119 Knob Hill Road, Mooresville; 704–663–5331). This combination museum/hall of fame/art gallery/gift shop is dedicated to all motorsports. You'll find Curtis Turner's No. 99, Davey Allison's No. 28 Havoline Ford, and a bevy of street muscle cars. And if you *really* need to get away from the fumes of the racetrack, you might want to spend a relaxing afternoon at **Lake Norman,** the largest man-made lake in the state. It's located about 18 miles northwest of Charlotte and offers golfing, fishing, and boating, as well as accommodations ranging from bed-and-breakfasts to resort hotels. Call the Lake Norman Chamber of Commerce and Visitor and Convention Bureau at (704) 892–1922, or visit www.lakenorman.org.

Where to Eat

Located in the shadows of Lowe's Motor Speedway is **Chris' Pit Board Grille** (5062 State Road 49 South, Harrisburg; 704–455–3944), always a hot spot for race fans. Chris's adds extra servers and cashiers to handle the crowds who come in droves for the cheeseburgers and chocolate milk shakes during race week.

Speaking of burgers, you have to try the Garbage Burger at **Max & Erma's** (8619 J. W. Clay Boulevard, Charlotte; 704–510–1025). It's topped with everything but the kitchen sink. Get the original ten-ouncer or the more demure six-ounce "Erma" version.

If you really want to mingle with the rich and famous, there's the **Speedway Club.** You don't have to be a member to dine in the massive tower overlooking the finish line at the racetrack, but you do have to make a reservation. The club starts taking nonmember calls for October race week in late August at (704) 455–3216. Up for a little spice? Check out the **Cajun Queen** (1800 East Seventh Street, Charlotte; 704–377–9017), where you can sup on crawfish and gumbo while tapping a jazzed-up foot to the Dixieland combo that plays every night.

Where to Stay

Accommodations aren't a problem in Charlotte, the undisputed capital of stock car racing. For affordable lodgings close to the track, try the **Holiday Inn Express** (704–979–7900) just off I–85 in Concord. There are plenty of restaurants nearby, and the manager's been known to throw a barbecue on race weekends.

Also right in Concord is the **Wisteria Bed & Breakfast Inn** (1900 Gold Hill Road; 704–792–1897), a Victorian farmhouse built in 1918 by the Lentz family. Relax on the big wraparound porch or sooth those tired post-qualifying cheek muscles in the Jacuzzi. Wisteria has two rooms with king-size beds, and a full Southern-style breakfast is served in the dining room each morning at 9:00 A.M.

In Charlotte you can make it a romantic race rally at **The Park Hotel** (2200 Rexford Road; 704–364–8220), a member of the Preferred Hotel collection known for its elegance and privacy. It's located across from SouthPark, one of Charlotte's ritziest shopping malls. You'll definitely get chocolate on the pillow of your king-size four-poster bed here. If you want to get a little golf in between race events, try the new **Ballantyne Golf Resort and Spa** (10000 Ballantyne Commons Parkway; 704–248–4000), on the Interstate 485 side of Charlotte. In addition to its own eighteen-hole course and PGA pro, it's got great tennis facilities and a terrific full-service spa.

Concord/Charlotte Area Restaurants

Alabama Grill	Amalfi Pasta 'N Pizza	Applebee's
8341 Concord Mills	8542 University City	8700 J. W. Clay Boulevard
Boulevard	Boulevard	Charlotte, NC
Concord, NC	Concord, NC	(704) 548–9219
(704) 979–7000	(704) 547–8651	

Applebee's
1240 Concord Parkway
    North
Concord, NC
(704) 795–6005

Bob Evans
7791 Gateway Lane
    Northwest
Concord, NC
(704) 979–8080

Cajun Queen
1800 East Seventh Street
Charlotte, NC
(704) 377–9017

Chili's
500 University City
    Boulevard
Charlotte, NC
(704) 510–0626

Chris' Pit Board Grille
5062 State Road 49 South
Harrisburg, NC
(704) 455–3944

Cracker Barrel
1175 Copperfield
    Boulevard Northeast
Concord, NC
(704) 792–0277

El Cancun
1225 Concord Parkway
    North
Concord, NC
(704) 786–8505

Hereford Barn Steak House
4320 Graham Street
Charlotte, NC
(704) 596–0854

Hops
729 McCullough Drive
Charlotte, NC
(704) 549–1585

Houlihan's
8760 J.M. Keynes Drive
Charlotte, NC
(704) 503–5512

The Italian Oven
1215 Concord Parkway
    North
Concord, NC
(704) 795–6836

Jillian's Entertainment
8361 Concord Mills
    Boulevard
Concord, NC
(704) 979–1700

Katubo Japanese Steak
    House
1001 East W. T. Harris
    Boulevard
Charlotte, NC
(704) 548–1219

Longhorn Steakhouse
351 Copperfield
    Boulevard Northeast
Concord, NC
(704) 795–1030

Luigi's Village
1704 Harris Houston Road
Charlotte, NC
(704) 547–1104

Max and Erma's
8619 J. W. Clay Boulevard
Charlotte, NC
(704) 510–1025

On the Border
8001 Concord Mills
    Boulevard
Concord, NC
(704) 979–9029

Outback Steakhouse
1015 Chancellor Park Drive
Charlotte, NC
(704) 598–7727

R&R Barbeque
5249 State Road 49
    South
Harrisburg, NC
(704) 455–9113

Razzoos Cajun Grill
8011 Concord Mills
    Boulevard
Concord, NC
(704) 979–0222

The Speedway Club
5555 Concord Parkway
    South
Smith Tower, Sixth Floor
Concord, NC
(704) 455–3216

Stock Car Cafe
20936 Torrence Chapel
    Road
Cornelius, NC
(704) 895–1003

Texas Roadhouse
7801 Gateway Lane
Concord, NC
(704) 979–3090

Texas Steakhouse &
    Saloon
290 Copperfield Boulevard
    Northeast
Concord, NC
(704) 792–1567

TGI Friday's
8041 Concord Mills
  Boulevard
Concord, NC
(704) 979–3043

TGI Friday's
409 West W. T. Harris
  Boulevard
Charlotte, NC
(704) 548–8113

Uno
8021 Concord Mills
  Boulevard
Concord, NC
(704) 979–0140

Concord/Charlotte Area Lodging

Adam's Mark
555 South McDowell
  Street
Charlotte, NC
(704) 372–4100

Ballantyne Golf Resort
  and Spa
10000 Ballantyne Com-
  mons Parkway
Charlotte, NC
(704) 248–4000

Brookwood Inn
1200 South Sugar Creek
  Road
Charlotte, NC
(704) 597–8500

Candlewood Suites
8812 University East Drive
Charlotte, NC
(704) 598–9863

Comfort Inn
3100 Cloverleaf Parkway
Concord, NC
(704) 786–3100

Comfort Suites UNCC
7735 University Boulevard
Charlotte, NC
(704) 547–0049

Days Inn Concord
5125 Davidson Highway
Concord, NC
(704) 786–9121

Doubletree Guest Suites
  SouthPark
6300 Morrison Boulevard
Charlotte, NC
(704) 364–2400

Drury Inn and Suites
415 W. T. Harris Boulevard
Charlotte, NC
(704) 593–0700

Four Points by Sheraton
201 South McDowell
  Street
Charlotte, NC
(704) 372–7550

Hampton Inn Charlotte
8419 North Tryon Street
Charlotte, NC
(704) 548–0905

Hampton Inn Concord
612 Dickens Place North-
  east
Concord, NC
(704) 793–9700

Hampton Inn and Suites
Speedway Boulevard and
  I–85
Concord, NC
(704) 979–5600

Hawthorn Suites
7800 Gateway Lane
  Northwest
Concord, NC
(704) 979–3800

Hilton Charlotte and
  Towers
222 East Third Street
Charlotte, NC
(704) 377–1500

Hilton Charlotte at University Place
8629 J. M. Keynes Drive
Charlotte, NC
(704) 547–7444

HoJo Inn by Howard
  Johnson
I–77 at Sunset Road
Charlotte, NC
(704) 598–7710

Holiday Inn Charlotte–City
  Center
230 North College Street
Charlotte, NC
(704) 335–5400

Holiday Inn Executive Park
8520 University Executive
    Park
Charlotte, NC
(704) 547–0999

Holiday Inn Express
1601 Concord Parkway
    North
Concord, NC
(704) 786–5181

Holiday Inn Express
7772 North Gateway Lane
    Northwest
Concord, NC
(704) 979–7900

Marriott City Center
100 West Trade Street
Charlotte, NC
(704) 333–9000

Marriott Executive Park
5700 Westpark Drive
Charlotte, NC
(704) 527–9650

Omni
132 East Trade Street
Charlotte, NC
(704) 377–0400

The Park Hotel
2200 Rexford Road
Charlotte, NC
(704) 364–8220

Sleep Inn
7821 Gateway Lane
Concord, NC
(704) 979–8800

Sleep Inn
8525 North Tryon Street
Charlotte, NC
(704) 549–4544

Sleep Inn
1120 Copperfield Boule-
    vard
Concord, NC
(704) 788–2150

SpringHill Suites by
    Marriott
8700 Research Drive
Charlotte, NC
(704) 503–4800

SpringHill Suites by
    Marriott
7811 Gateway Lane
Concord, NC
(704) 979–2500

Villager Lodge
State Road 16 and I–85
Charlotte, NC
(704) 393–8887

The Westin
601 South College Street
Charlotte, NC
(704) 375–2600

Wingate Inn
7841 Gateway Lane
    Northwest
Concord, NC
(704) 979–1300

Wisteria Bed & Breakfast
    Inn
1900 Gold Hill Road
Concord, NC
(704) 792–1897

Concord/Charlotte Area Camping

Charlotte/Fort Mill KOA
940 Gold Hill Road
Fort Mill, SC
(888) 562–4430

Fleetwood RV Racing
    Resort
6550 Speedway Boulevard
Concord, NC
(704) 455–4445

Statesville KOA
162 KOA Lane
Statesville, NC
(888) 562–5705

North Carolina Speedway:
The Rock

They call this place The Rock not just because it's short for Rockingham. The North Carolina Speedway, located in the Sandhills region of the state, is one tough racetrack. Rockingham is fast, unforgiving, and famous for wearing down drivers and equipment alike. The Rock traditionally hosts the second race on the NASCAR tour, giving teams a welcome respite from the pressure cooker of Daytona and a chance to just go racing. NASCAR stripped The Rock of its fall date, moving it to the Darlington Raceway 90 miles away. Having just one race here is a shame, since this place often serves up some of the best racing on the circuit.

Let's Go Racing

Measuring a tick over 1 mile, Rockingham stages some of the most competitive racing on the Nextel Cup circuit. Because there is more than one racing groove, drivers can run high, low, or in the middle—whichever lane suits their driving style and their car setup. The result is lots of side-by-side racing, with cars fighting door-to-door for several laps.

This speedway eats tires, forcing race teams to make strategic decisions that often win or lose the race. Fresh tires make a car tremendously faster than a competitor on worn tires, so the crews are constantly assessing when to pit, when to stay out, and when to take new tires. Exciting racing and critical pit decisions combine to make The Rock a touchstone of NASCAR racing.

Radio headphones tuned to the race broadcast will really help you enjoy a race at The Rock. Cars will try different pit stop strategies, which sometimes leaves the field jumbled with lapped cars—and some of the fastest cars trying to catch up after pitting for new tires. Better yet, bring a scanner to listen to the crew chiefs and drivers debate when to pit and what to do when they stop.

How to Get There

From Charlotte take North Carolina Highway 74 east to U.S. Highway 1 north in Rockingham. The track is 10 miles north on the right. From Raleigh take US 1 south. The track is on the left. From Greensboro take U.S. Highway 220 to NC 74 east to US 1 North at Rockingham. The track is 10 miles north on the right.

NORTH CAROLINA SPEEDWAY

Our Ratings

Racing: 🏁 🏁 🏁 🏁

Amenities: 🏁 🏁

Area Appeal: 🏁 🏁

Track Facts

1.0-mile oval

Seating capacity: 60,113

P.O. Box 500

Rockingham, NC 28380

(910) 582–2861

www.northcarolinaspeedway.com

Annual Events

One 400-mile Nextel Cup Series race, February

Companion events: Busch Grand National, February

Weather

Average High (F):   February 58.0

Average Low (F):   February 31.3

Top Gun

Richard Petty, 11 wins

Qualifying Record

Rusty Wallace, 158.035 mph

Best Seats in the House

For an excellent preview of the views from any seat at the speedway, visit the track's official Web site at www.northcarolinaspeedway.com and check out the 3-D interactive map. It works beautifully, panning left and right so that you can see exactly what you'll see from each section in the grandstands.

Our favorite seats are in Sections 37–47, where you'll have a great look at the cars negotiating the dogleg on the frontstretch and get into position as they slam into Turn 1. The grandstand on the backstretch is another good bet. The track really narrows up coming out of Turn 2; here you can watch the drivers working the wheel, trying to keep their cars from brushing the wall as they rocket down the backstretch.

Johnny Benson on Rockingham

"Rockingham is one of the best strategy shows for the fans," says Johnny Benson. "That's because of the importance of new tires and how they change your lap times. If you have new tires, you are a few seconds faster than a car still on the track with old tires. During the race you have to decide whether you want to risk pitting and falling down a lap or two or getting new tires and going a lot faster on the track.

"If you're leading the race and I pit for new tires ten laps before you do, I will be way ahead of you after you stop. But if the yellow falls between the time I stop and the time you stop, I will be one or two laps down. That's the gamble crew chiefs take there, and that's what the fans can always watch.

"Also, you will see something weird at Rockingham. I was leading the race there last year and had three cars pass me in the final laps because they had come in and got new tires. Now they were down a lap or two, but it was still tricky having them pass you. That doesn't happen too often.

"Winning my first Winston Cup race in the Valvoline Pontiac is my best memory of Rockingham. Second would be when we clinched the Busch title there in 1995. I think I broke there in 1998 on a day when I thought we could win the race. That might be my worst memory there."

Rockingham Memories

Curtis Turner, driving a Ford, won the first race here in 1965. **Ward Burton** took home his first Winston Cup race at The Rock, winning the fall 1995 race by 1.9 seconds. **Mark Martin** picked up his first win here in 1989. And **Johnny Benson** also won his first race at The Rock in 2002.

Make It a Vacation

The pastoral serenity of a golf course seems light years away from the thunder of a racetrack, but the **Pinehurst area,** just 30 miles from The Rock, offers some of the best golfing in the world. Contact the Pinehurst Visitors and Convention Bureau at (910) 692–3330 or visit www.homeofgolf.com.

The **Pinehurst Resort,** home of the world-famous Pinehurst No. 2, usually offers a package for golfers attending races at North Carolina Speedway. For the nonhackers the resort's spa is well above par. Call Pinehurst reservations at (800) 487–4653 and just mention NASCAR.

Away from the Track

Need a break from the sound and fury of the racetrack? Here are some family-friendly getaways within striking distance of North Carolina Speedway.

Especially popular with NASCAR fans is the **Richard Petty Museum** (311 Branson Hill Road, Randleman, North Carolina; 336–495–1143). **North Carolina Zoological Park** (4401 Zoo Parkway, Asheboro, North Carolina; 336–879–7000) is one of the best zoos you'll find anywhere.

Seagrove Potteries (Interstate 73 at US 220, exit 45), about 45 miles from the speedway on US 220, is home to the largest community of potters (outside Japan) in the world. Salt glazes, face jugs, animals, and decorative and art pottery are all hand-crafted in this village, settled by potters in the mid-eighteenth century.

Where to Eat

Everybody likes Mexican food, and Rockingham has its own version of an "authentic casa" in **Mi Casita Restaurante Mexicano** (1201 East Broad Street; 910–895–2222). It's one of seven in the small chain of Mi Casitas located in and around the Fayetteville area. Rockingham also boasts more than its fair share of the usual chains—steakhouses, fast-food joints, seafood places, and pseudo-Italian, so no one will go hungry.

In nearby Pinehurst **Dugans Pub** (2 Market Square; 910–295–3400) features a nautical decor to go with its selection of seafood, mainly from Carolina coastal waters, as decidedly non-publike entrees. Dugans also has live music on Friday and Saturday nights.

The best-kept secret in the Sandhills area? A lot of the "private" golf-haven country clubs open their dining room doors to nonmembers. The **Lakeview Dining Room** (Woodlake Boulevard; 910–245–4031) at Woodlake Country Club in Vass, North Carolina, has outside terraces offering casual and fine dining with—you guessed it—panoramic lake views. And the locals don't want you to discover the **Dunes Table Restaurant** (2115 Midland Road; 910–295–3240) at Midland Country Club, where seafood is the specialty.

AMTRAK
to the Track

Dreading the drive? Leave the car keys at home and let Amtrak drop you off at the station right across from North Carolina Speedway. The Rockingham Race Special runs nonstop from Raleigh. Call the speedway at (910) 582-2861, and ask about a Race and Rail package.

Where to Stay

For those who do the "train to the track" from the Raleigh-Durham area, the **Holiday Inn—Brownstone Hotel** (2424 Erwin Road, Durham; 919–286–7761) has a special rate of less than $100 a night, including transportation from the Amtrak station and back after the race. If you opt to stay in the lovely village of Pinehurst, the **Pine Crest Inn** (50 Dogwood Road; 910–295–6121) offers a wonderful option. Rates include breakfast and dinner for two, and the locals say the dining is just like coming home to Sunday dinner all the time. Another great golf combo can be had at the elegant **Knollwood House** (1495 West Connecticut Avenue; 910–692–9390) in nearby Southern Pines, North Carolina, which sits within glimpsing distance of the famous Donald Ross course at Mid-Pines. The Knollwood House golf package includes lodging in one of four suites with bath, greens fees, guaranteed tee times, swimming and tennis, and a full gourmet breakfast and dinner at your choice of nine top area restaurants.

Rockingham Area Restaurants

Applebee's
1403 Sandhills Boulevard
Aberdeen, NC
(910) 944–7422

The Barn
305 Rothney Avenue
Southern Pines, NC
(910) 692–7700

Becky's at Richmond
     Pines Country Club
US 1 North
Rockingham, NC
(910) 895–0207

Beefeaters
672 Southwest Broad
     Street
Southern Pines, NC
(910) 692–5550

Dugans Pub
2 Market Square
Pinehurst, NC
(910) 295–3400

Ellerbe Springs Inn
US 220 North
Ellerbe, NC
(910) 652–5600

Golden Corral
905 East Broad Avenue
Rockingham, NC
(910) 895–2023

Golden Corral
1859 U.S. Highway
15–501
Southern Pines, NC
(910) 695–9023

Holiday Restaurant
414 South Hancock Street
Rockingham, NC
(910) 895–2315

John's Barbeque
1910 US 15–501
Southern Pines, NC
(910) 692–9474

Little Bo Steakhouse
127 Little Bo Lane
Rockingham, NC
(910) 997–2171

Lob-Steer Inn
US 1 North
Southern Pines, NC
(910) 692–3503

Mi Casita Restaurante
Mexicano
1201 East Broad Avenue
Southern Pines, NC
(910) 895–2222

Peking Wok
1788 East Broad Avenue
Southern Pines, NC
(910) 895–8889

Raffaele's Restaurant
1550 US 1 South
Southern Pines, NC
(910) 692–1952

Ragazzi's
1640 US 1 South
Southern Pines, NC
(910) 692–4626

Rockingham Fish Camp
and Steak
532 East Broad Avenue
Rockingham, NC
(910) 997–4006

Seaboard Station
Restaurant
12 Charlotte Street
Hamlet, NC
(910) 582–1017

Theos Taverna
140 Chinquapin Road
Pinehurst, NC
(910) 295–0780

Vito's Ristorante
615 Southeast Broad
Street
Southern Pines, NC
(910) 692–7815

Rockingham Area Lodging

The Carolina
Carolina Vista Drive
Pinehurst, NC
(910) 295–6811

Condotels
305 North Page Road
Pinehurst, NC
(800) 272–8588

Comfort Inn
9801 US 15–501
Southern Pines, NC
(910) 215–5500

Comfort Suites
307 Green Street
Rockingham, NC
(910) 410–0077

Days Inn
408 West Broad Avenue
Rockingham, NC
(910) 895–1144

Hampton Inn
1675 US 1 North
Southern Pines, NC
(910) 692–9266

Holiday Inn—Brownstone
  Hotel
2424 Erwin Road
Durham, NC
(919) 286–7761

Holiday Inn Express
400 West Broad Avenue
Rockingham, NC
(910) 895–0099

Homewood Suites
250 Central Park Avenue
Pinehurst, NC
(910) 255–0300

Knollwood House
1495 West Connecticut
  Avenue
Southern Pines, NC
(910) 692–9390

Magnolia Inn
65 Magnolia Avenue
Pinehurst, NC
(800) 526–5562

Pine Crest Inn
50 Dogwood Road
Pinehurst, NC
(910) 295–6121

Pinehurst Resort
Carolina Vista Drive
Pinehurst, NC
(800) 487–4653

Regal Inn
130 West Broad Street
Rockingham, NC
(910) 997–3336

Regency Inn
710 Market Street
Cheraw, SC
(843) 537–2101

Residence Inn
105 Brucewood Road
Southern Pines, NC
(910) 693–3400

Royal Plaza
114 West Broad Street
Rockingham, NC
(910) 997–6636

Rockingham Area Camping

Heritage Camping and
  Recreation
353 Sadler Family Road
Carthage, NC
(910) 949–3433

Pinehurst RV Resort
288 Campground Road
Pinehurst, NC
(910) 295–5452

Racetrack Campground
490 Fox Road
Hamlet, NC
(910) 582–4673

Darlington Raceway:
Too Tough to Tame

Darlington. The very name conjures up ghosts of NASCAR's past. If NASCAR has a historical touchstone, Darlington is it. It's the circuit's oldest speedway, where Johnny Mantz won the inaugural Southern 500 in 1950. Darlington isn't sexy, it isn't new, it doesn't have cushy condos or skyboxes—but the place is steeped in history and serves up thrilling and unique racing.

What Darlington has is mystique—and the trickiest track to negotiate on the circuit. Drivers consider races here—particularly November's Southern 500—among the top prizes in the sport.

Sure, Darlington and the surrounding area don't have the lure of NASCAR's glamour tracks, but that's part of its charm. This track deserves a top spot on any fan's list of races to attend. And with NASCAR moving up to bigger markets, it's one of the last venues—a lot like baseball's Wrigley Field or Fenway Park—where you can still enjoy tradition along with the competition.

Let's Go Racing

Unlike the other ovals on the Nextel Cup circuit, Darlington isn't symmetrical. Builder Harold Brasington had to design the track around a minnow pond and allow for an adjacent tract of land whose owner wouldn't sell. The result: The radius of Turns 3 and 4 is tighter than Turns 1 and 2, giving the speedway an egg shape and making it a setup nightmare and wicked-tough for drivers to negotiate.

It's a frighteningly narrow racetrack, with a rough surface that chews up tires and makes pit strategy critical. But Darlington is a driver's track; only the most talented, smoothest racers win here. Some of them hate the place, but every stock car driver wants to put a Darlington win on his résumé. The track is so unforgiving that years ago, Darlington rookies— including the legendary A. J. Foyt—had to run test laps under the watchful eyes of veterans.

Simply put, Darlington Raceway wasn't built for today's speeds. A 170-plus mph qualifying lap at Darlington is a white-knuckle thrill ride. The track itself is extremely narrow, and the racing groove is even tighter. The fast line forces drivers to climb within inches of the outside wall in Turns 1 and 2. It's

DARLINGTON RACEWAY

Our Ratings	Racing: 🏁 🏁 🏁 🏁 🏁 Amenities: 🏁 🏁 🏁 Area Appeal: 🏁 🏁
Track Facts	1.366-mile egg-shaped oval Seating capacity: 65,000 P.O. Box 500 Darlington, SC 29540 (843) 395–8499 www.darlingtonraceway.com
Annual Events	Two NASCAR Nextel Cup races, March and November Companion events: Busch Series, March and November; NASCAR Craftsman Truck Series, March
Weather	Average High (F): March 67.3 November 67.0 Average Low (F): March 43.7 November 44.0
Top Gun	David Pearson, 10 wins
Qualifying Record	Ward Burton, 173.797 mph

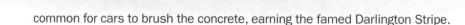

common for cars to brush the concrete, earning the famed Darlington Stripe.

As soon as the green flag falls, look for cars to try to get into line quickly. The first few laps at Darlington are some of the most exciting racing in the world as the drivers shuffle and maneuver to get to the inside. As the rubber is worn off the tires and the handling characteristics of the cars change, look for drivers to move around the track, high and low, hunting for a groove. Some will hug the concrete wall, while others will stick to the bottom of the track through the corners.

At various stages of a 400- or 500-mile race here, the leader will often pull far away from the pack. Don't get fixated on the leader when he's way out front by himself. Visually work your way back through the field to find hot battles and fast cars moving up through the field. As crews adjust their cars during pit stops, the best teams will start pushing toward the front.

The Southern 500 is the oldest—and most-revered—superspeedway race in NASCAR history. But after fifty-three years of enjoying a Labor Day weekend date, the sanctioning body decided to move the Labor Day weekend race to the California Speedway and shift the Southern 500 to a November date that used to belong to a race at the North Carolina Speedway.

How to Get There

From north or south: Take Interstate 95 (exit 164), and then take South Carolina Highway 52 (toward Darlington) to the SC 52 Bypass to South Carolina Highway 151/34. From east or west take Interstate 20 (exit 131) to South Carolina Highway 401 north to SC 151/34.

Best Seats in the House

Most fans assume the best seats are at the start/finish line, but that's not always the case. At Darlington the treacherous turns are where the action is. The first sections of the Pearson Tower—A, B, C—will give you a thrilling view of treacherous Turn 4 and a good shot of the pack as the cars accelerate onto the frontstretch on the way to the line. Also consider the Brasington Grandstand in Turn 2, where the cars often brush up—or worse—against the concrete wall. The tower seats are worth the money; otherwise your backstretch view will be blocked by the infield.

Joe Nemechek
on Darlington

"Probably the best spot to watch the race is around the Turn 4 area," says Joe Nemechek. "We run right up by the wall on both ends, but Turns 3 and 4 are where most of the passing ends up going on, because the high lane is the preferred lane and if you're going to pass, you've got to get a run underneath somebody. It's very competitive at Darlington. The track really wears the tires out. It makes for some pretty good racing."

Nemechek has come frustratingly close to a Darlington win, and, like most other drivers, a victory at the speedway known as "The Lady in Black" is at the top of his racing wish list. "I've come close to winning in the Busch Series a few times. In 1998 or 1999 we started midpack and took the lead by the first pit stop in the Winston Cup race. We ran really well all day, but the race got rain-shortened and we ended up finishing sixth. It was disappointing, but we showed that we had one of the best cars on the track that day."

Darlington Memories

Hollywood stuntman **Johnny Mantz** won the inaugural Southern 500, averaging a speedy 76 mph to outlast faster competitors in a six-hour marathon. Mantz, who never won another big-time stock car race, started in the back of the field in a six-cylinder Plymouth and beat seventy-four other cars—including Cadillacs and Lincolns—to the checkered flag.

In 1965's Southern 500, South Carolina hard-charging driver **Cale Yarborough**'s car tangled with another car in Turn 1, and he sailed over the wall into the parking lot. A few minutes later Yarborough climbed over the guardrail, unhurt and waving to the fans.

"Million Dollar Bill" Elliott made NASCAR history here in 1985 when he won the race to become the first driver to win the Winston Million—then a shocking amount of money that put the sport on the front pages of newspapers all across the country.

In April 2003 **Ricky Craven** and **Kurt Busch** slammed against each other repeatedly in a stirring run to the checkered flag, for one of the closest finishes in NASCAR history. Craven won the photo finish by less than 5 inches.

Make It a Vacation

The town of Darlington isn't exactly a top tourist destination on its own, but one of the most famous beach towns in the country, **Myrtle Beach,** is only 80 miles away. Attending a Darlington race is a great opportunity to combine your race experience with a week or two at the ocean. Myrtle Beach offers great beaches, nightlife, entertainment—and some of the best golfing around. Come to think of it, there's a pretty fair half-mile racetrack in Myrtle Beach, too. Contact the Myrtle Beach Area Chamber of Commerce at (800) 356–3016 or www.mbchamber.com.

Away from the Track

Need a break from the sound and fury of the racetrack? Here are some family-friendly getaways within striking distance of Darlington Speedway.

The National Motorsports Press Association **Stock Car Hall of Fame** and the **Joe Weatherly Museum** (1301 SC 151/34, Darlington; 843–395–8821) are located directly adjacent to Darlington Raceway. Here you'll find the 1950 Plymouth that Johnny Mantz drove to victory in the first Southern 500, along with many other historic stock cars in the Weatherly Museum. Both are open 8:30 A.M. to 5:00 P.M. daily.

For some local history, check out the **Darlington County Historical Museum** (204 Hewitt Street, Darlington; 843–398–4710), where you'll find early photos, historical items and genealogical materials. The museum is open Monday through Friday; free admission.

If you need some quiet time, try **Williamson Park,** off Spring Street in Darlington. It overlooks the historic city of Lancaster, with views across **Morecambe Bay** to the **Lakeland Fells.** The fifty-four acres of parkland can be explored by woodland walkways and broad avenues of attractive trees, shrubs, and flowers, with several resting places to sit and enjoy the peaceful atmosphere.

Where to Eat

In Darlington you should sit for a spell at **Jewel's Deluxe Restaurant** (32 Public Square; 843–393–5511) and enjoy the local home-style country cooking. Most of the other dining options are in nearby Florence, and you simply can't leave the state without sampling the local take on barbecue at **Roger's** (2004 Second Loop Road; 843–667–9291). For big appetites check out the country buffet at the **Thunderbird Inn,** also in Florence (2004 West Lucas Street; 843–669–1611). For formal dining, the clear choice is **P.A.'s Restaurant** (1534 South Irby Street, Florence; 843–665–0846). For a great breakfast anytime, stop by **Venus Pancake House** (471 West Palmetto Street, Florence; 843–669–9977). And if you're in the mood for some nightlife, put on your dancing shoes and head for **Club 231** (231 South Irby Street, Florence; 843–664–0231).

Where to Stay

Most fans find rooms in Florence, South Carolina, about 10 miles from the track. Rooms are scarce during race week, so make your reservations well in advance. The **Holiday Inn** (843–665–4555) at exit 164 off I–95 has a nice pool, and past guests have lauded it for its—believe it or not—"Southern hospitality and personal service."

Want a budget motel with a swimming pool, a complimentary full breakfast buffet, and a fitness room for about $40 a night? Then the **Country Hearth Inn and Suites** (831 South Irby Street, Florence; 800–558–7023) is for you. And the drive might be worth it for the **South of the**

One for
A Million

When Bill Elliott arrived at Darlington Raceway in 1985 for the Southern 500, he had armed guards provided by the South Carolina Highway Patrol. The area around his Ford was roped off with crime scene tape; cameramen and reporters were told to stay away.

For a humble North Georgia mountainman whose father built a small fortune by selling supplies to build chicken coops around their Dawsonville home, it was a bit overwhelming. His Huckleberry Finn demeanor seemed misplaced among the white-hot spotlight of a curious public that was compelled by a storyline that a man could win $1 million in a single afternoon.

The R. J. Reynolds Tobacco Company wanted to spice up the NASCAR circuit by offering $1 million to any driver who could win any three of the sport's Big Four events—the Daytona 500, Winston 500, World 600, or the Southern

500. Racing was making small inroads into television, but it needed something extra—a jumpstart if you will—to distinguish it from football, baseball, basketball, and hockey. Back in 1985, $1 million got everyone's attention.

Elliott won the Daytona 500 and came back nearly three months later in one of the most stirring comebacks in racing history to win the Winston 500. A broken oil line put him nearly two full laps down early in the race at the 2.66-mile Talladega Superspeedway, but he rallied back. It took him most of the afternoon, but he chipped 10 yards, then 20, then 30 yards or more a lap off Cale Yarborough's lead until he erased the entire 5-mile deficit. On that day he became Awesome Bill from Dawsonville.

With two down and one of two to go, the interest in the Winston Million program suddenly hit full stride at the World 600

near Charlotte, North Carolina. National media outlets, many unaccustomed to the passionate and unrefined nature of stock car racing, were on board for that race. Elliott won the pole position—one of eleven poles he won that year—but he had troubles that dropped him twenty-one laps off the pace and to an eighteenth-place finish.

That left Darlington as Elliott's last hope. And the games began.

"It wasn't really my idea," Elliott says of the police escort throughout the entire racing weekend. "I think they just did it more for the PR side of it. We had a pretty good plan when we came into [Darlington]. When we went to Charlotte, it was so unorganized and so many things were going on that it was hard to deal with. At that time I was more like a crew chief *and* a driver; I couldn't deal with everything. I was trying to think about what I wanted to do carwise, and everybody else had other opinions. But by the time we got [to Darlington], we had a plan. I didn't think the patrolmen were needed. The way we ended up setting up press conferences and things like that, it worked out fine."

And it got even better when Elliott won the race. Not only did he bring NASCAR into America's living room that afternoon, he earned yet another nickname: "Million Dollar Bill."

"I don't even believe I was thinking about the million dollars at the time," Elliott says. "Your main goal is to beat the competition, and all I was thinking about was how I was going to continue to stay ahead of the competition. Cale was very strong that day. He probably should have won the race. I remember [it] very well. [Dale] Earnhardt was good that day. [Harry] Gant was good that day. They all had problems. When you're in a race car, you concentrate on what's happening at that second. You don't think beyond it, and you don't think behind it."

NASCAR now hands out million-dollar checks like penny candy. The sport has evolved from its dusty backwoods past into prime-time slots on network television. A major step toward that evolution was the day Bill Elliott became the first driver to earn $1 million in a single season. Shoot, he earned it in a single day.

And the money's been piling up since.

Border Motor Hotel (I–95 and U.S. Highway 301, Dillon; 800–845–6011) if you don't mind staying about fifty minutes north of the track. South of the Border is a 370-acre theme park–like complex of schlocky Mexi-glitz just barely south of the North Carolina–South Carolina line. It defies description, except on the SOB billboards that blanket 99 miles of I–95 around Dillon, South Carolina, but trust me, the kids will die of sheer joy if you stay there.

In Florence you can try any one of the various hotel chains located at the I–95 and U.S. Highway 52 exit or one exit south at I–20/Business 20.

Fans coming from Atlanta and Augusta, Georgia, may want to consider staying in Columbia, South Carolina. There are plenty of hotel rooms there—in November plan in advance to make sure you don't conflict with University of South Carolina home football games—and it's only an hour's drive to the speedway.

Darlington Area Restaurants

Cromers Pizza
103 Pearl Street
Darlington, SC
(843) 393–3626

Don Jose
2020 West Palmetto
    Street
Florence, SC
(843) 673–6988

Juan Jose
1316 South Irby Street
Florence, SC
(843) 665–0866

Jewel's Deluxe Restaurant
32 Public Square
Darlington, SC
(843) 393–5511

Joe's Grill
306 Russell Street
Darlington, SC
(843) 393–9140

Michael's Italian
1937 Second Loop Road
Florence, SC
(843) 669–3771

P.A.'s Restaurant
1534 South Irby Street
Florence, SC
(843) 665–0846

Percy's and Willy's
2401 David McLeod
    Boulevard
Florence, SC
(843) 669–1620

Raceway Grill
SC 151/34
Darlington, SC
(843) 393–9212

Red Bone Alley
1903 West Palmetto
Florence, SC
(843) 673–0035

Roger's
2004 Second Loop Road
Florence, SC
(843) 667–9291

Takis
639 Pearl Street
Darlington, SC
(843) 393–8979

Town House Restaurant
317 South Irby Street
Florence, SC
(843) 669–5083

Venus Pancake House
471 West Palmetto Street
Florence, SC
(843) 669–9977

Victor's European Bistro
829 South Irby Street
Florence, SC
(843) 662–6311

Darlington Area Lodging

Best Western
1808 West Lucas Street
Florence, SC
(843) 678–9292

Country Hearth Inn and
    Suites
831 South Irby Street
Florence, SC
(800) 558–7023

Country Inn and Suites
I–95 and US 52
Florence, SC
(843) 317–6616

Courtyard by Marriott
2680 Hospitality Boulevard
Florence, SC
(843) 662–7066

Days Inn
I–95 and US 76
Florence, SC
(843) 665–8550

Days Inn
I–95 and US 52
Florence, SC
(843) 665–4444

Econo Lodge
1811 West Lucas Street
Florence, SC
(843) 665–8558

Fairfield Inn
140 Dunbarton Drive
Florence, SC
(843) 669–1666

Hampton Inn
1826 West Lucas Street
Florence, SC
(843) 662–7000

Hampton Inn Suites
3000 West Radio Drive
Florence, SC
(843) 629–9900

Holiday Inn
1819 West Lucas Street
Florence, SC
(843) 665–4555

Holiday Inn Express
150 Dunbarton Road
Florence, SC
(843) 664–2400

Howard Johnson's
I–95 and US 52
Florence, SC
(843) 669–1921

Motel 6
1834 West Lucas Street
Florence, SC
(843) 667–6100

Ramada Inn
2038 West Lucas Street
Florence, SC
(843) 669–4241

Red Roof Inn
2690 McLeod Boulevard
Florence, SC
(843) 678–9000

Rodeway Inn
3024 T.V. Road
Florence, SC
(843) 669–1715

Sleep Inn
1833 Florence Park Drive
Florence, SC
(843) 662–8558

South of the Border Motor
    Hotel
I–95 and US 301
Dillon, SC
(800) 845–6011

Super 8
1832 West Lucas Street
Florence, SC
(843) 661–7269

Thunderbird Inn
2004 West Lucas Street
Florence, SC
(843) 669–1611

Wingate Hotel
I–95 and US 52
Florence, SC
(843) 629–1111

Darlington Area Camping

KOA-Florence
1115 East Campground
    Road
Florence, SC
(843) 665–7007

Swamp Fox Camping
1600 Gateway Road
Florence, SC
(843) 665–9430

End of
An Era

Hamburger steaks and hand-cut fries will be served as always at the Raceway Grill during Labor Day weekend, but everyone around here admits they won't taste the same.

The restaurant, as much a fixture on the old NASCAR Winston Cup Series as the fabled Darlington Raceway next door, has prepared meals for locals and race teams since before any of the current drivers on the Nextel Cup Series were born. Since 1950 hamburger steaks and the Southern 500 have been a Labor Day ritual at Darlington, a tradition so steeped in storied reverence that it seemed to be immune to the whirlwind changes in the sport.

Until now.

The power of television—and its billion dollars' worth of clout—lured NASCAR to abandon the cornerstone of Darlington's racing season. The sport now spends Labor Day weekend under the lights at the California Speedway. While Darlington Raceway says it will keep the Southern 500 name at its new mid-November slot in the schedule, everybody agrees the aura is lost forever.

"At least for a few years, a lot of hearts will be at Darlington that (Labor Day) weekend," says Kyle Petty, who has spent every Labor Day weekend of his life at the speedway. "Things change, though. Sometimes it's for the good, sometimes not. But things change all the time."

International Speedway Corporation, which owns eleven speedways on the Nextel Cup Series schedule, including Darlington, California, and the North Carolina Speedway, stripped North Carolina of one of its two racing dates and moved it to California. California got Darlington's Labor Day weekend date—largely because Los Angeles doesn't have a National Football League team—and Darlington gained North Carolina's old date. Darlington insists it still has the Southern 500. But the new date is too much of a change for a sport that had so few traditions remaining.

For drivers like Petty and Dale Jarrett, the Labor Day weekend tradition had even more meaning—they grew up watching their fathers race before them.

"Knowing the history of this sport and being there with my dad when he won there in '65, yeah, this is the one on my résumé that is not there right now that I'd like to have," Jarrett says.

"I learned to play football there," Petty says of the games children used to play in the infield.

California added lights and plans to hold the Labor Day race during prime time. Darlington, which has struggled to fill its 65,000 seats for years, is also adding lights, with hopes of moving one of its events to night.

"I hate to see it moving," Derrike Cope says. "That Labor Day weekend race is the longest tradition we have in our sport. I think tradition is important. Everybody has his own agendas, I guess, and tradition doesn't seem to be as big a deal anymore—not just in racing, but anywhere. And that's a shame."

Ernest Scurry, who owns the Raceway Grill, doesn't like the change one bit. "We hate it," he says. "It's not going to be the same."

Cale Yarborough, one of Scurry's oldest customers, says it will take a long time to think about the Southern 500 at any other time than Labor Day weekend. "If you can get bigger crowds in other places, I understand that," he says. "But Labor Day and the Southern 500 have been around almost as long as NASCAR has."

Deep South Speed

I n NASCAR, it seems the farther south you go, the hotter and faster the racing gets. This group of four tracks boasts three of the fastest speedways on the circuit: Daytona, Talladega, and Atlanta. Throw in the season-ending, championship-crowning Homestead-Miami facility, and you have a race fan's Southern paradise.

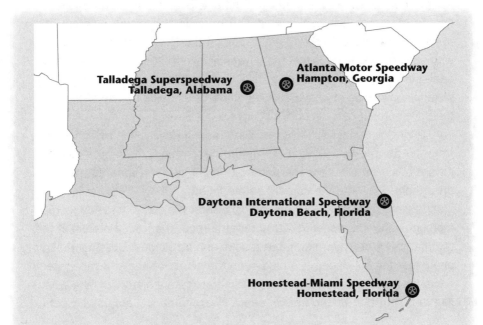

Talladega Superspeedway
Talladega, Alabama

Atlanta Motor Speedway
Hampton, Georgia

Daytona International Speedway
Daytona Beach, Florida

Homestead-Miami Speedway
Homestead, Florida

Atlanta Motor Speedway:
Southern Speed

Quick, name the fastest track in NASCAR. Most casual fans would say Daytona or Talladega, the Nextel Cup circuit's two monster superspeedways. But since NASCAR mandated carburetor restrictor plates to slow down cars at those two tracks, the speed trophy has been shared by the new Texas Motor Speedway and this lightning-fast circuit in Hampton, Georgia, about 30 miles south of Atlanta.

There are no speed restrictions here. Cars rocket around this 1.5-mile quad-oval at more than 190 mph. This is as fast and dangerous as stock car racing gets. Owner O. Bruton Smith—who also owns racetracks near Charlotte, North Carolina; Las Vegas; Fort Worth, Texas; Bristol, Tennessee; and Sonoma, California—has turned Atlanta into one of the showcase venues in the sport. Combine white-knuckle speed with some of the most competitive racing in the sport—this place has been the scene of many thrilling side-by-side finishes—and a visit to Atlanta makes for a can't-miss Southern celebration of racing.

Let's Go Racing

After owner O. Bruton Smith bought the track in 1990, he moved the finish line to what was the backstretch and repaved the racing surface. The result: Atlanta became the fastest track on the Nextel Cup Series circuit, with straightaway speeds teetering ever-so-close to 200 mph. Speeds have eased off slightly as the asphalt has aged and lost a bit of grip, but the slightly slower speeds have allowed some terrific side-by-side racing with the development of a second, higher racing groove.

During hot qualifying laps here, the fastest drivers don't lift their foot from the throttle—they're flat out all the way around. During the race the guys running up front are the ones with the fast cars—and the nerve to drive them deep into the corners before lifting.

Speeds approach 200 mph as cars enter the turns. It's a dangerous moment—and it's repeated 1,000 times a race. If anything breaks, if the throttle sticks or a tire blows, the results can be vicious. But Atlanta isn't about just flat-out speed; it's also been the scene of some of the closest racing on the circuit in recent years. This track has a history of long green-flag runs, but that doesn't mean a lack of excitement. Cars usually settle

ATLANTA MOTOR SPEEDWAY

Pit Road

START/FINISH

Our Ratings	Racing: 🏁 🏁 🏁 🏁 🏁
	Amenities: 🏁 🏁 🏁 🏁
	Area Appeal: 🏁 🏁 🏁
Track Facts	1.54-mile quad-oval
	Seating capacity: 124,000
	1500 U.S. Highways 19 and 41 South
	Hampton, GA 30228
	(770) 946–4211
	www.atlantamotorspeedway.com
Annual Events	Two 500-mile Nextel Cup Series races, March and October
	Companion events: Craftsman Truck Series, March; Busch Series, October
Weather	Average High (F): March 64.2 October 72.7
	Average Low (F): March 42.4 October 51.8
Top Gun	Dale Earnhardt, 9 wins
Qualifying Record	Geoffrey Bodine, 197.478 mph

into small groups here, so you'll frequently be watching three or four good battles for position.

This place is usually murder on engines, especially in the last 100 miles. Drivers who run up front or even pull away from the field early in the race often push their engines too far and aren't around to see the checkered flag fall.

How to Get There

The speedway is located on US 19/41, 30 miles south of downtown Atlanta, in Hampton. From the north: Take Interstate 75 and exit at US 19/41. From the south: Take I–75, exit at State Road 20, and follow the signs to the speedway.

An End to
Gridlock

It's no secret in NASCAR circles: The traffic in and out of Atlanta Motor Speedway is some of the worst anywhere. There's only one advertised way to get there, US 19/42 (Tara Boulevard), and the 11 miles from the interstate to the track are guaranteed to be clogged with race fans. If you go that way, bring a good book. But there is hope for frustrated race fans. Construction has started on a four-lane highway to connect the speedway with I–75.

Best Seats in the House

Our pick: the Petty grandstand at the exit of Turn 4. Row 20 or higher will provide a clear view of the action at the other end of the track, Turns 1 and 2, and you'll also have a good perspective of the action on pit road. If you'd prefer something closer to the finish line on the frontstretch, aim for about thirty rows up so that you will have an unobstructed view of the backstretch. No matter where you sit in the main grandstands, bring sunglasses and a hat; the frontstretch seats face the setting sun.

If you want to get down and dirty, Atlanta's infield offers one of the best views in the business. The racing surface is nearly 10 feet above the ground level of the infield, which allows just about everyone in the infield to see all the way around the track. Thirty years ago the Atlanta infield was notorious for drinking and lewd behavior, but it has been cleaned up considerably since Smith reconfigured the raceway and is now a lot more attractive as a grandstand alternative.

Atlanta Memories

Atlanta Motor Speedway's first NASCAR Cup race was the Dixie 300 held on July 31, 1960. Fans that year witnessed **Fireball Roberts** win. Because for many years the fall race here was the last event of the season, several championships have been decided at Atlanta. Perhaps the most exciting came in 1992, when **Alan Kulwicki, Davey Allison,** and **Bill Elliott** dueled for the title in what many consider the race that brought stock car racing into the world's consciousness. Elliott won the race, but the long-shot Kulwicki, driving his famous Ford "Underbird," finished second and won the season title by ten points. Kulwicki was killed the following April in a plane crash as he arrived for a race at Bristol, Tennessee. Allison died four months later in a helicopter crash at the Talladega Superspeedway.

Kevin Harvick won his first Nextel Cup Series race here in March 2001 after replacing **Dale Earnhardt,** following Earnhardt's fatal accident on the final lap of the Daytona 500 four weeks earlier. Harvick clipped **Jeff Gordon** in a thrilling side-by-side battle. The margin of victory was decided by a photo finish. The race was eerily similar to Earnhardt's photo-finish win over **Bobby Labonte** a year earlier.

Make It a Vacation

Transforming an Atlanta race trip into a full-blown vacation is easy. There are plenty of first-rate attractions in the area and plenty of opportunities for adventure downtown—try finding each of the fifty-plus Peachtree Streets. Plus there are more hotel rooms in Atlanta than almost any other city in the country.

Away from the Track

The first **NASCAR Thunder** retail store is located in the Gwinnett Place Mall, north of town on Interstate 85 (770–232–2808). Coca-Cola is based in Atlanta and, believe it or not, **The World of Coca Cola** (55 Martin Luther King Jr. Drive, Atlanta; 404–676–5151) makes for an entertaining morning or afternoon, especially in the taste-testing room. There is a charge for admission.

For you newshounds check out **CNN Center** (One CNN Center; 404–

827–2300; www.cnn.com/cnncenter) downtown, where a tour will give you a glimpse of the studio and the newsroom. There is an admission fee, and you'll need to call ahead for reservations.

Other getaways include the excellent **Zoo Atlanta** (800 Cherokee Avenue; 404–624–5600; www.zooatlanta.org), home to the famous panda pair Lun Lun and Yang Yang. **Stone Mountain Park** (Georgia Highway 78; 800–317–2006), 16 miles east of Atlanta, offers a peaceful respite from the city hustle. Or you can tour the battlefields that played a key part in Sherman's Atlanta campaign at **Kennesaw Mountain National Battlefield Park** (900 Kennesaw Mountain Drive; 770–427–4686), 26 miles north of Atlanta.

To satisfy the family's urge to shop, check out the city's two major malls, **Lenox Square** (Peachtree Street and Lenox Road) and **Phipps Plaza** (on the other side of Peachtree Street and Lenox Road). And if your pockets are really deep, head over to the very upscale **Buckhead** area.

If there's a train enthusiast among you, don't miss the **Southeastern Railway Museum** (Buford Highway; 770–476–2013) in Duluth, about 30 miles north of Atlanta.

Where to Eat

"What'll ya have, what'll ya have, have your order in mind and your money in your hand." That's just part of the legendary lingo at the **Varsity** (61 North Avenue Northwest; 404–881–1706; www.thevarsity.com), Atlanta's classic drive-in and the only one like it left in the world. Roll up your sleeves and try out the singsong: order a Heavyweight (a hot dog with mustard and extra chili), sideways (onions on the side) with bags of rags (potato chips) and an F.O. (a frosted orange, a secret Varsity formula). If you don't want the chili on the hot dog, just order a "naked" dog. Honest, they won't laugh. You just can't leave the city without getting some of the Varsity's greasy, wonderful food. Prices are a little more than McDonald's, but who cares?

Visit **Kyma** (3085 Piedmont Road; 404–262–0702; www.buckhead restaurants.com/kyma), a newer member of the Buckhead restaurant group and a contemporary Greek seafood tavern like no other. It's a bit costly, but not too costly for the dining delight you'll experience. If you want to stay toward town, be sure to try **Bones** (3139 Piedmont Road; 404–237–2663; www.bonesrestaurant.com), a trendy steakhouse in the Buckhead area, or the **Atlanta Fish Market** (265 Pharr Road; 404–262–3165), where the seafood is brought in fresh daily.

A little closer to the track, the best place to find a down-home country breakfast is at the **Country Bumpkin Cafe** (11714 Hastings Bridge Road; 770–478–0240) in Lovejoy. You can get country ham the size of a football as well as grilled bologna to go with your grits, hand-cut home fries, and biscuits and gravy. For lunch head to Jonesboro and get the special at **Dean's Barbeque** (9480 South Main Street; 770–471–0138). You can get two barbecue sandwiches, a bag of chips, and a soda or iced tea for about $6.00. And for dinner go south to Griffin or north to Jonesboro. The trip to **Manhattan's** (1707 North Expressway, Griffin; 770–228–5442), one of the top steakhouses south of Atlanta, is worth the fifteen-minute ride. **Mo Mo Ya Japanese Restaurant** (6987 Jonesboro Road, Jonesboro; 770–960–9988) is a favorite hangout for actor and former Rolex 24 Hours of Daytona winner Paul Newman.

And for that any-time-of-day snack, no trip to Atlanta would be complete without a stop at one of the five **Waffle Houses** on GA 19/41 between I–75 and the speedway, including one directly across from the raceway. Order like a local: hash browns scattered (spread out), covered (with cheese), smothered (with onions), chunked (with ham), and topped (with chili).

Where to Stay

If you're coming here for more than a day or two, consider staying downtown where the action is, unless you're camping or just don't plan on doing anything besides racing while you're in Atlanta. If you just want to stay out of the big city, there are accommodations in Jonesboro, Fayetteville, McDonough, and Peachtree City, all less than twenty minutes from the track. For a comprehensive guide to Atlanta hotels, surf over to www.best-atlanta-hotels.com or Vroomz.com, where you'll find hotels rated and grouped by price.

To get a taste of Atlanta history during your race visit, consider the **Shellmont Inn** (821 Piedmont Avenue, Atlanta; 404–872–9290) in historic Midtown, the city's theater, restaurant, and cultural district. Built in 1891, this restored Victorian touts itself as an oasis in downtown Atlanta.

The speedway works with Vroomz.com to lock up hotel rooms around the area. They also offer race packages that include three days' worth of tickets and a hotel room for two nights for as little as $400 for two people.

There is an abundance of hotels at Atlanta Hartsfield International Airport, including Marriott, Hilton, Renaissance, Red Roof Inn, Sheraton, and Radisson. In Jonesboro you'll find a few hotels, but you'll need to book rooms early. Choices include Comfort Inn, Econo Lodge, Holiday Inn, Scottish Inn, and Shoney's Inn. If those hotels are booked, ask the hotel chains' reservation departments to check Griffin, Fayetteville, and Peachtree City.

Atlanta Area Restaurants

Applebee's
6608 Tara Boulevard
Jonesboro, GA
(770) 968–1204

Atlanta Fish Market
265 Pharr Road
Atlanta, GA
(404) 262–3165

Azteca Grill
1140 Morrow Industrial
    Boulevard
Morrow, GA
(770) 968–0907

Bones
3139 Piedmont Road
Atlanta, GA
(404) 237–2663

Cheesecake Factory
3024 Peachtree Road
    Northeast
Atlanta, GA
(404) 816–2555

Chili's
2230 Mt. Zion Parkway
Morrow, GA
(770) 603–9900

Chili's
1740 Jonesboro Road
McDonough, GA
(770) 898–5774

Chops
70 West Paces Ferry Road
Atlanta, GA
(404) 262–2675

Country Bumpkin Cafe
11714 Hastings Bridge
    Road
Lovejoy, GA
(770) 478–0240

Dean's Barbeque
9480 South Main Street
Jonesboro, GA
(770) 471–0138

Golden Corral
8465 Tara Boulevard
Jonesboro, GA
(770) 477–0036

Hard Rock Cafe
215 Peachtree Street
Atlanta, GA
(404) 688–7625

Hooters of Fayetteville
750 North Glynn Street
Fayetteville, GA
(678) 817–6690

Hooters of Tara
6785 Tara Boulevard
Jonesboro, GA
(770) 478–2262

Kyma
3085 Piedmont Road
Atlanta, GA
(404) 262–0702

LongHorn Steakhouse
7882 Tara Boulevard
Jonesboro, GA
(770) 477–5365

Manhattan's
1707 North Expressway
Griffin, GA
(770) 228–5442

Mo Mo Ya Japanese
    Restaurant
6987 Jonesboro Road
Jonesboro, GA
(770) 960–9988

OB's BBQ
7045 Mt. Zion Circle
Morrow, GA
(770) 968–7601

OB's BBQ
725 Industrial Boulevard
McDonough, GA
(770) 954–1234

Olde Mill Steakhouse
1095 West Georgia
    Highway 54
Fayetteville, GA
(770) 460–6455

Olive Garden
1176 Mt. Zion Boulevard
Morrow, GA
(770) 968–4800

Outback Steakhouse
1375 Morrow Industrial
    Boulevard
Morrow, GA
(770) 961–6480

Red Lobster
6550 Tara Boulevard
Jonesboro, GA
(770) 968–8910

Red Lobster
1846 Jonesboro Road
McDonough, GA
(770) 898–2980

Ruby Tuesday's
2348 Southlake Mall
Morrow, GA
(770) 961–6422

Shoney's
955 Georgia Highway 155
McDonough, GA
(770) 914–8050

Southern Pit BBQ
2964 North Expressway
Griffin, GA
(770) 229–5887

The Varsity
61 North Avenue
    Northwest
Atlanta, GA
(404) 881–1706

Atlanta Area Lodging

Atlanta Airport Hilton
1031 Virginia Avenue
Atlanta, GA
(404) 767–9000

Club Hotel by Doubletree
3400 Norman Berry Drive
Atlanta, GA
(404) 763–1600

Comfort Inn
6370 Old Dixie Highway
Jonesboro, GA
(770) 961–6336

Country Hearth Inn
1078 Bear Creek
    Boulevard
Hampton, GA
(770) 707–1477

Drury Inn
6520 Lee Street South
Morrow, GA
(770) 960–0500

Econo Lodge
340 Upper Riverdale Road
Jonesboro, GA
(770) 991–0069

Four Seasons Hotel
75 Fourteenth Street
    Northeast
Atlanta, GA
(404) 881–9898

Hampton Inn Airport
1888 Sullivan Road
Atlanta, GA
(770) 996–2220

Hampton Inn McDonough
855 Industrial Boulevard
McDonough, GA
(770) 914–0077

Hampton Inn Peachtree
    City
300 Westpark Drive
Peachtree City, GA
(770) 486–8800

Hampton Inn Southlake
1533 Southlake Parkway
Morrow, GA
(770) 968–8990

Hampton Inn Stockbridge
7342 Hannover Parkway
   North
Stockbridge, GA
(770) 389–0065

Holiday Inn South
6288 Old Dixie Highway
Jonesboro, GA
(770) 968–4300

Ramada Inn Stockbridge
7265 Davidson Parkway
   North
Stockbridge, GA
(770) 474–1700

Ramada Limited Suites
357 Lee Street
Forest Park, GA
(404) 768–7799

Renaissance Atlanta Hotel
   Concourse
1 Hartsfield Centre Parkway
Atlanta, GA
(404) 209–9999

Ritz Carlton
181 Peachtree Street
   Northeast
Atlanta, GA
(404) 659–0400

Shellmont Inn
821 Piedmont Avenue
Atlanta, GA
(404) 872–9290

Sheraton Gateway Hotel
1900 Sullivan Road
College Park, GA
(770) 997–1100

Atlanta Area Camping

Atlanta Motor Speedway
US 19/41
Hampton, GA
(770) 946–4211

Atlanta South KOA
281 Mount Olive Road
McDonough, GA
(800) 443–1562

Talladega Superspeedway:
NASCAR's Most Competitive Track

It's the biggest, fastest racetrack, and the shows there are perhaps the most exciting you'll see all year. This 2.66-mile superspeedway, built by NASCAR founder Bill France in 1969 outside the small central Alabama town of Talladega, has always been synonymous with speed. Its blistering speeds and white-knuckle racing draw fans from all over the country.

This part of Alabama doesn't offer the amenities and activities of some of NASCAR's other destinations, but it's racing country. It's also beautiful country. You won't find any four-star hotels. But if hiking, hunting, fishing, or other outdoor activities are your idea of entertainment, you've come to the right place. And if you're a racing camper, this place is a dream. Talladega welcomes campers and RVers with open arms.

Let's Go Racing

Talladega means excitement, but there's not an abundance of strategy, subtlety, or sanity to the racing here. It's been that way since NASCAR required the use of restrictor plates on the engines to cut horsepower and slow down cars here and at Daytona. The move was triggered when Bobby Allison's car became airborne and nearly sailed over the catch fence and into the grandstand in a 1987 race here.

NASCAR immediately slowed things down to keep the cars on the ground. Cars now top out at about 30 mph slower than Elliott's record lap speed of 212.809 mph. Fans really don't notice the slower speeds, but the drivers sure feel the lack of horsepower. Gone are the days when a driver could pull out of the draft of the leading car and surge past.

Instead, the entire field often runs in one huge, frenetic pack of cars—inches apart and three-wide from first to last place. It's exciting for the fans; it's hell for the drivers. One bobble, one slip, one momentary lapse in concentration can trigger a wreck that takes out half the field. It's called The Big One, and it can happen on any lap, at any time.

Most drivers hate restrictor-plate racing. Ricky Rudd says that driving 500 miles at Talladega gives him a headache because he has to concentrate so hard, and it dries out his eyes because he's afraid to blink. The restrictor plate is the great equalizer, robbing the top teams of the horsepower edge they usually enjoy over their underfunded competitors. It also

TALLADEGA SUPERSPEEDWAY

START/FINISH

Pit Road

TURN 1

TURN 2

TURN 3

TURN 4

Our Ratings	Racing: ⚑ ⚑ ⚑ ⚑ ⚑
	Amenities: ⚑ ⚑ ⚑
	Area Appeal: ⚑
Track Facts	2.66-mile tri-oval
	Seating capacity: 143,000
	3366 Speedway Boulevard
	Talladega, AL 35160
	(256) 362–7223
	www.talladegasuperspeedway.com
Annual Events	Two 500-mile Nextel Cup Series races, April and October
	Companion events: Busch Series and International Race
	of Champions, April; ARCA Series, September
Weather	Average High (F): April 74.5 October 76.0
	Average Low (F): April 49.1 October 45.0
Top Gun	Dale Earnhardt, 10 wins
Qualifying Record	Bill Elliott, 212.809 mph

means that inexperienced drivers can mix it up with the veterans in the same pack, inches apart at 190 mph in a forty-car pack of traffic.

Drivers talk a lot about "track position," a concept that's as important here as it is anywhere. Because it's so hard to pass, teams will often gamble on pit strategy, taking on only two new tires instead of four to gain a few precious spots in the running order. Watch for these moves during both green- and caution-flag stops, then see how that driver fares on the track.

How to Get There

The superspeedway is easily accessible from Interstate 20, where the Speedway Boulevard exit funnels right into the track. Air travelers usually fly into Birmingham, about 50 miles away, or Atlanta, about 70 miles away. Speedway Boulevard runs parallel to I-20, so there's an exit west of the speedway if you're coming from Birmingham and an exit east of the track if you're coming from Atlanta. Traffic moves well at Talladega once you get out of the parking lot—the secret is not to park in the middle of one of the spacious lots. Park out front, where it's an easy exit onto Speedway Boulevard, even if it means walking a mile to your seats.

Sterling Marlin on Talladega

Sterling Marlin won the Diehard 500 here in 1995, backing it up with a win in the spring Talladega race the next year. "Winning at Talladega for the first time is my best memory from there. I've been going down there for the races close to all my life, and to get a win there is pretty cool," he said.

Marlin's advice to fans: "You'd better bring some binoculars."

Best Seats in the House

Tower seats are a must: the higher the better, here more than anywhere else on the NASCAR circuit. Even with a lofty perch, you won't be able to see all areas of this massive facility. The addition of giant TVs in the infield will help you keep track of what's going on.

Try first for tickets in the Tri-Oval Tower. This is an ideal vantage point; cars fan out three- and four-wide as they negotiate the tricky doglegs of the tri-oval. Seats here also give you a good view of pit road.

If you can't get seats in the tri-oval, try the Talladega Tower at the entrance to Turn 1. You'll have a great view of the scream off pit road, as well as the racing action as the field thunders into the first turn. These seats are premium because the finish line is at the end of pit road, not at the dogleg in the middle of the tri-oval.

Talladega Memories

In 1987 **Bill Elliott,** driving a Ford, set a Nextel Cup Series qualifying record at 212.809 mph at Talladega, breaking his own record set here the year before.

When this massive track opened in 1969, most of NASCAR's top teams refused to run the first Talladega 500, arguing that tire problems at the 195-plus mph speeds made the racing too dangerous. **Bobby Isaac** won the pole at 196.386 mph, and **Richard Brickhouse** won the race, his first and only Nextel Cup Series victory. Bill France broke the impromptu strike by inviting drivers from the ARCA Series. By the next year the tire problems were solved, and race teams haven't organized against NASCAR since.

Dale Earnhardt made one of his most stirring charges to the front here in October 2001, when he blasted through the pack in the final five laps. He was 16th with five to go, and he carved his way through traffic for one of his most memorable victories—and his last—in a stellar career than included seven championships.

The track is home to the famed **Alabama Gang: Bobby Allison,** his brother **Donnie Allison,** short-track ace **Red Farmer,** and **Neil Bonnett. Davey Allison,** Bobby's son, continued that legacy, winning the 1987 Winston 500 here for his first Cup win. He followed it up in the 1988 Daytona 500, finishing second to his father.

The proud group was mired in tragedy. Bobby Allison's career ended in a crash at Pocono in 1988 that left him with brain damage. Donnie Allison's career essentially ended with a crash at Charlotte, North Carolina, in 1982; and Neil Bonnett died in a crash at Daytona in 1994. Davey Allison died in a helicopter crash at Talladega in 1993.

Make It a Vacation

This part of Alabama may lack tourist attractions, but the region makes up for it with some of the prettiest scenery in the South. The Talladega National Forest contains two wilderness areas, **Dugger Mountain** and the **Cheaha Wilderness Area,** and both offer plenty of hiking, camping, boating, and fishing.

It's a surprisingly mountainous area, with peaks higher than 2,000 feet. For a taste of easy living, Alabama style, try **The Secret** bed-and-breakfast (2356 Alabama Highway 68 West; 256–523–3825) in Leesburg, about 62 miles from Talladega. Sitting atop Lookout Mountain, The Secret offers panoramic views of the surrounding countryside and Weiss Lake.

There are plenty of vacation rentals available in the Pell City area around Logan Martin Lake, about 20 miles northwest of Talladega. Not a bad way to spend a week: relaxing and fishing for a few days, with a couple days of racing action to break the peace.

Party Time on
Talladega Boulevard

It's not just the racing that gets wild at Talladega. While other aspects of NASCAR have toned down and buttoned up, the Talladega infield community is a throwback to the sport's rough and rowdy days. The infield atmosphere here is, well, lively. OK, it's downright insane.

At the heart of the infield madness is Talladega Boulevard, where race revelers really let it all hang out. It's a sort of Bourbon Street, Alabama style, complete with Mardi Gras-type beads—and the shouted requests for exposure associated with that street festival.

You probably don't want to take your girlfriend or your wife and kids on a tour of Talladega Boulevard. But if you want to bring the family to stay in the infield, don't let the rowdy boys keep you away. Track officials and security maintain areas that are safe and family friendly. The closer to the middle of the infield you get, the more controlled the atmosphere. But be aware that spots along the fences, especially in the third and fourth turns, are like a three-day fraternity party: a lot of drinking, loud music, and people in all stages of dress—and undress.

Away from the Track

If you can't wrap a vacation around your Talladega visit, here are a few side trips to keep you entertained between activities at the track.

At the top of any race fan's to-do list should be the **International**

Motorsports Hall of Fame (3366 Speedway Boulevard, Talladega; 256–362–5002). Aside from the hall of fame, the facility houses the Motorsports Museum, where you'll find a bevy of racing legends, including Richard Petty's famed STP Dodge Charger and Bill Elliott's 1985 Ford Thunderbird.

In Birmingham check out the **Barber Motorsports Park and Vintage Motorsports Museum** (Barber Motorsports Parkway, Birmingham, 205–327–7223; www.barber motorsports.com). The complex has a racetrack and the largest collection of vintage motorcycles in North America.

Also of interest are the **Birmingham Race Course** for greyhound racing (1000 John Rogers Drive, Birmingham; 205–838–7500); **Birmingham Zoo** (2630 Cahaba Road, Birmingham; 205–879–0409; www.birminghamzoo.com); **Alabama Sports Hall of Fame** (2150 Civic Center Boulevard, Birmingham; 205–323–6665; www.alasports.org); and **Brierfield Iron Works Historical Park** (240 Furnace Parkway, Brierfield; 205–665–1856; www.brierfieldironworks. com) all great getaways an hour from the racetrack. The **Talladega Short Track** (Speedway Boulevard; 256–831–1413; www.talladegashorttrack.com) is just across the street. The short track always has shows on Friday and Saturday nights of race week.

Where to Eat

Most of the local restaurants are twenty minutes away in Oxford and Anniston. In Anniston the best include the **Top O' the River** (3220 McClellan Boulevard, 256–238–0097), where they serve up fried dill pickles and "the world's largest seafood platter," and the **Victoria Inn** (1604 Quintard Avenue; 256–236–0503), which specializes in fine and local cuisine. While in Anniston you can also treat your taste buds at the **Mikado Japanese Steak House** (McClellan Plaza; 256–236–1616) or the **Old Smokehouse Bar-B-Q** (631 South Quintard Avenue; 256–237–5200), two other local favorites.

If you're adventurous and up for a drive, there are a couple great spots an hour from the speedway. Best of all are the famed **Dreamland Barb-B-Que** (5535 Fifteenth Avenue East, Tuscaloosa; 205–758–8135) and **Bob Sykes Barbeque** (1724 Ninth Avenue, Bessemer; 205–426–

1400). These places aren't for sissies. Bring an appetite—and be ready to get sauce up to your elbows.

Where to Stay

Hotel rooms can be a rare commodity in this part of Alabama, especially during race weeks. Since hotels are few and far between in the Talladega area, the handful of bed-and-breakfasts are a good option—if veteran race-goers haven't booked them for life.

The **Governor's House** (500 Meadowlake Lane, Talladega, 205–763–2186) bed-and-breakfast is only 4 miles from the speedway. Built in 1850 by former Alabama governor Lewis Parson, the house was later moved to its current location overlooking Logan Martin Lake.

Also in Talladega, 4 blocks from the town square, is the **Oakwood Bed and Breakfast** (715 North Street East; 256–362–0662), built in 1847 and an excellent example of Federal-style architecture.

Somerset House Bed and Breakfast (701 North Street E, Talladega; 256–761–9251) is another Talladega landmark. The colonial plantation-style home was originally built in 1905 and rebuilt in 1933. Located near the historic town square, the house now is listed on the National Registry of Historic Homes.

There are a lot of hotels in nearby Oxford and Anniston. If you plan early, you might get a room at the **Victoria Inn** (1604 Quintard Avenue, Anniston; 256–236–0503). Otherwise you'll have to settle for the regular hodgepodge of highway rest stops.

Hotels, big and small, abound at the Oxford/Anniston exit 20 miles east of the speedway—the gathering place for most fans and most of the race teams. But don't let these small Alabama towns fool you. They're no bumpkins. The sticker shock—you will pay four times the regular rate and be required to stay a minimum number of nights—can take a lot of the fun out of the trip. Don't be afraid to stay in Birmingham or Atlanta. They're both about an hour away, and it's an easy drive.

Camper's "Paradise"

About 900 acres are available for camping at the track. It is primitive camping—nothing but port-a-potties and garbage cans—but, hey, some of it's FREE! The campgrounds—450 acres for free camping; 450 for reserved lots—start filling up earlier every race, but people are still arriving on Saturday night, so get there when you can.

Inside the raceway, there are 210 more acres for camping.

Talladega Area Restaurants

Acapulco Mexican
Restaurant
Lenlock Shopping Center
Anniston, AL
(256) 820–9616

Applebee's
U.S. Highways 78 and 21
Oxford, AL
(256) 835–2434

The Ark
13030 US 78
Riverside, AL
(205) 338–7420

Brad's Bar-B-Q
1809 US 78
Oxford, AL
(256) 831–7878

Betty's Bar-B-Q
401 South Quintard
Avenue
Anniston, AL
(256) 237–1411

China Luck
503 Quintard Avenue
Oxford, AL
(256) 831–5221

Cracker Barrel
220 Morgan Road
Oxford, AL
(256) 835–6700

Diamond Lil's Restaurant
65600 Alabama
Highway 77
Talladega, AL
(256) 362–0900

Fincher's Catfish Kitchen
Renfroe Road
Talladega, AL
(256) 268–0255

Frontera Grill
1750 East Hamric Drive
Oxford, AL
(256) 835–9905

Fuji Japanese Cuisine
218 Davis Loop
Oxford, AL
(256) 835–8788

Garfield's
700 Quintard Mall
Oxford, AL
(256) 832–5453

Gateway
75333 AL77
Lincoln, AL
(256) 763–7231

Goal Post Barbecue
1910 Quintard Avenue
Anniston, AL
(256) 236–9280

Kathy's Stampede
Steakhouse
710 East Battle Street
Talladega, AL
(256) 315–0600

Logan's Roadhouse
40 Ali Way
Oxford, AL
(256) 835–3116

Lone Star Steak House
171 Colonial Drive
Oxford, AL
(256) 831–7441

Margarita's Mexican
Restaurant
103 Seventeenth Street
South
Talladega, AL
(256) 315–9711

Mata's Greek Pizza and
Grinders
1708 Quintard Avenue
Anniston, AL
(256) 237–3100

Matehuala Mexican
Restaurant
114 Court Square South
Talladega, AL
(256) 362–5754

Mikado Japanese Steak
House
McClellan Plaza
Anniston, AL
(256) 236–1616

Miller's Dinner Bell
136 North East Street
Talladega, AL
(256) 362–9955

Old Mill Restaurant
57900 AL77
Talladega, AL
(256) 761–0043

Old Smokehouse Bar-B-Q
631 South Quintard
    Avenue
Anniston, AL
(256) 237–5200

Outback Steakhouse
196 Springbranch Drive
Oxford, AL
(256) 835–4644

Parigi's Pizza
119 West Court Square
Talladega, AL
(256) 362–8663

Quizno's
1783 East Hamric Drive
Oxford, AL
(256) 831–4114

Red Lobster
515 Quintard Avenue
Oxford, AL
(256) 835–2013

Ruby Tuesday's
712 South Quintard
    Avenue
Anniston, AL
(256) 237–2229

Shack BBQ
7744 Stemley Bridge
    Road
Talladega, AL
(256) 268–2005

Top O' the River
3220 McClellan Boulevard
Anniston, AL
(256) 238–0097

Victoria Inn
1604 Quintard Avenue
Anniston, AL
(256) 236–0503

Western Sizzlin
200 Vaughn Lane
Pell City, AL
(205) 814–5665

Zack's Mesquite Grill
1613 East Snow Drive
Oxford, AL
(256) 831–9334

Talladega Area Lodging

Budget Inn
AL 77
Talladega, AL
(256) 362–0900

Comfort Inn
138 Elm Street
Oxford, AL
(256) 831–0860

Days Inn
1 Recreation Drive
Oxford, AL
(256) 835–0300

Days Inn
945 Speedway Industrial
    Boulevard
Lincoln, AL
(205) 763–8080

Econo Lodge
25 Elm Street
Oxford, AL
(256) 831–9480

Governor's House
500 Meadowlake Lane
Talladega, AL
(205) 763–2186

Hampton Inn
Alabama Highway 21
    South
Oxford, AL
(256) 835–1492

Hampton Inn
220 Vaughn Lane
Pell City, AL
(205) 814–3000

Holiday Inn Express
AL 77
Lincoln, AL
(205) 763–9777

Holiday Inn Express
160 Colonial Drive
Oxford, AL
(256) 832–4041

Holiday Inn
US 78 and 21
Oxford, AL
(256) 831–3410

Jameson Inn
161 Colonial Drive
Oxford, AL
(256) 835–2170

McCaig Motel
12155 Stemley Road
Lincoln, AL
(205) 763–7771

McCaig Motel
75333 AL 77
Lincoln, AL
(205) 763–7731

Oakwood Bed and
   Breakfast
715 North Street East
Talladega, AL
(256) 362–0662

Ramada Inn
300 Quintard Avenue
Anniston, AL
(256) 237–9777

Sleep Inn
88 Colonial Drive
Oxford, AL
(256) 831–2191

Somerset House Bed and
   Breakfast
701 North Street East
Talladega, AL
(256) 761–9251

Victoria Inn
1604 Quintard Avenue
Anniston, AL
(256) 236–0503

Villager Lodge
1015 Alabama
   Highway 431
Anniston, AL
(256) 237–2525

The Wingate Inn
143 Colonial Drive
Oxford, AL
(256) 831–1921

Talladega Area Camping

Logan Landing RV Resort
   and Campground
1036 Paul Bear Bryant
   Road
Alpine, AL
(256) 268–0045

Noccalula Falls Park and
   Campground
1500 Noccalula Road
Gadsden, AL
(256) 543–7412

Talladega Superspeedway
3366 Speedway Boulevard
Talladega, AL
(256) 362–7223

Daytona International Speedway:
World Center of Racing

When Bill France opened this speedway in 1959, there was nothing like it anywhere else in the world—a 2.5-mile, high-banked oval. And Daytona endures as the sport's showcase venue, despite Indianapolis Motor Speedway's prestige and Lowe's Motor Speedway's proximity to the majority of race shops.

If you go to only one NASCAR race, the Daytona 500 should probably be it. Or if you prefer spending the Fourth of July weekend at one of the world's most famous beaches, there's the Pepsi 400 in July.

Each of these two annual NASCAR events is a shining star on the circuit, but for different reasons. After the season winds up in November, the drivers and crews get a much-deserved break from the rigors of the Nextel Cup Series schedule. But for fans, the wait until February and Speed Weeks at Daytona is interminable. In February Daytona breaks the racing dry season with an explosion of high-speed thrills.

It's a very different atmosphere that greets the racing community in July for the Pepsi 400. It's the midpoint of the season; it's summer; it's the beach; it's under the lights. What more could you want?

Two terrific racing experiences await you in Daytona. Take your pick.

Let's Go Racing

The racing here has always been unique. It was at Daytona that drivers and teams first began to understand the aerodynamic aspect of their high-speed dance. A car traveling at such speeds creates a vacuum behind it, allowing a trailing car to "suck up" right behind the lead car. The effect of "the draft" means that two or more cars running in line are much faster than a single car running alone, since they can divide the wind resistance.

The draft has always defined racing here, but it's not what it used to be. In the old days, when horsepower ruled, the drivers used the slingshot maneuver—getting a running start in the tunnel of calm air behind the lead car—to rocket past the leader. Now, with carburetor restrictor plates cutting about 45 mph here and at Talladega, the cars lack the power to pull out and pass on their own. The result: a gigantic pack of cars inches apart, three-wide. It looks like rush hour on the freeway, except these cars are hurtling at 185 mph.

It's a testament to the skill of the drivers that they can run in these giant packs lap after lap without incident. But massive wrecks are almost

DAYTONA INTERNATIONAL SPEEDWAY

TURN 3

TURN 2

TURN 4

TURN 1

Pit Road

START/FINISH

Our Ratings	Racing: 🏁 🏁 🏁
	Amenities: 🏁 🏁 🏁 🏁 🏁
	Area Appeal: 🏁 🏁 🏁 🏁 🏁

Track Facts	2.5-mile tri-oval
	Seating capacity: 170,000
	P.O. Box 2801
	Daytona Beach, FL 32120
	(386) 253–7223
	www.daytonaintlspeedway.com

Annual Events	Two Nextel Cup Series races, February and July
	Companion events: ARCA Series and Craftsman Truck
	Series, February; Busch Series, February and July

| **Weather** | Average High (F): | February 69.4 | July 89.8 |
| | Average Low (F): | February 48.4 | July 72.5 |

| **Top Gun** | Richard Petty, 10 wins |

| **Qualifying Record** | Bill Elliott, 210.364 mph |

inevitable. One slip, one bobble can trigger a chain-reaction wreck that might take out half the field.

If the field can manage to avoid "the big one," the racers eventually will break apart into several drafting packs. It's a welcome respite for the drivers—and a chance for fans to see who's the fastest. A car's setup and handling characteristics come more into play here than at the slightly longer Talladega circuit. During long green-flag runs, the better handling cars will come to the front of the pack.

One problem with restrictor-plate racing is that the cars lack enough power to make passes without several cars working in tandem. Don't expect a lot of moves in the waning laps. The last time a car passed for the lead on the final lap at Daytona was the 1990 Daytona 500, when Dale Earnhardt blew a right-rear tire and Derrike Cope passed him in the third turn for one of racing's biggest upsets.

How to Get There

The speedway is located on International Speedway Boulevard (Florida Highway 92), just east of Interstate 95. If you're flying into Orlando, Daytona is about 50 miles east on Interstate 4.

If you have any local knowledge of the area, take U.S. Highway 1 off I–95 from the north and go into town. The traffic from the beach is a fraction of the backups out on the interstates. If you're coming from Orlando—and with Daytona Beach hotels charging as much as $300 a night for rooms, many fans stay in Orlando—skip over to New Smyrna Beach on Florida Highway 44, and approach from the south on I–95. If you use that back way into the speedway, get off at the Port Orange exit, head toward the beach, and turn left at Clyde Morris Boulevard. That road takes you to the back of the speedway.

Best Seats in the House

Aim as high as you can at this massive complex. As a rule, don't settle for anything below Row 25 or you'll be frustrated by the view. Consider the Superstretch along the backstretch, preferably Row 35 or higher. You'll be able to keep up with the action on a pair of huge TVs in this area.

Daytona Memories

Daytona has seen some of the most thrilling finishes in racing history, but the most memorable has to be the last-lap duel between arch rivals **Richard Petty** and **David Pearson** in 1976. The two had dominated the race and were running 1–2 on the last lap, with Petty in the lead. Pearson shot past Petty going into Turn 3, only to have Petty get back beside him coming through Turn 4. As Petty slipped ahead, the two cars banged together, sending both crashing hard into the wall and coming to rest a few hundred yards short of victory. Petty's engine stalled, but Pearson kept his engine running and crept across the finish line at about 20 mph. It was the only Daytona 500 win for Pearson, one of the sport's all-time greats.

The Daytona 500 historically has attracted some of the biggest stars from outside stock car racing circles. **Mario Andretti** won the 500 in 1967 then went on to win the Indianapolis 500 two years later, becoming the first driver to win both renowned races. In 1972 **A. J. Foyt** won at Daytona, one of his seven NASCAR wins.

Cale Yarborough duked it out—literally—with **Bobby** and **Donnie Allison** after Cale and Donnie crashed while fighting for the lead in the third turn of the final lap of the Daytona 500. It was 1979, and CBS was broadcasting the race live for the first time to nationwide audience. Many viewers got their first look at the passion and the rowdiness of Southern stock car racing that day—and they loved it.

Michael Waltrip
on Daytona

Daytona is a special place for everyone involved in NASCAR racing. For Michael Waltrip, though, the place is especially meaningful.

"Every year since I can remember, when February came around it was time to head to Daytona," Waltrip says. "We'd drive to Daytona in our Chevrolet Impala, which is always what my dad drove." As a ten-year-old from Owensboro, Kentucky, Waltrip came to watch older brother Darrell race. Decades later, the younger Waltrip would become an acknowledged master of Daytona.

But it's not just the racing that Waltrip loves about Daytona. It's the place. "I think the lead-time to the Daytona 500 is a huge part of the popularity of the 500," he says. "For so many families the entire week becomes a way of life."

Coming into the Daytona 500 in 2001, Waltrip's career had been a frustrating one. He'd had success, but a Nextel Cup win had eluded him in his first 462 starts. Once he got a job with Dale Earnhardt Inc., Waltrip had his best chance.

"He didn't care that I was 0 for 462," Waltrip says. "He just knew that I could win that race." Earnhardt was right: Waltrip won the 500, taking the checkered flag seconds after Earnhardt died in the fourth turn when his car slammed into the outside wall.

Waltrip again proved he was worthy of his late friend's confidence, winning the 500 for a second time in 2003.

Make It a Vacation

Daytona Beach, which is almost as famous for its wide beaches as it is for its three-wide racing, is a dream racing vacation. The track is just 4 miles from the ocean. In July you can spend the day at the beach, grab a quick dinner, then head to the track for racing under the lights.

Of course there's more to do in Central Florida than going to the beach. Orlando, with its many first-rate attractions like Walt Disney World, Sea World, and Universal Studios, is just 50 miles east; historic St. Augustine is about 50 miles north.

Away from the Track

You won't even have to leave the track to visit **Daytona USA** (386–947–6800), the official attraction of NASCAR. You can test your skills in live pit-stop competitions, lend your voice to a simulated broadcast call of a famous race, and take a tour of the speedway. The kids—and probably dad, too—will love Daytona Dream Laps, a motion-simulated thrill ride that puts you in the Daytona 500.

Just a mile from the speedway is **Mark Martin's Klassix Auto Attraction** (2909 West International Speedway Boulevard, Daytona Beach; 386–252–3800), where you'll see cars from racing and Hollywood fame, along with muscle cars, motorcycles, and other vehicles.

To get your own racing thrills, check out the outstanding go-cart tracks at **Speed Park** (201 Fentress Boulevard, Daytona Beach; 386–253–3278), located right across from the speedway.

For a superb view of Daytona Beach, climb the **Ponce De Leon Inlet Lighthouse** (4931 South Pennisula Drive, Daytona Beach; 386–761–1821). The lovely resort community of Ponce Inlet is a perfect place to wind down after the 500.

If you have a free day, it's definitely worth the 80 miles down the peninsula to visit the **Kennedy Space Center** (Cape Canaveral; 321–867–5000). You'll need a full day to immerse yourself in the history of America's space program. Highlights include the Air Force Museum, IMAX movies, and a walk-through full-size Space Shuttle display.

And what would a trip to Florida be without golf, especially in February? **LPGA International** (1000 Champions Drive, Daytona Beach; 386–274–5742), home base for the women's professional golf tour, is

Speed Weeks

If you're ready for complete NASCAR immersion therapy, then February Speed-Weeks at Daytona is the ticket. Make that *lots* of tickets. In the three weeks culminating in the Daytona 500, NASCAR's host track puts on an unparalleled festival of speed: The sports cars of the Rolex 24 Hours of Daytona, the Nextel Cup Series, the Craftsman Truck Series, the Goody's Dash Series, and the ARCA Series—they're all in action as the season starts with a bang.

five minutes from the speedway. The two courses there are true tests for men or women. Just look in the Yellow Pages—there are fifteen different golf courses within a half hour of the speedway.

Where to Eat

There are some great local secret dining spots in Daytona Beach. **Hampton's Restaurant** (1116 Mason Avenue, Daytona Beach; 386–253–3889) isn't fancy, but you'll get the best country-style breakfast and fried chicken in town. Just look for the orange Ponce Inlet lighthouse and you're a few steps away from **Down the Hatch Seafood Restaurant** (4884 Front Street, Ponce Inlet; 386–761–4831). All the seafood is fresh, but their trademarks are grouper bites and Buffalo shrimp appetizers. Order both and make it a meal. **Chart House** (1100 Marina Point Drive, Daytona Beach; 386–255–9022) is where the drivers hang out. You'll find four or five of them there every night, each poring over a fabulous salad bar and a great selection of steaks and seafood. Many of the boats in the marina belong to some of the sport's biggest stars. Teresa Earnhardt, Ward Burton, Rusty Wallace, Jeff Gordon, and Felix Sabates all have been known to drop anchor at the Chart House during SpeedWeeks. The chefs have won awards for their crab cakes and grouper at **Billy's Tap Room and Grill** (58 East Granada Boulevard, Ormond Beach; 386–672–1910). *NOTE:* During SpeedWeeks you need to make reservations at Chart House and Billy's Tap Room and Grill.

The food is great and the view incredible at **Famous Steve's Diner** (1620 South Atlantic, Daytona Beach; 386–252–9444), which serves breakfast on the beach. Lots of places cater to the sea and sun lovers, local and otherwise. Try **J's Island Patio Restaurant** on South Beach (831 East International Speedway, Daytona Beach; 386–238–1414). Or go for the wings with rasta sauce right on the beach at the **Ocean Deck** (127 South Ocean Avenue, Daytona Beach; 386–253–5224).

Of course there's as much nightlife in Daytona as you can stand. For a bit of the boot scoot boogie, check out **Billy Bob's Race Country USA** (2801 South Ridgewood Avenue, Daytona Beach; 386–756–2653). And if you need to stay in touch with nonracing sports, drop in for a cold one at the **Oyster Pub** (555 Seabreeze Boulevard, Daytona Beach; 386–255–6348). Locals and the biker crowd prefer the famed **Boot Hill Saloon** (310 Main Street, Daytona Beach; 386–258–9506). Located across the street from the city's cemetery, it's where movie stars like Peter Fonda and Dennis Hopper have bellied up to the bar and where Dickie Betts was inspired to write "In Memory of Elizabeth Reed" for the Allman Brothers Band. Bob Latford invented the current point system for the Nextel Cup Series on the back of a cocktail napkin while drinking beer here. The saloon's motto is as cool as its decor of women's underwear and biker apparel: "Order a drink and have a seat, you're better off here than across the street."

No matter how long you plan to stay around Daytona Beach, an 18-mile trip west to Deland is a must for the best sandwich on the entire circuit. **Belly Busters Restaurant** (930 North Woodland Boulevard, Deland; 386–734–1611) has an incredible cheesesteak that's worth the drive.

Where to Stay

With some 400 hotels in the area, finding accommodations isn't a problem. Paying for them, however, might be. Most hotels require minimum stays, usually five nights. If you're down for all of SpeedWeeks, that's not a problem. If you're the gambling type and are coming down just for the race without a reservation, hotels with vacancies on the day before the event will often negotiate the minimum stay.

If you're in Daytona for the week (and why wouldn't you be?), your best bet (if you can afford it) is a beachfront resort. If deluxe and oceanfront are at the top of your hotel wish list, we recommend the **Hilton** (2637 South Atlantic Avenue, Daytona Beach; 386–767–7350), or the **Daytona Beach Regency** (400 North Atlantic Avenue, Daytona Beach; 386–255–0251).

Frequent Daytona visitors prefer lesser known properties, including the **Talisman Lodge** (4311 South Atlantic Avenue, Daytona Beach; 386–761–0511). This little jewel is quiet, beautifully landscaped, and has some terrific views. For families you can't beat the **Sun Viking Lodge** (2411 South Atlantic Avenue, Daytona Beach; 800–815–2846). Another terrific value: the **Ocean Court** (2315 South Atlantic Avenue, Daytona Beach; 386–253–8185).

Even if your budget demands more modest accommodations, try to get a beachfront hotel. One big advantage, other than the view, is access to the speedway. From the beach you'll have relatively smooth sailing to the track on race day, while it's pure gridlock in other directions as fans pour into Daytona on major thoroughfares from the north, south, and west.

If you must stay inland—closer to the airport—the best of the lot are the **Holiday Inn Daytona Speedway** (2620 West International Speedway Boulevard, Daytona Beach; 386–258–6333) and the **Ramada Daytona Speedway** (1798 West International Speedway Boulevard, Daytona Beach; 386–255–2422).

If you're bringing the whole family, consider renting a vacation home. Call **Vacation Rentals** of Daytona Beach (386–760–5515).

Orlando is an hour away and has nearly 200,000 hotel rooms. Although race time is prime tourist season, you won't have a problem finding a room there. Titusville and Cocoa Beach, also an hour away, offer the same ocean views without the racing prices.

Daytona Beach Area Restaurants

Aunt Catfish's on the River
4009 Halifax Drive
Port Orange, FL
(386) 767–4768

Barnacles Restaurant
869 South Atlantic Avenue
Ormond Beach, FL
(386) 673–1070

Belly Busters Restaurant
930 North Woodland
   Boulevard
Deland, FL
(386) 734–1611

Bennigan's Ormond Beach
890 South Atlantic Avenue
Ormond Beach, FL
(386) 673–3691

Bertie's Luncheonette
2575 North Atlantic
   Avenue
Daytona Beach, FL
(386) 672–8656

Billy's Tap Room and Grill
58 East Granada Boulevard
Ormond Beach, FL
(386) 672–1910

Biscuits 'N Gravy
3500 South Nova Road
Daytona Beach, FL
(386) 304–9433

Carrabba's Italian Grill
2200 West International
   Speedway Boulevard
Daytona Beach, FL
(386) 255–3344

Chart House
1100 Marina Point Drive
Daytona Beach, FL
(386) 255–9022

Chi-Ling Chinese Restaurant and Sushi Bar
4085 South Ridgewood Avenue
Port Orange, FL
(386) 788-8858

Daytona Ale House
2610 West International Speedway Boulevard
Daytona Beach, FL
(386) 255-2555

Down the Hatch Seafood Restaurant
4884 Front Street
Ponce Inlet, FL
(386) 761-4831

Earl Street Grill
715 Earl Street
Daytona Beach, FL
(386) 239-8781

Famous Steve's Diner
1620 South Atlantic Avenue
Daytona Beach, FL
(386) 252-9444

Hampton's Restaurant
1116 Mason Avenue
Daytona Beach, FL
(386) 253-3889

J's Island Patio Restaurant
831 East International Speedway
Daytona Beach, FL
(386) 238-1414

Julian's
88 South Atlantic Avenue
Ormond Beach, FL
(386) 677-6767

Lone Star Steakhouse
1198 Dunlawton Avenue
Daytona Beach, FL
(386) 304-8518

MC K's Dublin Station
218 South Beach Street
Daytona Beach, FL
(386) 238-3321

Molly's Cafe
1728 South Nova Road
Daytona Beach, FL
(386) 760-3948

The Ocean Deck
127 South Ocean Avenue
Daytona Beach, FL
(386) 253-5224

Outback Steakhouse
1490 West International Speedway Boulevard
Daytona Beach, FL
(386) 253-6283

Outback Steakhouse
135 East Granada Boulevard
Ormond Beach, FL
(386) 676-1550

The Oyster Pub
555 Seabreeze Boulevard
Daytona Beach, FL
(386) 255-6348

Park's Seafood Restaurant
951 North Beach Street
Daytona Beach, FL
(386) 258-7272

Patches Restaurant
403 North U.S. Highway 1
Ormond Beach, FL
(386) 672-5697

Perkins Family Restaurant
1000 West Palm Coast Parkway
Palm Coast, FL
(386) 446-7747

Port Orange Steakhouse
3851 Nova Road
Port Orange, FL
(386) 756-2660

Pub 44
1889 Florida Highway 44
New Smyrna Beach, FL
(386) 428-6523

Red Lobster
2735 South Atlantic Avenue
Daytona Beach, FL
(386) 677-2235

Red Lobster
3162 South Atlantic Avenue
Daytona Beach Shores, FL
(386) 756-1550

Red Lobster
2625 West International Speedway Boulevard
Daytona Beach, FL
(386) 255-7596

Rossi's Diner
2240 South Ridgewood Avenue
South Daytona, FL
(386) 760-4564

Ruby Tuesday's
1808 West International Speedway Boulevard
Daytona Beach, FL
(386) 254-8828

Sapporo Japanese Steak
House
3340 South Atlantic
Avenue
Daytona Beach, FL
(386) 756–0480

Sweetwater's
3633 Halifax Drive
Port Orange, FL
(386) 761–6724

Takeya Japanese Steak
House
437 South Nova Road
Ormond Beach, FL
(386) 615–7600

Ted's Diner
855 South Nova Road
Ormond Beach, FL
(386) 673–1898

Teddy's Beachside Family
Restaurant
812 East Third Avenue
New Smyrna Beach, FL
(386) 428–0443

Tim's Corner
5664 Ridgewood Avenue
Ormond Beach, FL
(386) 788–2627

Daytona Beach Area Lodging

Acapulco Hotel and Resort
2505 South Atlantic
Avenue
Daytona Beach, FL
(386) 761–2210

Adam's Mark
100 North Atlantic Avenue
Daytona Beach, FL
(386) 254–8200

Beachcomer Daytona
Beach Resort
2000 North Atlantic
Avenue
Daytona Beach, FL
(386) 252–8513

Best Western LaPlaya
Resort
2500 North Atlantic
Avenue
Daytona Beach, FL
(386) 672–0990

Best Western Mayan Inn
103 South Ocean Avenue
Daytona Beach, FL
(386) 252–2378

Comfort Inn and Suites
730 North Atlantic Avenue
Daytona Beach, FL
(386) 255–5491

Days Inn Daytona on the
Beach
1220 North Atlantic
Avenue
Daytona Beach, FL
(386) 255–2745

Days Inn Daytona
Speedway
2900 West International
Speedway Boulevard
Daytona Beach, FL
(386) 255–0541

Days Inn Oceanfront
South Tropical Seas
3357 South Atlantic
Avenue
Daytona Beach, FL
(386) 767–8737

Daytona Beach Regency
400 North Atlantic Avenue
Daytona, FL
(386) 255–0251

Daytona Surfside Inn and
Suites
3125 South Atlantic
Avenue
Daytona Beach, FL
(386) 788–1000

Dream Inn
3217 South Atlantic
Avenue
Daytona Beach, FL
(386) 767–2821

Hampton Inn Daytona
Shores
3135 South Atlantic
Avenue
Daytona Beach, FL
(386) 767–8533

Hampton Inn Daytona
Speedway
1715 West International
Speedway Boulevard
Daytona Beach, FL
(386) 257–4030

Hawaiian Inn Oceanfront
Resort
2301 South Atlantic
Avenue
Daytona Beach, FL
(386) 258–2860

Hilton Daytona Beach
Oceanfront Resort
2637 South Atlantic
Avenue
Daytona Beach, FL
(386) 767–7350

Holiday Inn Daytona Beach
Shores
3209 South Atlantic
Avenue
Daytona Beach, FL
(386) 761–2050

Holiday Inn Daytona
Speedway
2620 West International
Speedway Boulevard
Daytona Beach, FL
(386) 258–6333

Holiday Inn Hotel Suites
930 North Atlantic Avenue
Daytona Beach, FL
(386) 255–5494

Howard Johnson
701 South Atlantic Avenue
Daytona Beach, FL
(386) 257–9122

Howard Johnson's Ocean-
front Resort
2560 North Atlantic
Avenue
Daytona Beach, FL
(386) 672–1440

Inn on the Beach
1615 South Atlantic
Avenue
Daytona Beach, FL
(386) 255–0921

La Quinta Inn
2725 West International
Speedway Boulevard
Daytona Beach, FL
(386) 255–7412

Ocean Court
2315 South Atlantic
Avenue
Daytona Beach, FL
(386) 253–8185

Ocean's Eleven Resort
2025 South Atlantic
Avenue
Daytona Beach, FL
(386) 257–1950

Oceanside Inn
1909 South Atlantic
Avenue
Daytona Beach, FL
(386) 255–0394

Ocean Walk Resort
300 North Atlantic Avenue
Daytona Beach, FL
(386) 323–4800

Plaza Resort and Spa
600 North Atlantic Avenue
Daytona Beach, FL
(386) 255–4471

Quality Inn Ocean Palms
2323 South Atlantic
Avenue
Daytona Beach, FL
(386) 255–0476

Radisson Resort
640 North Atlantic Avenue
Daytona Beach, FL
(386) 239–9800

Ramada Daytona
Speedway
1798 West International
Speedway Boulevard
Daytona Beach, FL
(386) 255–2422

Ramada Limited on the
Beach
1000 North Atlantic
Avenue
Daytona Beach, FL
(386) 239–9795

Rodeway Inn and Suites
Oceanfront
333 South Atlantic Avenue
Daytona Beach, FL
(386) 255–0123

Suburban Hotel
220 Bill France Boulevard
Daytona Beach, FL
(386) 274–4337

Sun Viking Lodge
2411 South Atlantic
Avenue
Daytona Beach, FL
(800) 815–2846

Talisman Lodge
4311 South Atlantic
Avenue
Daytona Beach, FL
(386) 761–0511

Travelodge Daytona Beach
2250 West International
Boulevard
Daytona Beach, FL
(386) 255–3661

Travelodge Daytona Beach
Ocean Jewels
935 South Atlantic Avenue
Daytona Beach, FL
(386) 252–2581

Treasure Island Resort
2025 South Atlantic
Avenue
Daytona Beach, FL
(386) 255–8371

Tropical Winds Motel
1398 North Atlantic
Avenue
Daytona Beach, FL
(386) 258–1016

Daytona Beach Area Camping

Bulow RV Resort and
Campground
3345 Old Kings Road
South
Flagler Beach, FL
(800) 782–8569

Daytona Beach
Campground
4601 Clyde Morris
Boulevard
Daytona Beach, FL
(386) 761–2663

Harris Village and RV Park
1080 North US 1
Ormond Beach, FL
(386) 673–0494

International RV Park and
Campground
3175 West International
Speedway Boulevard
Daytona Beach, FL
(386) 239–0249

Nova Family Campground
1190 Herbert Street
Daytona Beach, FL
(386) 767–0095

Orange Isle Campground
3520 Nova Road
Port Orange, FL
(386) 767–9170

Rose Bay Travel Park
5200 South Nova Road
Daytona Beach, FL
(386) 767–4308

Spruce Creek Park
6250 South Ridgewood
Avenue
Port Orange, FL
(386) 322–5133

Tomoka State Park
2099 North Beach Street
Ormond Beach, FL
(386) 676–4050

Racing on The Beach

You probably had to see it to believe it, but they actually used to race stock cars on the beach here at Daytona Beach. The 4.1-mile circuit included a stretch on the sand, with the rest of the track running on famed U.S. Highway A–1A. NASCAR founder Bill France organized the first races there.

In 1951 Tim Flock and his hotrod Lincoln became the first driver to qualify at more than 100 mph on the beach, clocking in at 102.200 mph. Visitors can still drive on a 16-mile stretch of beach here, but we recommend obeying the posted speed limit.

Homestead–Miami Speedway:
Championship Weekend

The Homestead–Miami Speedway has the distinction of closing the season, not only for the Nextel Cup Series, but also for the Busch and Craftsman Truck Series as well—three championships in one glorious weekend.

The South Florida location makes Homestead a terrific racing vacation destination. The only drawback has been the racetrack itself. For the third time in seven years, the owners tore up the pavement and made it more conducive to side-by-side racing. Gone are the flat-banked corners, replaced with more-sweeping turns that, hopefully, will end years of follow-the-leader racing.

Built in 1995, the track has had something of a troubled childhood. Redesigned first following the 1997 season (the Nextel Cup Series first raced here in 1999), Homestead underwent an even more drastic face-lift in 2003, taking away the 6-degree banked turns and replacing them with an innovative variable banking system with a maximum 20-degree bank.

Let's Go Racing

It's anyone's guess what the racing will be like at the reconfigured Homestead–Miami Speedway. One thing's for sure: It has to be more exciting than the follow-the-leader, single-file races of the past. The banked corners may offer some immediate help, but it will take years for the pavement to cure before a true second groove opens up. Until then, Homestead will remain an exercise in futility.

How to Get There

From the north: Take the Florida Turnpike to Speedway Boulevard (Southwest 137th Avenue), then go east on Speedway Boulevard to the main entrance. From the east: Take U.S. Highway 1 to Palm Drive (Southwest 144th Avenue), then head east on Palm Drive for approximately 2.5 miles (past the baseball stadium) to Southwest 142nd Avenue. Go left on Southwest 142nd Avenue to the main entrance.

If you're coming from the south, you probably arrived by boat, since the speedway is just a few minutes from the bottom tip of the Everglades and Florida Bay.

HOMESTEAD–MIAMI SPEEDWAY

START/FINISH

TURN 1

TURN 4

Pit Road

TURN 2

TURN 3

Our Ratings

Racing: 🏁 🏁 🏁 🏁

Amenities: 🏁 🏁 🏁 🏁

Area Appeal: 🏁 🏁 🏁 🏁 🏁

Track Facts

1.5-mile oval

Seating capacity: **72,000**

1 Speedway Boulevard

Homestead, FL **33035**

(**305**) **230–7223**

www.homesteadmiamispeedway.com

Annual Events

Season-ending races in November for Nextel Cup, Busch, and Craftsman Truck Series

Weather

Average High (F): November 81.0

Average Low (F): November 64.6

Top Gun

Tony Stewart, 2 wins

Qualifying Record

Jamie McMurray, 181.111 mph

Best Seats in the House

To ensure a view of the entire 1.5-mile track, buy tickets as high up in the grandstand as you can afford. The new turns promise to be the hot areas of the reconfigured track, so consider seats at the exit of Turn 4 or near the entrance of Turn 1. You'll get to watch the competition in the corners up close and still be able to see the action on pit road.

South Florida remains a rare hotspot for open-wheeled racing. While the rest of the country has thrown its interest—and dollars—at stock cars, South Florida's diverse culture has deep Formula One and CART Champ Car World Series roots, especially in the Latin quarters. Because of that, the Nextel Cup Series remains a hard sell. Good tickets generally are available throughout the racing weekend.

Homestead Memories

NASCAR's top series has only been racing here since 1999, so there haven't been many incredible racing moments. In the first Nextel Cup Series race here, **Dale Jarrett,** driving a Ford, clinched the 1999 championship with a fifth-place finish at Homestead when it was positioned next-to-last in the schedule.

Homestead eventually hopes to have the kind of championship race that Atlanta enjoyed in 1992, but its incredible weather is a good consolation prize.

In 2002 **Tony Stewart** wrapped up his first Cup championship with an eighteenth-place finish here, beating **Mark Martin** for the title. **Kyle Busch** won the race, his third victory in the last five races of the season. Stewart, who was NASCAR's Rookie of the Year in 1999, previously won a championship in 1997 in the IRL IndyCar Series. Stewart, who won two of the first three Cup events at the track, is probably the only driver who liked the old, flat configuration just fine.

Make It a Vacation

Along with Las Vegas, Sonoma (San Francisco), and Daytona Beach, the Homestead–Miami Speedway ranks as one of the top vacation destinations on the NASCAR Nextel Cup Series circuit. All the activities and attractions that South Florida has to offer—the beaches, the Florida Keys, fishing, the alligators, and the Everglades—add up to a memorable racing vacation.

Here's one way to get the most out of a week at Homestead: Stay in **Key Largo,** about 30 miles to the south. The location for the classic Bogart/Bacall movie, this jumping-off point for the Florida Keys has everything you'd expect: fishing, diving, or just plain lounging and soaking up the unique, laid-back atmosphere of the Keys.

For luxury accommodations try the **Key Largo Bay Marriott Beach Resort** (103800 Overseas Highway, Key Largo; 305–453–0582). Suites can accommodate up to five persons, and most rooms have private balconies overlooking Florida Bay. You'll find the usual trappings of resort life, including golf, tennis, a private beach, a health spa, and a gambling cruise ship available to guests.

If you prefer a more local flavor—and lower rates—check out **Popp's Motel** (95500 Overseas Highway, Key Largo; 305–852–5201), a Key Largo institution and a favorite of veteran visitors. This little bayfront jewel of a resort has ten cottages, simply but nicely furnished.

Away from the Track

Can't spring for a resort vacation? There's plenty to do right in the Homestead area.

Believe it or not, the **Fruit and Spice Park** (24801 Southwest 187 Avenue, Homestead; 305–247–5727) in the Redlands area of Homestead is a real treat—literally. Almost everything in this thirty-two-acre tropical paradise—more than 500 varieties of fruits, herbs, spices, and nuts—is edible. And they actually encourage you to sample the flora.

If you've ever wanted to snorkel, here's your chance. Spend a day at **Biscayne National Park** (9700 Southwest 328 Street, Homestead; 305–230–1100), where it's easy to enjoy stunning underwater views in a shallow bay by snorkeling, diving, or glass-bottom boat.

For the landlubbers, **Monkey Jungle** (14805 Southwest 216th Street, Miami; 305–235–1611) is a truly unique experience, with the humans inside the fence and more than 500 primates running wild. In a rare role reversal, the monkeys are on the outside and the humans are in caged walkways. The primates fuss and flirt—and drop little baskets down chutes for the humans to fill with raisins. There's serious primate research going on here, but for visitors it's just monkey business.

For a quick taste of the Everglades, check out **Everglades Alligator Farm** (40351 Southwest 192nd Avenue, Florida City; 305–247–2628). It's home to about 3,000 alligators, large and small. When you're done pondering the big carnivores, hop on an airboat for a quick excursion into the Everglades.

Adults have a variety of ways to spend—or win—money at any one of the area's wagering playgrounds. **Miami Jai Alai** (3500 Northwest Thirty-seventh Avenue, Miami; 305–633–6400; www.fla-gaming.com) is a landmark; **Calder Race Course** (21001 Northwest Twenty-seventh Avenue, Opa Locka; 305–625–1311; www.calderracecourse.com) offers a full horse-racing program Wednesday through Monday; and **Flagler Dog Track Sports and Entertainment Center** (Northwest Thirty-seventh Avenue, Miami; 305–649–3000; www.flaglerdogs.com) is one of the country's biggest kennel clubs.

Where to Eat

The most popular restaurant in South Florida is **Joe's Stone Crab** (227 Biscayne Street, Miami Beach; 305–673–0365). You can expect to stand in line and spend a day's pay for a plate of stone crabs, but most claim it's worth the effort.

Popular hangouts in Homestead, a little closer to the speedway, include **Flagler Station Restaurant and Lounge** (28 South Krome Avenue; 305–242–0712); **Casita Tejas** Mexican restaurant (27 North Krome Avenue; 305–248–8224); **Redland Rib House** (24856 Southwest 177 Avenue; 305–246–8866); and **Sam's Country Kitchen** (1320 North Krome Avenue; 305–246–2990). Or head over to Florida City and the **Mutineer Restaurant/Wharf Lounge** (11 Southeast First Avenue, Florida City, 305–245–3377).

Where to Stay

You'll find plenty of budget hotels in the Homestead area, but it may be hard to get a reservation during race week. For those who can't get into **Best Western Gateway to the Keys** (411 South Krome Avenue, Florida City; 305–246–5100); **Comfort Inn** (333 Southeast First Avenue, Florida City; 305–248–4009); **Everglades International Hostel** (20 Southwest Second Avenue, Homestead; 305–248–1122); or **Hampton Inn** (124 East Palm Drive, Florida City; 305–247–8833), it's an easy trip down from Miami or over from South Beach. The Florida City hotels are of the no-frills variety, fine for the weekend but probably not what you want in a vacation getaway. If you want excitement and nightlife in your racing visit, look north and east.

The young and trendy will like to hang out at South Beach, and the **Holiday Inn at South Beach** (2201 Collins Avenue, Miami Beach; 800–356–6902) is a good value. For a more romantic experience, the **Aqua Hotel** (1530 Collins Avenue, Miami Beach; 305–538–4361) comes highly recommended. It's very chic and just a block from the beach.

If you're more interested in getting in and out of the speedway without any problems, check all the major hotel chains for rooms around Miami International Airport. There are enough rooms there to put up the entire race crowd.

Homestead–Miami Area Restaurants

Angie's Place
404 Southeast First
    Avenue
Florida City, FL
(305) 245–8939

Cafe Largo
99530 Overseas Highway
Key Largo, FL
(305) 451–4885

Canton Chinese
1657 Northeast Eighth
    Street
Homestead, FL
(305) 248–9956

Capri Restaurant
935 North Krome Avenue
Florida City, FL
(305) 247–1542

Casita Tejas
27 North Krome Avenue
Homestead, FL
(305) 248–8224

Chez Jean-Claude
1235 North Krome
  Avenue
Homestead, FL
(305) 248–4671

Denny's
401 Southeast First
  Avenue
Florida City, FL
(305) 246–0029

El Toro Taco
1 South Krome Avenue
Homestead, FL
(305) 245–8182

Farmer's Market Restaurant
300 North Krome Avenue
Florida City, FL
(305) 242–0008

Flagler Station Restaurant
  and Lounge
28 South Krome Avenue
Homestead, FL
(305) 242–0712

International House of
  Pancakes
399 South Homestead
  Boulevard
Homestead, FL
(305) 248–1990

Italian Fisherman
Mile Marker 104
Key Largo, FL
(305) 451–4471

Joe's Stone Crab
227 Biscayne Street
Miami Beach, FL
(305) 673–0365

Keg South of Homestead
27591 South Dixie
  Highway
Homestead, FL
(305) 248–0959

Main Street Cafe
128 North Krome Avenue
Homestead, FL
(305) 245–7099

Miami Subs
60 East Palm Drive
Florida City, FL
(305) 248–1513

Mutineer Restaurant
11 Southeast First Avenue
Florida City, FL
(305) 245–3377

Nikko Japanese
  Restaurant
827 North Homestead
  Boulevard
Homestead, FL
(305) 242–8772

Pizza Hut
28640 South Dixie
  Highway
Homestead, FL
(305) 247–6100

Pollo Tropical
915 Homestead Boulevard
Homestead, FL
(305) 245–0410

The Quay
102050 Overseas
  Highway
Key Largo, FL
(305) 451–0943

Redland Rib House
24856 Southwest 177
  Avenue
Homestead, FL
(305) 246–8866

Rosita's Restaurant
199 West Palm Drive
Florida City, FL
(305) 246–3114

Sam's Country Kitchen
1320 North Krome
  Avenue
Homestead, FL
(305) 246–2990

Shiver's Bar-B-Q
28001 South Dixie
  Highway
Homestead, FL
(305) 248–2272

Snapper's Saloon and Raw
  Bar
139 Seaside Avenue
Tavernier, FL
(305) 852–5956

Sports Page Pub
113 South Homestead
  Boulevard
Homestead, FL
(305) 246–3633

Sundays on the Bay
5420 Crandon Boulevard
Key Biscayne, FL
(305) 361–6777

Tiffany's
22 Northeast Fifteenth
Street
Homestead, FL
(305) 246–0022

White Lion Cafe
146 Northwest Seventh
Street
Homestead, FL
(305) 248–1076

Homestead–Miami Area Lodging

Aqua Hotel
1530 Collins Avenue
Miami Beach, FL
(305) 538–4361

Best Western Gateway to
the Keys
411 South Krome Avenue
Florida City, FL
(305) 246–5100

Best Western Suites at
Key Largo
201 Ocean Drive
Key Largo, FL
(305) 451–5081

Biltmore Hotel
1200 Anastasia
Coral Gables, FL
(305) 445–1926

Cheeca Lodge
Mile Marker 82
Islamorada, FL
(305) 664–4651

Comfort Inn
333 Southeast First
Avenue
Florida City, FL
(305) 248–4009

Dadeland Marriott
9090 South Dadeland
Boulevard
Miami, FL
(305) 670–1035

Doubletree Grand Hotel
1717 North Bayshore
Drive
Miami, FL
(305) 372–0313

Dupont Plaza Hotel
300 Biscayne Boulevard
Miami, FL
(305) 358–2541

Everglades International
Hostel
20 Southwest Second
Avenue
Homestead, FL
(305) 248–1122

Flamingo Lodge in Ever-
glades National Park
1 Flamingo Lodge Highway
Flamingo, FL
(941) 695–3101

Hampton Inn
124 East Palm Drive
Florida City, FL
(305) 247–8833

Holiday Inn at South
Beach
2201 Collins Avenue
Miami Beach, FL
(800) 356–6902

Key Largo Bay Marriott
Beach Resort
103800 Overseas
Highway
Key Largo, FL
(305) 453–0582

Marriott Biscayne Bay
1633 North Bayshore
Drive
Miami, FL
(305) 374–3900

Marriott Key Largo
Mile Marker 104
Key Largo, FL
(305) 453–0582

Miami Airport Marriott
1201 Northwest LeJeune
Road
Miami, FL
(305) 649–5000

Miami Beach Ocean
Resort
3025 Collins Avenue
Miami Beach, FL
(305) 534–0505

Miccosukee Resort
500 Southwest 177th
  Avenue
Miami, FL
(305) 925–2555

Popp's Motel
95500 Overseas Highway
Key Largo, FL
(305) 852–5201

Radisson Mart Plaza Hotel
711 Northwest Seventy-
  second Avenue
Miami, FL
(305) 261–3800

Radisson Miami Hotel
1601 Biscayne Boulevard
Miami, FL
(305) 374–0000

Ramada Limited
990 North Homestead
  Boulevard
Homestead, FL
(305) 247–7020

Redland Inn
5 South Flagler Avenue
Homestead, FL
(305) 246–1904

Sheraton Biscayne Bay
  Hotel
495 Brickell Avenue
Miami, FL
(305) 373–6000

Travelodge Motel
409 Southeast First
  Avenue
Florida City, FL
(305) 248–9777

Villager Lodge
1020 North Homestead
  Boulevard
Homestead, FL
(305) 248–2121

Westin Beach Resort
Mile Marker 97
Key Largo, FL
(305) 852–5553

Homestead–Miami Area Camping

Calusa Camp Resort
325 Calusa
Key Largo, FL
(305) 451–0232

Florida City Campsite and
  RV Park
601 Northwest Third
  Avenue
Florida City, FL
(305) 248–7889

Florida Keys RV Resort
106003 Overseas
  Highway
Key Largo, FL
(305) 451–6090

Four Seasons RV Park
220 Northeast Twelfth
  Avenue
Homestead, FL
(305) 248–4114

Goldcoaster RV Park
34850 Southwest 187th
  Avenue
Homestead, FL
(305) 248–5462

Key Largo Campground
  and Marina
101551 Overseas
  Highway
Key Largo, FL
(305) 451–1431

Miami/Homestead KOA
20675 Southwest 162nd
  Avenue
Homestead, FL
(800) 562–7732

Southern Comfort RV
  Resort
345 East Palm Drive
Florida City, FL
(305) 248–6909

Invasion of the North

Some old-school NASCAR fans decry the sameness of the newest tracks, mostly 1.5-mile layouts modeled after Lowe's Motor Speedway in Charlotte, North Carolina. Well, welcome to NASCAR Northeast style, where no two tracks are the same. In fact, these four tracks are all unique on the circuit—from the coat hanger–shaped layout at Pocono to the twisting road course at Watkins Glen to the high-banked torture test at Dover and the challenging flat oval in New Hampshire.

New Hampshire International Speedway
Loudon, New Hampshire

Watkins Glen International
Watkins Glen, New York

Pocono Raceway
Long Pond, Pennsylvania

Dover International Speedway
Dover, Delaware

New Hampshire International Speedway: The Magic Mile

A week before NASCAR's traveling circus comes to town, tiny Loudon, New Hampshire, has a population of 4,481 people. The week of its two stock car races, however, the population climbs to 100,000 strong.

This is a vacation haven, a place where folks from the Northeast corridor come to listen to the birds, watch the deer, swat mosquitoes, and spend glorious summer days on the lake. The sounds of an 800-horsepower race engine would seem out of place amid this splendor if these same people weren't also race fans. A day at the races in New Hampshire is like taking a vacation from your vacation. And the best part is, by Monday morning the crowds have gone and the tranquility returns.

In 1993 Rusty Wallace won the first race at this track, which started as a road course for motorcycle racing. Track owner Bob Bahre, one of the most-beloved figures in the sport, has continually tinkered with the layout to make it more competitive, and it remains a work in progress.

Bahre had only one annual date when he gave NASCAR a much-needed presence in the Boston-area market, and he conspired with Speedway Motorsports Inc. chairman O. Bruton Smith to buy the North Wilkesboro Speedway in 1996. As soon as they bought that track—and its two racing dates on the Nextel Cup Series calendar—they closed it and sent one of the dates to Smith's new Texas Motor Speedway and the other to New Hampshire, giving Bahre two races a year.

The September race comes as the White Mountain National Forest and the tiny hamlets surrounding Lake Winnipesaukee prepare to change into their autumn colors. It's a show that shouldn't be missed.

Let's Go Racing

For all its beauty and grandeur, New Hampshire International still has trouble coming up to speed. The first race here in 1993 was mired by crumbling pavement that had to be replaced as soon as the race was over. The 1990 season was the speedway's worst when Adam Petty, the fourth-generation driver from the most famous family in stock car history, and Kenny Irwin both died in separate, but alarmingly similar, accidents in the third turn. Both died after a mechanical failure sent them into the outside wall at full speed. NASCAR reacted by making a restrictor plate mandatory to reduce speeds, but all that did was eliminate most passing and allow

NEW HAMPSHIRE INTERNATIONAL SPEEDWAY

START/FINISH

TURN 1

TURN 4

Pit Road

TURN 2

TURN 3

Our Ratings	Racing: 🏁 🏁
	Amenities: 🏁 🏁 🏁
	Area Appeal: 🏁 🏁 🏁 🏁

Track Facts

1.058-mile oval
Seating capacity: 91,000
1122 Route 106 North
Loudon, NH 03307-7888
(603) 783–4931
www.nhis.com

Annual Events

Two NASCAR Nextel Cup Series events, July and September
Companion events: Busch Series, July; NASCAR Craftsman
Truck Series, September

Weather

Average High (F):	July 83.0	September 72.0
Average Low (F):	July 57.0	September 47.0

Top Gun

Jeff Burton, 4 wins

Qualifying Record

Ryan Newman, 132.241 mph

Jeff Burton to lead all 300 laps in the September race. That put an end to the plates.

The speedway then decided to redesign the inside groove at both ends of the track to create a more sweeping entrance and exit with hopes of promoting more side-by-side racing. It helped, but new patches where they did the work broke into pieces a year later, triggering a near-revolt by the drivers.

The Bahres went back to work and replaced the racing surface again. All that's needed now is time for the asphalt to cure. Until then, the races are as frustrating for the drivers to drive as they are for the fans to watch.

Bob Bahre is known for being true to his convictions—including being against alcohol consumption—and he backs that up by not allowing beer sales at his track, giving up millions in beer sales to be true to his beliefs.

How to Get There

The problem with inviting 100,000 of your best friends to a town of fewer than 5,000 is that the roads aren't ready for the rush. New Hampshire Highway 106 connects Laconia and Concord, with the speedway in the middle. Traffic can be heavy from both directions, so be prepared.

From Boston; Manchester, New Hampshire; and Providence, Rhode Island: Take Interstate 93 north to Interstate 393 north in Concord. Turn left onto NH 106 and the speedway is 14 miles north of Concord.

From Laconia and the Lake Winnipesaukee area: Take NH 106 south to the raceway. An alternative route from the lake is to take New Hampshire Highway 107 south to New Hampshire Highway 129 south to the speedway.

The biggest problem with traffic after the race is the huge backups on I–93 at the tollbooths between Concord and Boston. Our suggestion is to avoid some of the traffic and enjoy the scenery along U.S. Highway 3 south.

Best Seats in the House

The size and shape of the track makes just about every seat a good one. The garage area is low, so the view to the backstretch and third-turn area is unobstructed. A section of the infield is a wildlife protected area, so there's nothing to block the view of the entire backstretch. The grandstands were smartly built with a gradual slope. That means there's not much difference between the views from one of the cheaper seats in the fifteenth row and the more expensive fortieth-row seats.

Ward Burton on New Hampshire

Although Ward Burton had won the Daytona 500 five months earlier, he couldn't figure out why his season turned out so bad. Then while winning the New England 300 in 2002, it hit him: "We didn't break, and that's what has been killing us all year," he said.

On a day when the pavement was chewed into marbles at both ends of the speedway, Burton found a way to keep his Dodge pointed in the right direction. He trailed Matt Kenseth by 50 yards, but he made up the deficit in less than two laps when Kenseth had trouble.

"I saw Matt get loose off [the second turn], and we gained on him," Burton says. "I saw him get loose again off Turn 4 and we gained on him a little more. We got into Turn 1 and he got extremely loose, and that's when I figured there was something wrong."

That something was a flat tire. Kenseth's misfortune proved fortunate for Burton, who had gone without a top-five finish after the Daytona 500 victory until he won at New Hampshire.

"You've got to be in position to win them, and we were in position," Burton says. "We ran all day, and that's what you have to do."

Doing Deluxe

New Hampshire is one of the few racetracks that sell seats in the Corporate Suites to the general public. Each suite has air-conditioning and a clear view of the entire raceway. They also have bars and rest rooms and can accommodate as many as sixty fans.

If you have a suite tooth, remember this important catch: You have to rent it for the entire year.

New Hampshire Memories

Drivers always say the most memorable victory is the first one. **Robby Gordon** took that adage to a new level. Not only was his win here in the 2001 season finale a first in his stock car–racing career, but it came at the expense of **Jeff Gordon.** Robby Gordon won with a late-race bump that nearly sent Jeff Gordon into the fourth turn wall, and after the race Robby wasn't in the mood to apologize.

"That's why they call it racing," Robby Gordon says. "I got into him a bit, but I didn't spin him. I just moved him up the racetrack a little bit. I had to go."

The Gordons aren't related. And after their late-race antics, it's not likely either will get a Christmas card from the other. During a late-race caution, Jeff Gordon ran his Chevrolet into Robby's Chevrolet in retaliation, drawing a black flag from NASCAR and a one-lap penalty.

"I didn't expect that from Jeff," Robby says. "I didn't wreck him. I could see it if I'd wrecked him and he'd hit the wall. He had a car still good enough to win the race, and he took himself out. Once he ran into me and didn't wreck me, I knew there wasn't another car out there as fast as ours."

Make It a Vacation

Start looking now to rent a cottage anywhere on Lake Winnipesaukee, and plan to stay a week or two. The area is where On Golden Pond and What About Bob? were filmed, and it is more breathtaking in real life than on the movie screen.

There's not a lot to do at the lake—and that's exactly the point. We advise spending the day playing on the shore, cruising or sailing, or simply sitting on the dock with your toes in the water. Getting back to nature has never felt so good.

For a jump on finding a house or cottage to rent, contact any of the following companies that specialize in rentals: **Century 21 Lakes Region Realty** (888–359–3858), **Preferred Properties, Inc.** (603–253–4345), **Roche Realty Group, Inc.** (603–279–7046), and **Village at Winnipesaukee** (603–366–4878).

Away from the Track

If you only have a day or two, spend at least half of it driving and exploring the Lake Winnipesaukee area. There are hundreds of little shops around the lake and just as many little sandwich shops and ice-cream parlors that are open only during the summer vacation months.

Weirs Beach is a popular hangout. You can take a boat tour of the lake or while away an afternoon sitting in the shade of a gazebo. Or play a round of miniature golf, take some swings in the batting cage, or make a splash at the water park.

The mansion known as **Castle in the Clouds** (New Hampshire Highway 171, Moultonborough; 603–476–2352) is a great place to ride horses or enjoy the view overlooking the mountains.

For a more historical perspective of the area, you can spend the day exploring the **Christa McAuliffe Planetarium** (3 Institute Drive, Concord; 603–271–7831) or the **Museum of New Hampshire** (6 Eagle Square, Concord; 603–228–6688).

A great way to spend the afternoon is taking a day cruise on the **M/S Mt. Washington** (Weirs Beach; 603–366–5531). It makes stops at Weirs Beach, Alton Bay, and Wolfeboro. You can also take a dinner cruise out of Weirs Beach on Friday and Saturday.

Where to Eat

The first big meal everyone has in New England is lobster. One choice is **Makris Lobster and Steak House** (354 Sheep Davis Road, Concord; 603–226–6588), just down the road from the speedway, or **Weathervane Seafoods** (379 Dover Road, Chichester; 603–225–4044), a few minutes farther away. Drivers make appearances at Makris; Weathervane has an exceptional seafood menu. You can't go wrong with either place.

Near the lake we recommend trying **Nothin' Fancy** (306 Lakeside Avenue, Weirs Beach; 603–366–5764); **Cherrystone Lobster House** (40 Weirs Road, Gilford; 603–293–7390); **Hart's Turkey Farm** (New Hampshire Highways 3 and 104, Meredith; 603–279–6212); **Weirs Beach Lobster Pound** (70 Endicott North, Laconia; 603–366–2255); **Pop's Clam Shell** (New Hampshire Highway 11, Alton Bay; 603–875–6363); and **Alan's of Boscawen** (133 North Main Street, Boscawen; 603–753–6631).

In Concord **Cheers** (17 Depot Street, Concord; 603–228–0180); **Red Blazer** (72 Manchester Street, Concord; 603–224–4101); **Angelina's Ristorante Italiano** (11 Depot Street, Concord; 603–228–3313); **Harry's Steakhouse** (61 South Main Street, Concord; 603–229–0004); and **Kansas City Steak House** (172 North Main Street, Concord; 603–224–0400) are local favorites.

Where to Stay

Most of the hotels are south of the speedway in Concord or Manchester.

In Concord start with **Fairfield Inn by Marriott** (603–224–4011); **Best Western Inn and Suites** (603–228–4300); **Comfort Inn** (603–226–4100); **Days Inn** (603–224–2511); **Holiday Inn** (603–224–9534); and **Courtyard by Marriott** (603–225–0303).

In Manchester try the **Sheraton Four Points** (603–668–6110); **Ash Street Inn** (603–668–9908); and the **Highlander Inn** (603–625–6426).

If you work at it, you might find a place up at the lake. Here are some suggestions: **Lovejoy Farm Bed and Breakfast** (268 Lovejoy Road, Loudon; 603–783–4007); **Bayside Inn** (New Hampshire Highway 11–D, Alton Bay; 603–875–5005); **The Margate** (76 Lake Street, Laconia; 603–524–5210); and **Naswa Resort** (1086 Weirs Boulevard, Laconia; 603–366–4341).

New Hampshire Speedway Area Restaurants

Alan's of Boscawen 133 North Main Street Boscawen, NH (603) 753–6631	The Barley House 126 North Main Street Concord, NH (603) 228–6363	Brookside Pizza NH 106 Brookside Mall Loudon, NH (603) 783–4550
Angelina's Ristorante Italiano 11 Depot Street Concord, NH (603) 228–3313	Beefside 106 Manchester Street Concord, NH (603) 228–0208	The Capital Grille 1 Eagle Square Concord, NH (603) 228–6608

Cat 'N Fiddle
118 Manchester Street
Concord, NH
(603) 228–8911

Cheers
17 Depot Street
Concord, NH
(603) 228–0180

Cherrystone Lobster
    House
40 Weirs Road
Gilford, NH
(603) 293–7390

Chili's
221 Loudon Road
Concord, NH
(603) 226–3830

Cityside Grill
25 Manchester Street
Concord, NH
(603) 227–0884

The Common Man
29 Water Street
Concord, NH
(603) 228–3463

Egg Shell Restaurant
NH 106 Brookside Mall
Loudon, NH
(603) 783–4060

Fratello's
799 Union Avenue
Laconia, NH
(603) 528–2022

Ginger Garden
161 Loudon Road
Concord, NH
(603) 226–8866

Harry's Steakhouse
61 South Main Street
Concord, NH
(603) 229–0004

Hart's Turkey Farm
NH 3 and 104
Meredith, NH
(603) 279–6212

Hermanos Cocina
    Mexicana
11 Hills Avenue
Concord, NH
(603) 224–5669

Kansas City Steak House
172 North Main Street
Concord, NH
(603) 224–0400

King's Chinese Restaurant
NH 106 Brookside Mall
Loudon, NH
(603) 783–3316

Longhorn Steakhouse
217 Loudon Road
Concord, NH
(603) 228–0655

Makris Lobster and Steak
    House
354 Sheep Davis Road
Concord, NH
(603) 226–6588

Margaritas
1 Bicentennial Square
Concord, NH
(603) 224–2821

McGillicuddy's
Fox Pond Plaza
Loudon, NH
(603) 798–3737

Moritomo
32 Fort Eddy Road
Concord, NH
(603) 224–8363

99 Restaurant and Pub
60 D'Amante Drive
Concord, NH
(603) 224–7399

Nothin' Fancy
306 Lakeside Drive
Weirs Beach, NH
(603) 366–5764

Olive Garden
219 Loudon Road
Concord, NH
(603) 228–6886

Oliver's
NH 3
Tilton, NH
(603) 286–7379

Pop's Clam Shell
NH 11
Alton Bay, NH
(603) 875–6363

The Red Blazer
72 Manchester Street
Concord, NH
(603) 224–4101

Weathervane Seafoods
New Hampshire Highway 4
Chichester, NH
(603) 225–4044

Weirs Beach Lobster
    Pound
70 Endicott North
Laconia, NH
(603) 366–2255

New Hampshire Speedway Area Lodging

Ash Street Inn
118 Ash Street
Manchester, NH
(603) 668–9908

B. Mae's Resort Inn
Junction New Hampshire
   Highway 11 at 11B
Gilford, NH
(603) 293–7526

Bay Side Inn
NH 11D
Alton Bay, NH
(603) 875–5005

Bedford Village Inn
2 Village Inn Lane
Bedford, NH
(603) 472–2001

Best Western Inn and
   Suites
97 Hall Street
Concord, NH
(603) 228–4300

Black Swan Inn
354 West Main Street
Tilton, NH
(603) 286–4524

Centennial Inn
96 Pleasant Street
Concord, NH
(603) 227–9000

Comfort Inn
71 Hall Street
Concord, NH
(603) 226–4100

Courtyard by Marriott
70 Constitution Avenue
Concord, NH
(603) 225–0303

Days Inn
406 South Main Street
Concord, NH
(603) 224–2511

Fairfield Inn
4 Gulf Street
Concord, NH
(603) 224–4011

Hampton Inn
515 South Street
Bow, NH
(603) 224–5322

Highlander Inn
2 Highlander Way
Manchester, NH
(603) 625–6426

Holiday Inn
172 North Main Street
Concord, NH
(603) 224–9534

Lakeview Bed and
   Breakfast
6 Winnisquam Avenue
Belmont, NH
(603) 528–3129

Lovejoy Farm Bed and
   Breakfast
268 Lovejoy Road
Loudon, NH
(603) 783–4007

The Margate
76 Lake Street
Laconia, NH
(603) 524–5210

Misty Harbor Resort
NH 11B
Gilford, NH
(603) 293–4500

Naswa Resort
1086 Weirs Boulevard
Laconia, NH
(603) 366–4341

Red Roof Inn
519 NH 106 South
Loudon, NH
(603) 225–8399

Shalimar Resort
NH 3
Winnisquam, NH
(603) 524–1984

Sheraton Four Points
55 John E. Devine Drive
Manchester, NH
(603) 668–6110

Super 8 Motel
7 Tilton Road
Tilton, NH
(603) 286–8882

Tara Wayfarer Inn
121 South River Road
Bedford, NH
(603) 622–3766

Tilton Manor
40 Chestnut Street
Tilton, NH
(603) 286–3457

New Hampshire Speedway Area Camping

Bay Hill Campground and
Cabins
Alton Bay, NH
(603) 875–0528

Clearwater Campground
26 Campground Road
Meredith, NH
(603) 279–7761

Gunstock Campground
NH 11A
Laconia, NH
(603) 293–4341

Hack-Ma-Tack Campground
RFD 3
Laconia, NH
(603) 366–5977

Meredith Woods Year-
Round RV Park
26 Campground Road
Meredith, NH
(603) 279–5449

Paugus Bay Campground
96 Hillard Road
Laconia, NH
(603) 366–4757

Roberts Knoll Campground
New Hampshire Highway 1
Alton Bay, NH
(603) 875–6388

Viewland Campground
Bay Hill Road
Alton Bay, NH
(603) 875–7100

Weirs Beach Tent and
Trailer Park
RFD 3
Laconia, NH
(603) 366–4747

Willey Brook Campground
883 Center Street
Wolfeboro, NH
(603) 569–9493

Wolfeboro Campground
61 Haines Hill Road
Wolfeboro, NH
(603) 569–9881

Watkins Glen International:
Thunder Road

In its glory, Watkins Glen International was a world-class road course. But that was a long time ago. The track, located at the southern tip of Seneca Lake, used to be a favorite playground for drivers like Jackie Stewart, Graham Hill, and Mark Donahue and the Formula One circuit. Now, more than fifty-five years after it opened, it's a shell of its former glory.

Carved among the Finger Lakes, lush farmland, and the awe-inspiring scenery of upstate New York, the track is part of the International Speedway Corporation family. Since the same family that owns and operates ISC—the Frances—also owns and operates NASCAR, the track isn't in danger of losing its annual date on the Nextel Cup Series calendar.

The grandstands are old and don't offer much in the way of entertainment; the facility lacks many of the basic amenities that racing fans have come to expect. The saving grace for the entire experience is the surrounding area.

Let's Go Racing

Unlike the other road course at Sonoma, California, there are places to pass at Watkins Glen. Traffic moves in a clockwise direction, and there are three straightaways where drivers can drag race to the corners. The track is very fast considering that a driver has to shift ten times a lap and work the brakes just as often.

After J. D. McDuffie was killed in a horrific collision at the end of the fastest straightaway leading into the fifth turn, the speedway added a chicane—a turnoff that includes a quick right, a quick left, and a quick right back onto the racetrack—to slow the cars down. The speedway also added huge gravel pits at the end of the straightaways to keep cars from sliding through the grass and hitting the walls head-on.

The gravel pits are a great place to watch because they're almost certain to get action. Cars generally get stuck in the gravel and have to be pulled out with a wrecker. Most of the time, it costs a driver at least one lap to the leader.

As with most races, fuel mileage has become an important factor at The Glen. Despite the number of places to make a pass, teams still prefer to gain track position with a pit strategy that requires less time on pit road.

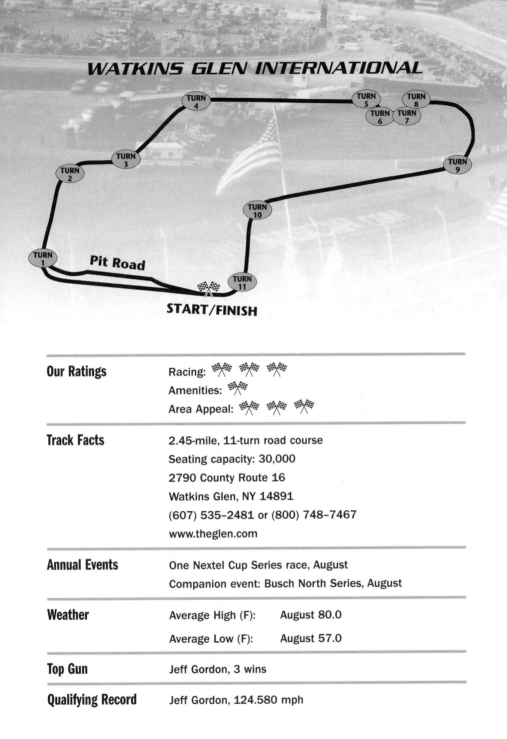

WATKINS GLEN INTERNATIONAL

TURN 4
TURN 5
TURN 8
TURN 6
TURN 7
TURN 3
TURN 2
TURN 9
TURN 10
TURN 1

Pit Road

TURN 11

START/FINISH

Our Ratings	Racing: 🏁 🏁 🏁
	Amenities: 🏁
	Area Appeal: 🏁 🏁 🏁

Track Facts	2.45-mile, 11-turn road course
	Seating capacity: 30,000
	2790 County Route 16
	Watkins Glen, NY 14891
	(607) 535–2481 or (800) 748–7467
	www.theglen.com

| **Annual Events** | One Nextel Cup Series race, August |
| | Companion event: Busch North Series, August |

| **Weather** | Average High (F): | August 80.0 |
| | Average Low (F): | August 57.0 |

| **Top Gun** | Jeff Gordon, 3 wins |

| **Qualifying Record** | Jeff Gordon, 124.580 mph |

How to Get There

The drive into Watkins Glen is beautiful, which is a good thing, since it takes a long time to move traffic on a two-lane country road.

From Elmira: Take New York Highway 14 north to County Road 64 east. Make a right onto NY 14 north (Westinghouse Road), a left onto West South Street, a right onto South Genesee Street, and a left onto County Road 16 to the speedway.

From Corning: Take New York Highway 414 north to County Road 19 (Beaver Dam Road), and turn left. Turn right onto CR 16 to the speedway.

From Rochester: Take Interstate 90 east to NY 14 (exit 42) and turn toward Geneva. Make a right onto New York Highway 318, then a right onto NY 14. At NY 414 turn right, then make another right onto CR 16 to the speedway.

From Syracuse: Take Interstate 81 south to New York Highway 13 (exit 11) and drive toward Ithaca. Turn right onto NY 13, right onto NY 224, and left onto NY 14. Turn right onto West South Street, and make another right onto Genesee Street. Make a left onto CR 16 to the speedway.

Jeff Gordon on Watkins Glen

Jeff Gordon became NASCAR's King of the Road by winning a series record seven road course races in a span of five years. Four of those wins came at Watkins Glen.

He won the 2001 race here with a gutsy pass of Jeff Burton heading into the chicane—not considered a smart place to pass. Gordon drove hard all the way to the turnoff, then he wrestled with his Chevrolet to complete the right-left-right turn without flying off course.

"I drove in there real deep, and that's not my favorite place to pass," Gordon says. "That's a corner that you have to overdrive in and compensate. I clipped the curb and the car jumped up and down a little bit and got sideways. You just have to take advantage of your momentum there, and I had a little momentum going into it."

Best Seats in the House

Most of the grandstand seats are located on the main straightaway and in Turns 1, 2, and 3. By design, road courses don't cater to the big picture, so the people in those seats are limited to seeing a car for only a handful of seconds each lap.

The Tower Suites between the second and third turns may provide the best view, since you can see nearly three-quarters of a mile of the raceway.

Most people, however, will find a spot in the infield or along the grassy knolls on the outside of the track. A general admission ticket means sitting on the ground—unless you bring your own chair—but offers the same view as the higher-priced grandstand seats.

Watkins Glen Memories

Buck Baker won the first stock car race at The Glen in 1957. The series didn't come back until 1964, with **Billy Wade** taking the checkered flag. After the 1965 race, NASCAR decided to leave the road course for twenty-one years. It made its third return in 1986, with **Tim Richmond** winning before 88,000 stock car racing–starved fans, and it's been back every year since.

Jeff Gordon has developed into the master of making left and right turns here, completing an impressive run of four victories in five races starting in 1997.

As a native New Yorker, **Steve Park** couldn't have picked a better place to win his first NASCAR Nextel Cup Series race. He led the final twenty-seven laps, and he showed no signs of slowing down after the race—he sprayed everyone, including car owner Dale Earnhardt, with champagne. "We had to race our guts out to win it and beat a guy **(Mark Martin)** known for winning a lot of races on road courses," Park says.

After going winless in his first seventy-six Nextel Cup Series starts, Park squelched any criticism that he didn't know how to win. The fact that the win came in his home state only intensified his satisfaction. "If you had asked me three years ago where I'd get my first win, I would only have hoped it would come at Watkins Glen," he says. "This is the place where it seems I got my start. This place got me noticed."

Make It a Vacation

The Finger Lakes region is a wonderful retreat, and **Seneca Lake** in the summer is a mecca for boating, skiing, sailing, and fishing.

While there aren't a lot of resorts in the area, we recommend enjoying a few days at one of the quaint hotels in the area, spending the day on the lake, or exploring one of the nearby state parks.

The **Anchor Inn and Marina** (3425 Salt Pond Road, Watkins Glen; 607–535–4159); **Benjamin Hunt Inn** (305 Sixth Street, Watkins Glen; 607–535–6659); **Colonial Inn and Motel** (701 North Franklin Street, Watkins Glen; 607–535–7545); **Seneca Lodge** (Watkins Glen State Park, Watkins Glen; 607–535–2014); and the **Glen Motor Inn** (Seneca Lake Road, Watkins Glen; 607–535–2706) are some cozy places with a local flavor.

Away from the Track

There are two great ways to kill an afternoon during a race weekend. You can visit some of the wineries in the area, or you can explore the splendor of **Watkins Glen State Park** (1005 North Franklin Street, Watkins Glen; 607–535–4511), where there is a massive gorge, 300-foot-tall shale and sandstone cliffs, and nineteen waterfalls. The park, which also offers an Olympic-sized pool, allows camping.

Tours through the **Knapp Vineyards Winery and Restaurant** (277 County Road 128, Romulus; 800–869–9271); **Fox Run Vineyards** (670 NY 14, Penn Yan; 800–636–9786); **Glenora Wine Cellars** (5435 NY 14, Dundee, 800–243–5513); and the **Seneca Lake Wine Trail** (100 North Franklin Street, Watkins Glen; 877–536–2717) can be informative and entertaining.

Where to Eat

You won't find big-chain restaurants in this area, but you can find a lot of well-cooked meals in some of the smallest places. Some of the best in the region are **Bianco's Daughters** (401 East Fourth Street, Watkins Glen; 607–535–2863); **Curly's Family Restaurant** (2780 NY 14, Watkins Glen; 607–535–4383); **Franklin Street Grille** (413 North Franklin Street, Watkins Glen; 607–535–2007); **Glen Mountain Market** (200 North Franklin Street, Watkins Glen; 607–535–6900); **Boomers Bistro** (58 West Market Street, Corning; 607–936–1408); **Grapevine Deli and Cafe** (418 North Franklin Street, Watkins Glen; 607–535–6141); **Moretti's** (800 Hatch Street, Elmira; 607–734–1535); **Palm's Restaurant** (1157½ North Main Street, Elmira; 607–734–5599); and the **Wildflower Cafe** (301 North Franklin Street, Watkins Glen; 607–535–9797).

Where to Stay

If you're looking for name-brand hotels, you'll have to stay in Elmira, Corning, or farther away from the track. Rooms are at a premium, especially in Watkins Glen, so expect to pay four times what they're worth. All of a sudden, Elmira, Corning, and farther away don't look so bad.

Comfort Inn (607–962–1515), **Days Inn** (607–936–9370), **Fairfield Inn by Marriott** (607–937–9600), and **Radisson Hotel Corning** (607–962–5000) highlight what's available in Corning. **Econo Lodge** (607–739–2000), **Holiday Inn Elmira-Riverview** (607–734–4211), and the **Mark Twain Motor Inn** (607–733–9144) head the list in Elmira. **Best Western** (607–272–6100), **Hilton Garden Inn** (607–795–1111), **Country Inn and Suites** (607–739–9205), **Holiday Inn Horseheads** (607–739–3681), **Howard Johnsons** (607–739–5636), **Knights Inn** (607–739–3807), **Motel 6** (607–739–2525), and **Red Carpet Inn** (607–739–3831) aren't too far away in Horseheads.

Watkins Glen Area Restaurants

Applebee's
877 County Route 64
Elmira, NY
(607) 739–1959

Bianco's Daughters
401 East Fourth Street
Watkins Glen, NY
(607) 535–2863

Boomers
35 East Market Street
Corning, NY
(607) 962–6800

Boomers Bistro
58 West Market Street
Corning, NY
(607) 936–1408

Curly's Family Restaurant
2780 NY 14
Watkins Glen, NY
(607) 535–4383

Franklin Street Grill
413 North Franklin Street
Watkins Glen, NY
(607) 535–2007

Glen Mountain Market
200 North Franklin Street
Watkins Glen, NY
(607) 535–6900

Grapevine Deli and Cafe
418 North Franklin Street
Watkins Glen, NY
(607) 535–6141

Jerlando's Pizza Co.
400 North Franklin Street
Watkins Glen, NY
(607) 535–4254

London Underground
69 East Market Street
Corning, NY
(607) 962–2345

Market Street Brewing
  Company
63 West Market Street
Corning, NY
(607) 936–2337

Moretti's
800 Hatch Street
Elmira, NY
(607) 734–1535

Olive Garden
3288 Chamber Road
Horseheads, NY
(607) 796–5228

Outback Steakhouse
200 Colonial Drive
Horseheads, NY
(607) 795–1224

Palm's Restaurant
1157½ North Main Street
Elmira, NY
(607) 734–5599

Pelham's Upstate
Tuna Co.
73 East Market Street
Corning, NY
(607) 936–8862

Spencer's Restaurant
359 East Market Street
Corning, NY
(607) 936–9196

Wildflower Cafe
301 North Franklin Street
Watkins Glen, NY
(607) 535–9797

Pierce's 1894
228 Oakwood Avenue
Elmira Heights, NY
(607) 734–2022

Watkins Glen Area Lodging

Anchor Inn and Marina
3425 Salt Point Road
Watkins Glen, NY
(607) 535–4159

Days Inn
23 Riverside Drive
Corning, NY
(607) 936–9370

Holiday Inn Corning
NY 15 and NY 417
Painted Post, NY
(607) 962–5021

Benjamin Hunt Inn
305 Sixth Street
Watkins Glen, NY
(607) 535–6659

Econo Lodge
New York Highway 17,
exit 51
Elmira, NY
(607) 739–2000

Holiday Inn Elmira-
Riverview
760 East Water Street
Elmira, NY
(607) 734–4211

Best Western Lodge on
the Green
New York Highways 15
and 417
Painted Post, NY
(607) 962–2456

Fairfield Inn by Marriott
3 South Buffalo
Corning, NY
(607) 937–9600

Holiday Inn Horseheads
NY 14 and NY 17
Horseheads, NY
(607) 739–3681

Colonial Inn and Motel
701 North Franklin Street
Watkins Glen, NY
(607) 535–7545

Glen Motor Inn
Seneca Lake Road
Watkins Glen, NY
(607) 535–2706

Holiday Inn Ithaca
222 South Cayuga Street
Ithaca, NY
(607) 272–1000

Comfort Inn
66 West Pultney Street
Corning, NY
(607) 962–1515

Hampton Inn
9775 Victory Highway
Painted Post, NY
(607) 936–3344

Howard Johnsons
Horseheads Junction
Horseheads, NY
(607) 739–5636

Country Inn and Suites
205 East Mall Road
Horseheads, NY
(607) 739–9205

Hilton Garden Inn
35 Arnot Road
Horseheads, NY
(800) 445–8667

Knights Inn
2707 Westinghouse Road
Horseheads, NY
(607) 739–3807

Mark Twain Motor Inn
1996 Lake Street
Elmira, NY
(607) 733–9144

Motel 6
4133 Route 17
Horseheads, NY
(607) 739–2525

Radisson Hotel Corning
125 Denisson Parkway
East
Corning, NY
(607) 962–5000

Red Carpet Inn
3325 South Main Street
Horseheads, NY
(607) 739–3831

Seneca Lodge
Watkins Glen State Park
1005 North Franklin
Street
Watkins Glen, NY
(607) 535–2014

Watkins Glen Area Camping

Cayuta Lake Camping
County Route 6
Alpine, NY
(607) 594–2366

Watkins Glen KOA Campground
NY 14 South
Watkins Glen, NY
(607) 535–7404

Watkins Glen State Park
1005 North Franklin
Street
Watkins Glen, NY
(607) 535–4511

W.W. Clute Memorial Park
541 East Fourth Street
Watkins Glen, NY
(607) 535–4438

Pocono Raceway:
Fire in the Mountains

The Pocono Raceway was carved out of a spinach patch, which helps explain why it looks like a giant coat hanger. And when it comes to being different, that's only the beginning.

Pocono's six-lane-wide, 3,740-foot-long front straightaway is the widest and longest in the sport. The first turn is a 14-degree-banked hairpin; the second turn—called the "tunnel turn"—is a gradual 8-degree-banked corner common to a superspeedway; and the third turn is a 6-degree-banked sweeper that wouldn't be out of place on a road course.

Doctors Joseph and Rose Mattioli, perhaps the most gracious owners in all of racing, survived years of struggle and the threat of bankruptcy to be on the ground floor of the sport's methodical rise to popularity. Their dogged dedication is one of the reasons the NASCAR circuit not only was able to sustain an existence in the Northeast but also flourish. Dr. Joseph has been seen directing traffic into the tunnel; Dr. Rose is famous for her genuine handshakes and hugs. The racetrack is far more than a business for the family; it's a sense of duty.

Richard Petty christened the place with a victory in 1974, and the crazy stories have piled up ever since. Flagman Harold Kinder once stuck both thumbs into his ears and wiggled his fingers to signal the drivers that a deer was running across the track. Another year, a crazed man ran out onto the track while the cars were at full speed, only to disappear over the second turn wall and into the thick woods. He got so lost that he set a fire to signal the police.

Let's Go Racing

No matter how hard they try, drivers cannot master all three turns at Pocono. A car that's good in Turns 1 and 2 usually has to tip-toe through Turn 3. Since the third turn sets up the nearly mile-long run down the main straightaway, most drivers try to make the car work in the third turn and make do everywhere else.

In the past ten years, crew chiefs have gone to an overdrive gear to handle the abuse on the engine on the long run down the frontstretch. Rules allow four forward gears and one reverse, so teams have forfeited second gear and installed an overdrive to keep the RPMs at or below the 9,000 range.

POCONO RACEWAY

START/FINISH

🏁

Pit Road

TURN 1

TURN 3

TURN 2

Our Ratings	Racing: 🏁 🏁 🏁 🏁
	Amenities: 🏁 🏁
	Area Appeal: 🏁 🏁 🏁
Track Facts	2.5-mile, triangle-shaped oval
	Seating capacity: 65,000 seats
	Long Pond Road
	Long Pond, PA 18334
	(800) 722–3929
	www.poconoraceway.com
Annual Events	Two Nextel Cup Series races, June and August
	Companion events: ARCA Re/Max Series, June and August
Weather	Average High (F): June 73.0 August 76.0
	Average Low (F): June 51.0 August 54.0
Top Gun	Bill Elliott, 5 wins
Qualifying Record	Tony Stewart, 172.391 mph

Even with the safety net of an overdrive gear, transmissions and engines still take a beating here. It's common for as much as 20 percent of the field to finish on a wrecker's hook.

The best place to pass is at the end of the front straightaway as the four-, five-, and sometimes six-wide racing funnels into two racing grooves in the first turn. The car on the inside groove has the best angle to make the run down the Long Pond straightaway leading up to the tunnel turn.

Bobby Labonte on Pocono

Bobby Labonte said he saw a "light at the end of the tunnel" after his team made final adjustments on his Pontiac and he started the long and tedious task of reeling in Dale Earnhardt Jr. during the July 2001 race. That light proved to be the tunnel turn.

That's where Labonte caught the third-generation driver and made the winning pass with two laps to go. The key, he says, was making sure the car wasn't too good in one corner at the expense of another. Once he found a rare balance to get through all three turns without a lot of trouble, he was able to track down and pass young Earnhardt without much of a fight.

"I told [crew chief] Jimmy [Makar], 'I see the light at the end of the tunnel'; we just needed to know if it was a train or not," Labonte says. "I wanted it pretty bad because it had been a while since we'd been that close to a checkered flag without fifteen cars passing before us.

"[Earnhardt Jr.] was being pursued that whole time, trying to hit his marks just right, and I was catching him. I felt pretty good that our car was going to be good toward the end of the run."

How to Get There

Pocono is in the mountains. That makes getting there a little more of a challenge on race day.

Fans coming from Philadelphia and Allentown will drive north on the Pennsylvania Turnpike (Pennsylvania Highway 9) to the Lake Harmony exit. Although traffic signs will tell you to follow Interstate 80 east to the speedway, here's a great way to bypass a lot of traffic: After exiting the turnpike, turn left onto Pennsylvania Highway 940 to Blakeslee. Turn right at Pennsylvania Highway 115 and follow that to the speedway.

From Scranton: Take Interstate 380 south to I–80 west. From I–80 exit at PA 115 south to the speedway.

From New York: Take Interstate 84 west to I–380 south. Get off at I–80 west and take it to PA 115; follow PA 115 south to the speedway.

Best Seats in the House

The size and shape of the speedway doesn't create a great view. Fans in the upper half of the grandstands have a clear view of the Turn 3 exit, the frontstretch, and the entrance to Turn 1. People in the lower half of the bleachers are limited to the frontstretch.

What distinguishes Pocono from other racetracks is its enormous infield. While Daytona and Talladega also are 2.5-mile raceways, they've dedicated a lot of the infield space to large garage and hospitality areas. Most of Pocono's infield is wide open for the largest infield throng of the year. The exodus to the infield is at full speed shortly after the ARCA Re/Max Series race ends on Saturday. By race time on Sunday, it's wall-to-wall campers, cars, and pup tents. Fans at the center of the infield are more than a quarter-mile away from the track, and many will spend the entire weekend without ever seeing a race car. Spending a day in the infield is the true meaning of roughing it.

Pocono also offers vantage points that come with a hot buffet and cold drinks. There are Luxury Sky Boxes for sale, as well as Pit Side Suites that face the frontstretch from the infield and the Chalet Village, where corporate hotshots mingle before the race.

Pocono Memories

It wasn't often that anyone got the better of **Dale Earnhardt.** Even more amazing was the way **Jeremy Mayfield** lived to talk about it.

Mayfield used an old Earnhardt trick—a bump-and-run maneuver—in the final turn of the last lap to win the June 2000 race. Earnhardt led the race and was about a third of a mile away from victory when Mayfield used the front bumper of his Ford to pry Earnhardt's Chevrolet off the bottom groove to open up the door for a daring pass.

Earnhardt's car bobbled and nearly hit the wall. His problems allowed **Dale Jarrett** and **Ricky Rudd** also to pass for second and third place, respectively, but he regrouped to finish fourth.

Junkyard 500

None of the cars in the annual Junkyard 500 could pass NASCAR inspection. And that, according to host Jimmy Spencer, is what makes his invitation-only race so special.

There are no race officials, no inspection lines, and no manners when drivers from the Nextel Cup Series meet at Spencer's family junkyard in Berwick, Pennsylvania, about forty-five minutes away from the Pocono Raceway. Winners don't thank their sponsors—they thank their lucky stars they survived a night of beating and banging far away from the television cameras and race queens.

The Junkyard 500 was the name given to a race among some of racing's biggest names. The course is a one-eighth-mile dirt track around the piles of rusted and abandoned cars; the cars used in this night of racing and demolition are one step away from the crusher.

Spencer is picky about who can drive in the Junkyard 500. The competitors have to be tough in nature, the kind of men who love dishing out—and receiving—rumpled fenders without complaining. Drivers who hide behind public relations specialists and have all their corporate sponsors memorized for Victory Lane have never driven a 1973 Ford Pinto in Spencer's backyard—and they never will.

This is old-school racing. And for those who've cut laps in the wobbly-wheeled jalopies, it's a night that takes them back to their roots. It's dirty, loud, and fulfilling. "You want to find out who's the best, don't you?" Spencer said of his annual private party a couple nights before the June race at Pocono. "This track tests every talent and skill God ever gave you."

Dale Earnhardt, Richard Childress, Benny Parsons, Tony Stewart, and Buddy Baker are some of the legendary drivers who've taken a night away from personal appearances for a night of fun in the junkyard. Their tales are legendary, too.

One of Spencer's favorite memories is

the night Baker was knocked off the track and into a swamp. "Me and Dale Earnhardt ran him off the track right into the swamp pit," Spencer said.

How Spencer and Earnhardt were riding together when they crashed Baker is a story of its own. One of the tires on Earnhardt's cars went flat, but he continued to race with it. Once the rubber burned away, he sent a shower of sparks around the track racing on the rim. Then the rim broke, shearing off part of the front suspension. The next step for that car was the crusher the next morning.

"That was the last straw for the car, because it came to a complete stop," Spencer said. "I'm coming around the turn in my car, and I see [Earnhardt] standing on the roof of his car yelling for someone to stop. So I pulled over, and he slid in. He wanted to drive, so we were wrestling for the steering wheel. He eventually forced me out of the driver's seat. We were riding along and started to catch Baker. I said to Earnhardt, 'When you get over there to Turn 3, push Baker into the swamp.' We started laughing, and sure enough we proceeded to run Baker straight into the swamp pit. The next time we drove by we glanced down there and saw Baker just sitting in his car in the middle of the swamp, trying to figure out how he was going to get out of the car. My brother drove up in a big Caterpillar tractor with forks on the front to pick him up. My brother slid the forks underneath the car, lifted the car 8 feet in the air with Baker still in it, backed the car out, and set it down on the ground.

"Baker said it was awful. Take my word for it: you don't want to go (into the pit). There are snakes everywhere. About the time my brother pulled Baker out, our cars were pretty much junk. None of them were running anymore, and the race was history. So we went back to the house and ate steaks.

"Earnhardt used to say it was illegal to have that much fun."

Another tale coming from the Junkyard 500 involved Childress, a former driver who is now one of the most successful car owners in NASCAR history. Shortly after Childress's car was crashed, he went to the parking lot to find another. He wound up with the station wagon that belonged to Spencer's mother. The problem was, it was her personal car.

"All of the cars end up in the crush pile," Spencer said. "All except my mother's car. We had to fix that one."

Earnhardt had little to say about the move, especially since many of his wins came in the same manner. The bump-and-run was so common to Earnhardt's success that drivers still call a rear-end collision "getting Earnhardted."

"I just wanted to rattle his cage a little bit," Mayfield said, echoing the same thing Earnhardt said ten months earlier when he crashed **Terry Labonte** on the final lap at Bristol to win a race. "I had one last shot at him. I came off (Turn) 2 and had a good run going. It looked like he pushed up a little bit and slowed down a little. When we went into (Turn) 3 he really backed off. We had a good run going in, and he got a little loose and slid up. It was just hard-nosed racing. You've got to do what you've got to do to win."

Earnhardt showed amazing grace in defeat. "I got beat," he said. "I got in the corner and shoved a little bit. It felt like he hit me. I don't know if he did or not."

Mayfield said the payback didn't erase all the times he got Earnhardted. But it was a good start. "I hadn't forgotten about the ten times he got me," he said at the time. "I'm not intimidated by Dale Earnhardt; I never will be."

Make It a Vacation

Known as a honeymoon hideaway and a summer retreat, the Poconos are a terrific place to escape the fast lane. The area is famous for its resorts, and most of them provide opportunities to spend a week lounging in a spa, playing a round of golf, riding horses, or swimming. And, yes, many resorts come with heart-shaped tubs.

Caesar's Pocono Resorts (Pennsylvania Highway 611, Scotrun; Pennsylvania Highway 590, Lakeville; PA 940, Mt. Pocono; and Pennsylvania Highway 209, Marshalls Creek; 800–805–3559); **Pocono Manor Inn and Golf Resort** (Pennsylvania Highway 314, Mount Pocono; 570–839–7111); **Skytop Lodge** (One Skytop, Skytop; 570–595–7401); **Pocmont Resort and Conference Center** (Bushkill Falls Road, Bushkill Falls; 570–588–6671); **Resort at Water Gap Country Club** (Mountain Road, Delaware Water Gap; 570–476–0300); **Big Boulder and Jack Frost Resorts** (PA 940, Blakeslee; 800–468–2442); **Chateau at Camelback** (300 Camelback Road, Tannersville; 570–629–5900); **Mountain Laurel Resort** (White Haven; 570–443–8411); and **Split Rock Resort** (1 Lake Drive, Lake Harmony; 570–722–9111) are all outstanding options.

Away from the Track

There are more than trees and bears in these woods. The more than one hundred stores at **The Crossings Factory Stores** (285 Crossings Outlet Square, Tannersville; 570–629–4650) attract many of the race teams, as does the town of **Stroudsburg,** rich in Pennsylvania Dutch history. Nearby **Pocono Downs** (1280 Pennsylvania Highway 315, Wilkes-Barre; 570–825–6681) is home to harness racing and live simulcast wagering. For something very different, check out the **Houdini Tour and Magic Show** (1433 North Main Avenue, Scranton; 570–342–5555), dedicated to one of the greatest magicians of all time.

Where to Eat

The best places to stay are within a 50-mile radius of the speedway, and so are the best places to eat.

There are a couple outstanding places close to the track. A German delicacy called the **Edelweiss Restaurant** (PA 940, Blakeslee; 570–646–3938) is a favorite of the drivers. At **Robert Christian's** (PA 940, Pocono Lake; 570–646–0433) steaks, seafood, and pasta are served in a family atmosphere. Other good bets include **Amadeo's Pizza-Deli** (PA 940 and Pennsylvania Highway 423, Pocono Pines; 570–646–4540); **Bailey's Grille**

and Steakhouse (PA 611 and Pocono Boulevard, Mount Pocono; 570–839–9678); and **Van Gilder's Jubilee Restaurant** (PA 940, Pocono Pines; 570–646–2377), where giant breakfast platters are served daily from 7:00 A.M. to 3:00 P.M.

A little farther out, try the **Steak and Rib Inn** (PA 209, Bushkill; 570–588–9466); **Petrizzo's Italian American Restaurant** (5789 Milford Road, East Stroudsburg; 570–588–6414); **Ramblers Ranch** (Maury Road, Jim Thorpe; 570–325–3060); and the **Bear Creek Inn** (5505 PA 115, Bear Creek; 570–472–9045). The scenic rides to each of these local favorites are just as good as the food.

Where to Stay

For this year you'll need to have made reservations a year in advance or plan to stay an hour away from the track. If you want to get started for next year, we suggest trying these hotels: **Best Western Inn** (PA 115, Blakeslee; 570–646–6000); **Comfort Inn** (PA 940, White Haven; 570–443–8461); **Harmony Lake Shore Inn** (Lakeshore Drive, Lake Harmony; 570–722–0522); **Ramada Limited** (Pennsylvania Highway 715 and I–80, Tannersville; 570–629–4100); **Ramada Inn Pocono** (PA 940, Lake Harmony; 570–443–8471); **The Blakeslee Inn and Restaurant** (PA 940, Blakeslee; 570–646–1100); **The Inn at Jim Thorpe** (24 Broadway, Jim Thorpe; 570–325–2599); **Clarion** (1220 West Main Street, Stroudsburg; 570–420–1000); and **Woodlands Resort** (PA 315, Wilkes-Barre; 570–824–9831).

Pocono Area Restaurants

Amadeo's Pizza-Deli PA 940 and PA 423 Pocono Pines, PA (570) 646–4540	Beaver House PA 611 Stroudsburg, PA (570) 424–1020	Casa di Pasta PA 940 Blakeslee, PA (570) 643–2222

Bailey's Grille and
  Steakhouse
PA 611 and Pocono
  Boulevard
Mt. Pocono, PA
(570) 839–9678
	Brandi's Pizzeria and
	  Italian Restaurant
	6A Foxmoor Village
	East Stroudsburg, PA
	(570) 223–1600
		Dansbury Depot
		50 Crystal Street
		East Stroudsburg, PA
		(570) 476–0500

	Brownie's in the Burg 700 Main Street Stroudsburg, PA (570) 421–2200	Dario's Brass Door PA 314 Pocono Manor, PA (570) 839–7386

Edelweiss Restaurant
PA 940
Blakeslee, PA
(570) 646–3938

Friendly's Restaurant
PA 611
Tannersville, PA
(570) 619–8877

Garris Log Cabin
   Restaurant
Pennsylvania Highway 1
Bushkill, PA
(570) 588–6398

Hanna's Ugly Mug
   Restaurant
217–219 Main Street
White Haven, PA
(570) 443–7141

High Elevations
PA 940
White Haven, PA
(570) 443–8899

J.R.'s Greenscene
   Restaurant
I–80, exit 51
East Stroudsburg, PA
(570) 424–5451

Memorytown Restaurant
NC 10 Grange Road
Mt. Pocono, PA
(570) 839–1680

Petrizzo's Italian American
   Restaurant
5789 Milford Road
East Stroudsburg, PA
(570) 588–6414

Powerhouse
PA 940
White Haven, PA
(570) 443–4480

Ramblers Ranch
Maury Road
Jim Thorpe, PA
(570) 325–3060

Robert Christian's
PA 940
Pocono Lake, PA
(570) 646–0433

Smuggler's Cove
PA 611
Tannersville, PA
(570) 629–2277

Steak and Rib Inn
PA 209
Bushkill, PA
(570) 588–9466

Van Gilder's Jubilee
   Restaurant
PA 940
Pocono Pines, PA
(570) 646–2377

Village Squire
PA 115
Blakeslee, PA
(570) 646–3446

Pocono Area Lodging

Best Western
700 Main Street
Stroudsburg, PA
(570) 421–2200

Best Western
PA 115
Blakeslee, PA
(570) 646–6000

Big Boulder and Jack Frost
   Condos
PA 940
Blakeslee, PA
(800) 468–2442

The Blakeslee Inn and
   Restaurant
PA 940
Blakeslee, PA
(570) 646–1100

Budget Motel
I–80, exit 308
East Stroudsburg, PA
(570) 424–5451

Caesars Paradise Stream
PA 940
Mt. Pocono, PA
(800) 805–3559

The Chateau at Camelback
300 Camelback Road
Tannersville, PA
(570) 629–5900

Clarion Hotel
1220 West Main Street
Stroudsburg, PA
(570) 420–1000

Comfort Inn
PA 940
White Haven, PA
(570) 443–8461

Fernwood Hotel and Resort
PA 209
Bushkill, PA
(570) 588–9500

Harmony Lake Shore Inn
Lakeshore Drive
Lake Harmony, PA
(570) 722–0522

The Inn at Jim Thorpe
24 Broadway
Jim Thorpe, PA
(570) 325–2599

Mountain Laurel Resort
White Haven, PA
(570) 443–8411

Penn's Wood Motel and
    Cottages
PA 611
Tannersville, PA
(570) 629–0131

Pocmont Resort
Bushkill Falls Road
Bushkill, PA
(570) 588–6671

Pocono Days Inn
100 Park Avenue
Stroudsburg, PA
(570) 424–1771

Pocono Manor Inn
PA 314
Mount Pocono, PA
(570) 839–7111

Pocono Super 8 Motel
HCR 1
Mt. Pocono, PA
(570) 839–7728

Pocono View Inn
PA 209
Sciota, PA
(570) 992–4167

Ramada Inn Pocono
PA 940
Lake Harmony, PA
(570) 443–8471

Ramada Limited
PA 715 at I–80
Tannersville, PA
(570) 629–4100

Resort at Water Gap
    Country Club
Mountain Road
Delaware Water Gap. PA
(570) 476–0300

Skytop Lodge
One Skytop
Skytop, PA
(570) 595–7401

Split Rock Resort
1 Lake Drive
Lake Harmony, PA
(570) 722–9111

Sullivan Trail Motel
PA 940
Pocono Lakes, PA
(570) 646–3535

Value Inn
5219 Milford Road
East Stroudsburg, PA
(570) 588–1100

Whispering Hills Motel
    and Cottages
Grange Road
Mt. Pocono, PA
(570) 839–9219

Woodlands Resort
PA 315
Wilkes-Barre, PA
(570) 824–9831

Pocono Area Camping

Delaware Water Gap KOA
RR 6 Hollow Road
East Stroudsburg, PA
(570) 223–8000

Mountain Vista
    Campground
RR 2
East Stroudsburg, PA
(570) 223–0111

Dover International Speedway:
The Monster Mile

Dover is one of the most unusual and toughest tracks on the NASCAR circuit. Difficult racetracks usually have nicknames, and the high-banked concrete oval at Dover has earned two: the Monster Mile and White Lightning.

Aside from some fast and furious racing action, Dover International Speedway is also home to a ⅝-mile harness racing track called Dover Downs and the Dover Slots, a gaming venue. To make it fit, the track owners put the harness track inside the stock car track. The frontstretch for the harness track is the backstretch for car races; the frontstretch for car races is the backstretch for the horses.

Combine intense, interesting racing with the revitalized area surrounding the track, then throw in a bit of on-site gambling, and Dover adds up to one of the best-kept secrets in NASCAR racing.

Let's Go Racing

The track opened its gates in 1969, changing to a concrete racing surface in 1994 and earning the nickname White Lightning. But whether it's asphalt or concrete, Dover is one of the toughest, most physically demanding tracks on the circuit.

It's one of the fastest oval tracks on the NASCAR circuit, thanks to 24 degrees of banking in the turns and 9 degrees on the straights—some of the steepest banking outside Talladega, Daytona, and Bristol. The result: Cars rip around the track, leaving drivers exhausted and putting equipment to an extreme test. Drivers will tell you that there are no easy hits here; when cars slam the wall at Dover, they really pound it.

Aside from the speed and ferocity of action here, Dover's brand of racing is some of the most strategically fascinating in all of NASCAR. As is the case at most other tracks, the bottom groove is the fast way around here, but it's a challenge to get the car to stick down low, especially after the tires get worn.

At the start of the race, and after teams pit for fresh tires, everyone wants the low groove—and they'll fight and crash to keep that line. About twenty laps into a run, as the tires begin to lose some grip, cars will drift higher and higher toward the outside wall. You'll see drivers using every conceivable line around the track, from the bottom to high up the banking right

DOVER INTERNATIONAL SPEEDWAY

Pit Road

START/FINISH

Our Ratings	Racing: 🏁 🏁 🏁 🏁
	Amenities: 🏁 🏁
	Area Appeal: 🏁 🏁
Track Facts	1.0-mile oval
	Seating capacity: 142,000
	1131 North DuPont Highway
	Dover, DE 19903
	(800) 441–7223
	www.doverspeedway.com
Annual Events	Two Nextel Cup Series races, June and September
	Companion events: NASCAR Craftsman Truck Series, June;
	Busch Series, June and September
Weather	Average High (F): June 83.7 September 80.1
	Average Low (F): June 61.9 September 58.8
Top Gun	Richard Petty and Bobby Allison, 7 wins
Qualifying Record	Rusty Wallace, 159.964 mph

against the wall, and everywhere in between. The low groove is still the pre-ferred line, but only the best-handling cars are able to stay down there.

Because drivers are forced to hunt for the line that works best for their particular setups, Dover is the scene of some of the most stirring side-by-side battles you'll see anywhere.

How to Get There

If you drive, it's worth the $20 to park next door at the mall. Getting your car out there after the race will be much less stressful. For those who don't mind inching along for a couple hours, here's how to get all the way to the track:

From Philadelphia and Wilmington, Delaware: Take Delaware Highway 1 south to U.S. Highway 13. Turn left to the speedway.

From the southern peninsula: Take US 13 north to the speedway.

From Baltimore and Washington, D.C.: Take U.S. Highways 50/301 east across the Bay Bridge, then take US 301 north to Maryland Highway 302. Turn right to Maryland Highway 454 at Templeville. The road becomes Delaware Highway 8 at the state line. Follow DE 8 into Dover then turn left onto US 13 to the speedway.

Monster Mile
Express Train

There's no denying it: Traffic flow is just plain awful in and out of Dover Downs, especially where US 13 and DE 1 converge a couple miles south of the raceway. One relaxing solution is to let Amtrak take you there by rail on the Monster Mile Express. If you're coming here from New York or Washington, this is the ticket. Amtrak, which doesn't normally offer service to Dover, has been running the race train for the past few years. The Monster Mile Express departs from New York's Penn Station, making stops in Newark, Trenton, Philadelphia, and Wilmington on its way to Dover. Race fans from the Washington and Baltimore areas can connect to Wilmington and meet the Express. The Amtrak ticket includes bus service from the station to the speedway. Ride along and smile as you glide past the bumper-to-bumper traffic. Contact Amtrak at (800) 872-7245.

Best Seats in the House

There aren't any truly bad seats here, but generally the higher in the grand-stands the better. Because of the steep banking, if you sit too close to the track you'll have trouble seeing the action right in front of you. The enclosed and air-conditioned grandstands on the backstretch are comfortable, but the views of the track from there aren't the best. Take some sun-screen and sit as high in the turns as you can.

Dover also offers a family seating area—an alcohol- and tobacco-free area in the desirable Turn 4 grandstands.

Doing Deluxe

Even if you can't watch the race from the comfort of the trackside hotel, Dover still has several ticket packages worth considering. About $200 will get you great seats, catered food and drink, and some souvenirs to boot.

Dover Memories

Harry Gant was a master at Dover, with four of his eighteen career wins coming at the fast, tricky oval. In September 1991 Gant reeled off four vic-tories in a row with wins at Darlington, Dover, Richmond, and Martinsville. He almost ran the streak to five at North Wilkesboro the following week, only to lose his brakes while leading in the closing laps and lose to a hard-charging **Dale Earnhardt.**

All-time greats **Richard Petty** and **Bobby Allison** each scored seven wins here. Petty won the first two Dover races, in 1969 and 1970, with the 1969 win coming at the wheel of a Ford in the season Petty strayed from his traditional Dodge and Plymouth rides in favor of the faster Fords. Bobby Allison notched the first of his seven Dover victories in 1971, when the Alabaman led the way in a rare caution-free 500-mile race.

In seven races from 1996 to 1999 **Mark Martin** dominated Dover, winning three and posting six top-five finishes. But his win in September 1999 was sweeter, ending a twenty-five-race winless string.

It was here that NASCAR raced for the first time since the terrorist attacks of September 11, 2001, with **Dale Earnhardt Jr.** thrilling the ecstatic crowd by charging to the lead late in the race to win the Cal Ripken Jr. 400, named in honor of the retiring baseball great.

Jimmie Johnson on Dover

To say that Jimmie Johnson quickly developed a knack for the Monster Mile is an understatement. During his rookie season of 2002, he swept both 400-mile races at Dover, joining Jeff Gordon, Tony Stewart, Dale Earnhardt, Bill Elliott, Rusty Wallace, and Bobby Allison as the only drivers since 1969 to win both main events during the same year.

"It's just as easy to lose these things as it is to win them," Johnson says. "I was just trying to pass whoever was in front of me. Then I looked up and the only one left was [Ricky] Rudd. After that, I said, 'Hey, we made it.' This is incredible. Everything just came together. I wish we could bottle this up and keep it for a hundred years. Six months ago I was shaking a little bit, wondering what the season was going to hold for me."

Make It a Vacation

The truth is, this isn't much of a vacation spot. The biggest things in town are the racetrack and Dover Air Force Base.

The best beaches are a little farther south; the big city nightlife is 100 miles north. If you're not planning to spend a weekend watching a race or sitting behind a slot machine, it's probably best to look elsewhere for a vacation option.

Away from the Track

There are some things to do when you need an escape from the routine of screaming engines and the clanging bells of a slot machine. The **Bombay Hook National Wildlife Refuge** is 16,000 acres of marsh and wetlands.

As the capital of Delaware and birthplace of the U.S. Constitution, Dover is rich in history. Delaware earned its nickname "The First State" on December 7, 1787, when it became the first state to ratify the constitution at the **Golden Fleece Tavern on the Green** (State and Green Streets).

There are other sites in Dover dedicated to the nation's history, such as **Constitution Park** (South State Street), a minipark with a 12-foot bronze quill on a 4-foot cube inscribed with a copy of the U.S. Constitution. The tavern is just 1 block south of the park. Other points of interest are the **Christ Episcopal Church** (South State and Water Streets), where there's a monument of Caesar Rodney, a signer of the Declaration of Independence, and the **Delaware Public Archives** (121 Duke of York Street, Dover; 302–744–5000), where visitors can study the state's archives and culture.

Dover Air Force Base is home to the Air Mobility Command Museum (1301 Heritage Road, Dover; 302–677–5938), dedicated to vintage and historical warplanes, including a C–47, a C–141, and a B–17G Flying Fortress. Be sure to call ahead to find out what security measures are in effect that day.

Gambling

OK, so it's not exactly Las Vegas, but you can play the slots and maybe even see Wayne Newton at the Dover Downs Hotel and Conference Center. The $60 million complex, which opened in spring 2002, brings a bit of Vegas glitz to the decidedly blue-collar atmosphere of Dover.

Where to Eat

No visit to Dover would be complete without a trip to **Sambo's Tavern** (Front Street, Leipsic; 302–674–9724), where they serve up huge platters of steamed shrimp, crabs, crab cakes, and mussels. The gang from the Motor Racing Network are regulars here.

On Friday and Saturday the **Sheraton Inn** (1570 North DuPont Highway, Dover; 302–678–8500) has a pretty impressive seafood buffet.

For good barbecue try **Wally's Bar-Ba-Cue** (244 South Main Street, Smyrna; 302–653–7515). For incredible prime rib topped off with great cheesecake for dessert, go to **Cool Springs Fish Bar and Restaurant** (2463 South State Street, Dover; 302–698–1955). Another spot for prime rib and steaks is the **Iron Gate Inn** (1151 South Bay Road, Dover; 302–678–9666), and you can always get a good cup of soup at **WT Smithers Restaurant** (140 South State Street, Dover; 302–674–8875).

Where to Stay

The best place to stay here is the **Dover Downs Hotel,** which towers over the backstretch of the track. But unless you work for NASCAR or one of the television networks, forget it. For the rest of us, it can be difficult to sift through the list of small, grossly overpriced hotels in town.

Most places throughout the Delaware peninsula are sold out a year in advance, making it tough to find a room. And when you do find one, expect to pay four or five times the normal rate. If you're not on a renewal list, your best bet may be as far north as New Castle, Delaware, as far west as Annapolis, Maryland, or as far south as Milford or Seaford, Delaware.

If you want to try Dover, start with the **Hampton Inn** (302–736–3500), **Comfort Suites** (302–736–1204), **Best Western Galaxy Inn** (302–735–4700), **Fairfield Inn** (302–677–0900), **Holiday Inn Express** (302–678–0600), **Sheraton Inn** (302–678–8500), **Super Lodge** (302–678–0160), **Ramada Inn** (302–734–5701), and the **Relax Inn** (302–734–8120).

Dover Area Restaurants

Blue Coat Inn
800 North State Drive
Dover, DE
(302) 674–1776

The Boondocks
825 Lighthouse Road
Smyrna, DE
(302) 653–6962

Chinatown Buffet
1071 North DuPont
  Highway
Dover, DE
(302) 678–8868

Cool Springs Fish Bar and
  Restaurant
2463 South State Street
Dover, DE
(302) 698–1955

La Tolteca
247 South DuPont Highway
Dover, DE
(302) 734–3444

The Lobby House
9 East Loockerman Street
Dover, DE
(302) 741–2420

Long Star Steaks
365 North DuPont Highway
Dover, DE
(302) 736–5836

Olive Garden
263 North DuPont Highway
Dover, DE
(302) 734–5837

Paradiso Restaurant
1151–B East Lebanon
  Road
Dover, DE
(302) 697–3055

Roma Italian Restaurant
Delaware Highway 113
Dover, DE
(302) 678–1041

Sambo's Tavern
Front Street
Leipsic, DE
(302) 674–9724

Shucker's Pier 13
889 North DuPont Highway
Dover, DE
(302) 674–1190

Wally's Bar-Ba-Cue
244 South Main Street
Smyrna, DE
(302) 653–7515

Where Pigs Fly
US 13 and Loockerman
  Street
Dover, DE
(302) 678–0586

WT Smithers Restaurant
140 South State Street
Dover, DE
(302) 674–8875

Dover Area Lodging

Best Western Galaxy Inn
1700 East Lebanon Road
Dover, DE
(302) 735–4700

Comfort Inn of Dover
US 13 at Loockerman
  Street
Dover, DE
(302) 674–3300

Comfort Suites
1654 North DuPont
  Highway
Dover, DE
(302) 736–1204

Days Inn
272 North DuPont Highway
Dover, DE
(302) 674–8002

Dover Budget Inn
1426 North DuPont
  Highway
Dover, DE
(302) 734–4433

Dover Downs Hotel
1131 North DuPont
  Highway
Dover, DE
(866) 473–7378

Fairfield Inn
655 North DuPont Highway
Dover, DE
(302) 677–0900

Hampton Inn
1568 North DuPont
  Highway
Dover, DE
(302) 736–3500

Hampton Inn
799 North Dual Highway
Seaford, DE
(302) 629–4500

Holiday Inn Express
1780 North DuPont
  Highway
Dover, DE
(302) 678–0600

Howard Johnson
561 North DuPont Highway
Dover, DE
(302) 678–8900

Inn at Meeting House
  Square
305 South Governors
  Avenue
Dover, DE
(302) 734–1583

Little Creek Inn Bed and
  Breakfast
2623 North Little Creek
  Road
Dover, DE
(302) 730–1300

Ramada Inn
348 North DuPont Highway
Dover, DE
(302) 734–5701

Red Roof Inn
652 North DuPont Highway
Dover, DE
(302) 730–8009

Relax Inn
640 South Dupont
    Highway
Dover, DE
(302) 734–8120

Sheraton inn
1570 North DuPont
    Highway
Dover, DE
(302) 678–8500

Super 8
729 Bay Road
Milford, DE
(302) 422–2777

Super 8
17010 South DuPont
    Highway
Harrington, DE
(302) 398–4206

Super Lodge
Delaware Highway 13
Dover, DE
(302) 678–0160

Dover Area Camping

Three Seasons RV Resort
727 Country Club Road
Rehoboth Beach, DE
(800) 635–4996

Racing in the Heartland

The Heartland is proof that stock car racing has evolved from its Southern roots. The raceways in the Midwest—Chicagoland, Indianapolis Motor, Kansas, and Michigan International Speedways—all share a passion for speed. All four tracks also enjoy continual sellouts, proving again that NASCAR has no boundaries when it comes to its fan base.

Michigan International Speedway
Brooklyn, Michigan

Chicagoland Speedway
Joliet, Illinois

Indianapolis Motor Speedway
Indianapolis, Indiana

Kansas Speedway
Kansas City, Kansas

Michigan International Speedway:
Detroit's Backyard

The smokestacks of Ford, General Motors, and Daimler-Chrysler assembly plants and worldwide headquarters are less than an hour away, so a manufacturer that can win at the Michigan International Speedway has bragging rights.

It's also important to the race teams here because this is a speedway that demands the very best engine, pit stops, fuel strategy, chassis setup, and driving ability. The place is so wide, so smooth, so fast, there's a workable racing groove for everyone. It's no secret that Michigan is one of the most popular speedways on the NASCAR schedule among those in the know—the drivers.

Cale Yarborough won the first NASCAR Nextel Cup Series race at Michigan by averaging 139.254 mph in the 1969 Motor State 500. David Pearson won a track-record nine races here, but Bill Elliott also had an impressive run by winning seven of eleven starts between 1984 and 1989, including four in a row.

The speedway is positioned among the tall evergreens and mishmash of lakes that make up the Irish Hills. The scenery is spectacular; the air is crisp, clean, and a refreshing change from the big city that's about 60 miles away. Its remote location is both good and bad: It's a great escape from Detroit, but the roads leading into the racetrack are small, narrow, and antiquated. As long as the shows remain some of the best in the business, though, we feel it's worth the trouble.

Let's Go Racing

Michigan International Speedway was ahead of its time when it opened in 1969. It was one of the first raceways to include variable-degree banking. It also was the first to use a polymer-enhanced asphalt, developed to handle both the high-banked racing and the cruel Michigan winters.

The lower groove near the track apron isn't banked as steep as the higher grooves. While the bottom groove is the shortest way around the track, it's easier to keep a head of steam in the higher grooves. A car with a perfect setup can run on the bottom; a car with a fast engine can run against the outside wall. It's common to see cars fan into two, three, or four lanes of traffic in the turns, then all fall right back in line like a high-speed ballet as they exit the turns and head down the straightaway.

MICHIGAN INTERNATIONAL SPEEDWAY

START/FINISH

Pit Road

TURN 1

TURN 2

TURN 3

TURN 4

Our Ratings	Racing: 🏁 🏁 🏁 🏁 🏁
	Amenities: 🏁 🏁
	Area Appeal: 🏁 🏁 🏁

Track Facts	2.0-mile tri-oval
	Seating capacity: 136,373
	12626 U.S. Highway 12
	Brooklyn, MI 49230
	(517) 592–6666
	www.mispeedway.com

| **Annual Events** | Two 500-mile Nextel Cup races, June and August |
| | Companion events: ARCA, June; Busch Series, August |

| **Weather** | Average High (F): | June 79.0 | August 80.0 |
| | Average Low (F): | June 55.0 | August 58.0 |

| **Top Gun** | David Pearson, 9 wins |

| **Qualifying Record** | Dale Earnhardt Jr., 191.149 mph |

While the different race grooves make for great racing, the finishes often are the result of number crunching on pit road. Half the races in the past ten years have been determined by fuel mileage. Some cars are equipped with gas-efficient engines designed to squeeze an extra lap or two out of each tank of gas like a Hyundai in the middle of the desert; others rely on gas-guzzling engines designed for unadulterated speed. The winning car will either coast across the finish line on fumes or rocket to the checkers at full throttle.

Since the speedway's so far away from a major city, this might be a good time to dig that old tent out of the attic or fire up the RV. There's plenty of room to camp across from the speedway. And when you're that close, you don't have to worry about race-day traffic.

How to Get There

No matter what compass point you come from, it's hard not to think you're lost before you finally find the Michigan International Speedway. Don't worry; as long as you follow the directions, you will get there. If you don't follow directions, good luck.

From Detroit: Take Interstate 94 west to U.S. Highway 12 west (exit 181A). The track is about 40 miles on the right.

From Ann Arbor: Take U.S. Highway 23 south to US 12. Turn right (west); the speedway is about 36 miles away.

From Jackson: Take U.S. Highway 127 south to US 12. Turn left; the speedway is just a couple miles away on your left.

From Toledo: Take US 23 north to Michigan Highway 50 north to the speedway.

Best Seats in the House

There are grandstands with views that cover about a mile and a third of the 2-mile racetrack. While there are plenty of seats with myriad viewing angles, we have some suggestions to enhance your experience. The higher the better, so look for seats in the second or third sections, anything between Rows 19 and 53 in the center grandstands.

If you can't get upper seats in the center grandstands, try the grandstands in the second turn, Sections 91 to 99. Anything above Row 31 is ideal because it gives you a great view of the main straightaway, the first and second turns, and the backstretch. Most of the crashes happen in the second turn, since it's the most abrupt of the four and sets up the long run down the backstretch.

If Plans A and B don't work out, get the highest seat possible in any of the grandstands.

Michigan Memories

While **Dale Jarrett**'s side-by-side finish with **Davey Allison** in 1991 was his first career win and gave Michigan a real Kodak moment, no victory was more significant than **Sterling Marlin**'s ten years later.

Just a couple weeks after Daimler-Chrysler laid off several thousand employees, company officials finally had reason to cheer on August 19, 2001, when Marlin won the rain-shortened Pepsi 400.

Dodge, which hadn't won a NASCAR Nextel Cup Series race since 1977, bailed out of the circuit in 1985. The car company returned sixteen years later and was counting on its presence in the popular stock car series to boost sales. Daimler-Chrysler officials were so excited about being back that they developed a slick two-word promotion to mark the occasion: "It's Time." Before Dodge could test the adage "Win on Sunday, Sell on Monday," it needed to get to Victory Lane.

It took Dodge, with its Intrepid model, twenty-three races into the season to get that first victory. "We just kept hammering away," Marlin says. "We had a real good car here in June and had a chance to win the race, but it got away from us. Then Indy got away from us. We should have won three or four races."

Marlin needed an assist from Mother Nature in this one. Moments after he took the lead at Michigan, rain forced NASCAR officials to pull the plug on the race. Marlin was declared the winner. The weather didn't keep Daimler-Chrysler officials from celebrating. The party eventually moved to inside the garage area, and it lasted well into the night.

Johnny Benson on Michigan

Michigan has a special meaning for Johnny Benson, a native of Grand Rapids.

"All our races are pretty important, but the Michigan International Speedway is important to me because it is in my home state," he says. "It's a place where you have an opportunity to pass if your car is running good. What I like most about Michigan is that it becomes a two- or three-groove track immediately after the green flag drops, which gives the driver a ton of options."

Since Michigan is his home track, Benson has to guard against creating more pressure on himself than is usual for drivers. It took him 226 starts to win his first race—the 2002 fall race at Rockingham, North Carolina—so winning at any track would be special.

"You hear guys say all the time that they want to do really well at their home track. Heck, I want to do well at every track where we race. I don't know if going home to race gives you any extra, but it does let you know that you have a lot of great fans there rooting for you. A win would be big. Whether it is at Rockingham, where we won our first race, or Michigan or Daytona or Indy.

"You have to have a lot of momentum, and that means getting through the center of the corner there. That makes you fast coming off the corner and getting down the long straightaways. Man it's fast—a lot faster than most everybody realizes."

Make It a Vacation

The area around the speedway is where the people from Detroit come to get away from it all. Here hundreds of small lakeside cottages and several state parks help you to get back to nature.

The conditions are a bit primitive, but that's the whole point. You can spend the day on the lake on boats or just sit still with a fishing line in the water. In fact, there seems to be three speeds up here when the race cars aren't in town: slow, slower, and glacial. Internet hookups are difficult to find, and there's not a Starbuck's within 50 miles.

One of the best places to kick up your feet and forget about the TV remote is **Walter J. Hayes State Park** (1220 Wamplers Lake Road, Onsted; 517–467–7401), with 710 acres for camping, games, picnics, swimming, boating, and fishing.

If the only driving you want to do on your camping trip is on a golf course, then try the **Greenbriar Golf Course and Campground** (14820 Well-wood, Brooklyn; 517–592–6952). There's also a basketball court, heated pool, horseshoe pit, and a children's fishing pond.

Away from the Track

Unless you want to get far away from the track, the only thing to do is hike, camp, or play golf, perhaps an occasional round of miniature golf. We recommend spending the afternoon walking through scenic **Hidden Lake Gardens** (6280 Munger Road, Tipton; 517–431–2060) or playing golf at the **Hills Heart O' the Lakes Golf Course** (500 Case Road, Brooklyn; 517–592–2110).

If you don't mind driving 90 minutes, you can head into Detroit. Two casinos—**MGM Grand Detroit Casino** (1300 John C. Lodge, Detroit; 877–888–2121) and **MotorCity Casino** (2901 Grand River Avenue, Detroit; 877–777–0711)—and Major League Baseball's **Detroit Tigers** at Comerica Park (2100 Woodward Avenue, Detroit; 248–258–4437) are all within a couple blocks of one another.

During the August racing weekend, the city of Detroit also hosts the largest gathering of classic cars and hot rods with the **Woodward Dream Cruise.** Hundreds of thousands of spectators line Woodward Avenue on Saturday to watch an all-day parade of classic cars.

Where to Eat

You have to break down your dining choices into two categories: cozy places minutes from the raceway and bigger places that require a little travel. Here's our picks of both:

The **Stagecoach Stop** complex within **Walter J. Hayes State Park** is a collection of shops featuring antiques, glass-blowing, a blacksmith, and a sawmill. There's also an amusement park, petting zoo, ice-cream parlor, and wedding chapel. But our favorites here are the **Longhorn Saloon** (517–467–2300) and the **Golden Nugget** (517–467–2190). The Longhorn has the coldest beer in the Irish Hills; the Golden Nugget specializes in steaks and pork chops. Both are located at 7203 US 12, Onsted.

Our other local favorites include **Old Town** (109 South Main Street, Brooklyn; 517–592–8007); **Artesian Wells Sports Bar** (US 12 at US 127, Brooklyn; 517–547–8777); **Poppa's Place** (208 South Main Street, Brooklyn; 517–592–4625); and **The Beach Bar** (3505 Ocean Beach Road, Clark Lake; 517–529–4211).

A little farther down the road, **Gilbert's Steak House** (2323 Shirley Drive, Jackson; 517–782–7135) specializes in prime rib and Great Lakes perch. Or you might enjoy the **Red Moose Inn** (145 West Pearl, Jackson; 517–784–7662); **Bella Notte Ristorante** (137 West Michigan Avenue, Jackson; 517–782–5727); **Bullinger's** (501 Longfellow at Wildwood, Jackson; 517–783–3768); **Brass Lantern** (1853 West Maumee Street, Adrian; 517–263–0411); and **Chop House** (322 South Main Street, Ann Arbor; 734–669–9977).

Where to Stay

Just like finding a meal, you have to decide whether it's worth finding rooms within 20 miles of the speedway—most of the rooms are very expensive and reserved well in advance—or worth fighting traffic from outside the 20-mile radius. We think it's best to stay as far away as Ann Arbor or at the Detroit Metro Airport and leave early on race day to beat the traffic.

If you're lucky enough to find a hotel within 20 miles, it's likely to be one of the following: **BayMont Inn** (2035 Service Drive, Jackson; 517–789–6000); **Colonial Inn** (6027 Ann Arbor Road, Jackson; 517–764–3820); **Days Inn–Adrian** (1575 West Maumee Street, Adrian; 517–263–5741); **Clearwater Hotel** (6150 U.S. Highway 223, Addison; 517–547–7472); **Super 8–Adrian** (1091 US 223, Adrian; 517–265–8888); **Carlton Lodge** (1629 West Maumee Street, Adrian; 517–263–7000); **Hampton Inn** (2225 Shirley Drive, Jackson; 517–789–5151); and **Holiday Inn Express–Adrian** (1077 West US 223, Adrian; 517–265–5700).

For the rest of us, there's a glut of rooms in Ann Arbor and at the Detroit Metro Airport. **Comfort Inn** (877–424–6423) has three hotels in that area. **Marriott Hotels** (800–228–9290) has six, and **Hilton Hotels** (800–774–1500) and **Holiday Inn** (800–465–4329) each have two.

Michigan Speedway Area Restaurants

Applebee's
1396 South Main Street
Adrian, MI
(517) 263–3344

Artesian Wells Sports Bar
US 12 at US 127
Brooklyn, MI
(517) 547–8777

The Beach Bar
3505 Ocean Beach Road
Clark Lake, MI
(517) 529–4211

Bella Notte Ristorante
137 West Michigan
    Avenue
Jackson, MI
(517) 782–5727

Big Boy Restaurant
126 North Broad Street
Adrian, MI
(517) 266–6600

Big Boy Restaurant
329 South Main
Brooklyn, MI
(517) 592–3212

Big Boy Restaurant
1213 North West
Jackson, MI
(517) 787–5566

Bill Knapp's Restaurant
2155 Holiday Inn Drive
Jackson, MI
(517) 783–2701

Brass Lantern
1853 West Maumee
    Street
Adrian, MI
(517) 263–0411

Bullinger's
501 Longfellow
Jackson, MI
(517) 783–3768

Chop House
322 South Main Street
Ann Arbor, MI
(734) 669–9977

The Common Grill
112 South Main Street
Chelsea, MI
(734) 475–0470

Cracker Barrel
2494 Airport Road
Jackson, MI
(517) 783–5300

Daryl's Downtown
151 West Michigan
    Avenue
Jackson, MI
(517) 782–1895

El Chapulin Restaurant
118 South Winter Street
Adrian, MI
(517) 265–6670

Ed's Main Street Station
149 North Main Street
Adrian, MI
(517) 263–2365

Finley's
1602 West Michigan
    Avenue
Jackson, MI
(517) 787–7440

Giglio's Italian Restaurant
2241 Brooklyn Road
Jackson, MI
(517) 787–5025

Gilbert's Steak House
2323 Shirley Drive
Jackson, MI
(517) 782–7135

Golden Nugget
7203 US 12
Onsted, MI
(517) 467–2190

Graham's Steakhouse
610 Hilton Boulevard
Ann Arbor, MI
(734) 761–7800

Ground Round
Jackson Grossing Mall
Jackson, MI
(517) 782–3330

Hudson's Grill
2900 Springport Road
Jackson, MI
(517) 784–4773

Hunt Club
1514 Daniel Street
Jackson, MI
(517) 782–0375

Knight's Steak House
2125 Horton Road
Jackson, MI
(517) 783–2777

L.A. Cafe
4460 Maumee Street
Adrian, MI
(517) 263–8788

Lone Star Steakhouse
3510 O'Neill Drive
Jackson, MI
(517) 768–0884

Longhorn Saloon
7203 US 12
Onsted, MI
(517) 467–2300

Main Street Stable and
    Tavern
116 North Main Street
Blissfield, MI
(517) 486–2144

Old Country Buffet
1230 Jackson Crossing
    Boulevard
Jackson, MI
(517) 789–3098

Old Town
109 South Main Street
Brooklyn, MI
(517) 592–8007

Olive Garden
445 East Eisenhower
    Parkway
Ann Arbor, MI
(734) 663–6875

Olive Garden
3500 O'Neill Drive
Jackson, MI
(517) 787–2388

Outback Steakhouse
1501 Boardman Road
Jackson, MI
(517) 784–7700

Poppa's Place
208 South Main Street
Brooklyn, MI
(517) 592–4625

Red Lobster
1420 South Main Street
Adrian, MI
(517) 263–3811

Red Lobster
2400 Clinton Road
Jackson, MI
(517) 787–7820

Red Moose Inn
145 West Pearl
Jackson, MI
(517) 784–7662

Shoopers Grill and Pub
11551 Brooklyn Road
Brooklyn, MI
(517) 592–4107

Steak 'n Shake
2655 Airport Road
Jackson, MI
(517) 841–9390

Tom's Grill and Pub
3705 Ann Arbor Road
Jackson, MI
(517) 764–4210

Village Creamery
140 North Main Street
Brooklyn, MI
(517) 592–8284

Weber's
3050 Jackson Road
Ann Arbor, MI
(734) 665–3636

Yenking Chinese
   Restaurant
2100 Holiday Inn Drive
Jackson, MI
(517) 787–8701

Zig's Kettle and Brew
6020 Ann Arbor Road
Jackson, MI
(517) 764–5010

Michigan Speedway Area Lodging

Amerihost Inn
111 Waterstradt Com-
   merce Drive
Dundee, MI
(800) 434–5800

Arbor Hills Motel
3330 Spring Arbor Road
Jackson, MI
(517) 782–6282

BayMont Inn
2035 Service Drive
Jackson, MI
(517) 789–6000

Best Motel
1725 North West Avenue
Jackson, MI
(517) 789–9051

Cadet Motor Inn
443 East Chicago Street
Coldwater, MI
(517) 278–5617

Campus Inn
615 East Huron Street
Ann Arbor, MI
(734) 769–2200

Carlton Lodge
1629 West Maumee
Adrian, MI
(517) 263–7000

Clarion Hotel
3600 Dunkel Drive
Lansing, MI
(517) 351–7600

Clearwater Hotel
6150 US 223
Addison, MI
(517) 547–7472

Clinton Inn
104 West Michigan
   Avenue
Clinton, MI
(517) 456–4151

Colonial Inn
6027 Ann Arbor Road
Jackson, MI
(517) 764–3820

Comfort Inn
1645 Commerce Park
   Drive
Chelsea, MI
(734) 433–8000

Comfort Inn
2455 Carpenter Road
Ann Arbor, MI
(734) 973–6100

Country Hearth Inn
1111 Boardman Road
Jackson, MI
(517) 783–6404

Country Inn and Suites
665 Tecumseh Street
Dundee, MI
(734) 529–8822

Courtyard
3205 Boardwalk Drive
Ann Arbor, MI
(734) 995–5900

Courtyard by Marriott
2710 Lake Lansing Road
Lansing, MI
(517) 482–0500

Crowne Plaza
610 Hilton Boulevard
Ann Arbor, MI
(734) 761–7800

Days Inn
1575 West Maumee
   Street
Adrian, MI
(517) 263–5741

Days Inn
2380 Carpenter Road
Ann Arbor, MI
(734) 971–0700

Days Inn
3241 Carleton Road
Hillsdale, MI
(517) 439–3297

Days Inn
27644 C Drive North
Albion, MI
(517) 629–9411

Doubletree Hotel
31500 Wick Road
Romulus, MI
(734) 467–8000

Econo Lodge
884 West Chicago Street
Coldwater, MI
(517) 278–4501

Evans Lake Resort
1237 West US 12
Tipton, MI
(517) 431–2233

Fairfield Inn
2395 Shirley Drive
Jackson, MI
(517) 784–7877

Fairfield Inn
3285 Boardwalk
Ann Arbor, MI
(734) 995–5200

Governor's Inn and Conference Center
6133 South Pennsylvania
Lansing, MI
(517) 393–5500

Hampton Inn
2225 Shirley Drive
Jackson, MI
(517) 789–5151

Hilton Garden Inn
31800 Smith Road
Romulus, MI
(734) 727–6000

Holiday Inn
17201 Northline Road
Southgate, MI
(734) 283–4400

Holiday Inn Campus
3600 Plymouth Road
Ann Arbor, MI
(734) 769–9800

Holiday Inn Express
630 East Chicago Street
Coldwater, MI
(517) 279–0900

Holiday Inn Express
100 White Tail Drive
Dundee, MI
(734) 529–5100

Jackson Travelodge
901 Rosehill Drive
Jackson, MI
(517) 787–1111

Joy Motel
7657 Ann Arbor Road
Jackson, MI
(517) 522–8402

Knights Inn Motel
400 B Drive North
Albion, MI
(517) 629–3966

McCamly Plaza
50 Capital Avenue
   Southwest
Battle Creek, MI
(616) 963–7050

Motel 6
830 Royal Drive
Jackson, MI
(517) 789–7186

Motel Somerset
13980 East Chicago Road
Somerset, MI
(517) 547–7241

Pine Motel
3895 South Adrian
   Highway
Adrian, MI
(517) 263–2444

Pinecrest Motel
516 West Chicago Street
Jonesville, MI
(517) 849–2137

Quality Inn and Suites
3750 Washtenaw Avenue
Ann Arbor, MI
(734) 971–2000

Ramada Inn
1000 Orleans Boulevard
Coldwater, MI
(517) 278–2017

Red Roof Inn
348 South Willowbrook
   Road
Coldwater, MI
(517) 279–1199

Red Roof Inn
7412 West Saginaw
    Highway
Lansing, MI
(517) 321–7246

Red Roof Inn
3621 Plymouth Road
Ann Arbor, MI
(734) 996–5800

Super 8
1091 US 223
Adrian, MI
(517) 265–8888

Super 8
2001 Shirley Drive
Jackson, MI
(517) 788–8780

Tecumseh Inn
1445 West Chicago
    Boulevard
Tecumseh, MI
(517) 423–7401

Three Rivers Inn
U.S. Highway 131 and
    Broadway Street
Three Rivers, MI
(616) 273–9521

Travel Inn and Suites
1440 North Dixie Highway
Monroe, MI
(734) 289–4000

Weber's Inn
3050 Jackson Road
Ann Arbor, MI
(734) 769–2500

Michigan Speedway Area Camping

Apple Creek Family
    Camping
11185 Orban Road
Grass Lake, MI
(517) 522–3467

Bernie's Campground
14335 US 12
Brooklyn, MI
(517) 592–8221

Brookfest
13122 US 12
Brooklyn, MI
(517) 592–5050

Greenbriar Campground
14820 Wellwood
Brooklyn, MI
(517) 592–6952

Greenwood Acres
    Campground
2401 Hilton Street
Jackson, MI
(517) 522–8600

Indian Creek
9415 Tangent Highway
Tecumseh, MI
(517) 423–5659

Jado Campground
5603 US 12
Tipton, MI
(517) 431–2111

Juniper Hills Campground
13500 US 12
Brooklyn, MI
(517) 592–6803

Sauk Valley
10750 Prospect Hill
    Highway
Brooklyn, MI
(517) 467–2061

Sequoia Camping
2675 Grady Road
Adrian, MI
(517) 264–5531

Somerset Beach
    Campground
9822 Brooklawn Court
Somerset, MI
(517) 688–3783

Victory Family Campground
13191 Michigan Highway 50
Brooklyn, MI
(517) 592–2128

Walter J. Hayes State Park
1220 Wamplers Lake
    Road
Onsted, MI
(517) 467–7401

Chicagoland Speedway:
Get Your Kicks on Route 66

Chicagoland Speedway and the adjacent Route 66 Raceway are quietly cut among miles of silo-tall fields of corn, and they offer a stark contrast to the serenity of the fertile farmland that seems to stretch well beyond the horizon in all directions.

Joliet is about an hour from downtown Chicago, where they used to race along the lakefront as far back as 1985. Joliet used to be famous only for the state prison that once housed Jake and Elwood Blue, but the addition of Chicagoland, a miniature version of the Daytona International Speedway, and the drag strip and dirt track next door at Route 66 changed all that. Chicagoland offers the best of both Daytona and Indianapolis— electric speeds that rival both Daytona and the Brickyard—but with the kind of sight lines neither can offer. At 1.5 miles, the racing action never gets too far from the grandstands.

Chicagoland wasn't so quick to come to speed with the drivers, but it was an instant hit with the fans, many of whom were honed on the fumes of that staple of Midwest racing, open-wheeled sprint cars. As the pavement matured since its debut in 2001 and slowly surrendered newer racing grooves, it became just as popular with the drivers.

Every Nextel Cup Series race has been sold out here since the speedway opened, and most tickets are sold as part of their Track Packs promotion that promises the same seat for Nextel Cup, Busch Series, ARCA, and IRL IndyCar Series races. The speedway starts a waiting list for season tickets the following year as soon as the Nextel Cup Series leaves town in July, so plan ahead. The cost for each seat ranges from $270 to $350, and payment must be submitted with the request.

Let's Go Racing

Chicagoland is fast, and, thanks to a few harsh winters that cured the asphalt, the racing surface has lost a lot of its grip. While that sounds bad, it's good for racing because it means that drivers have to slow down while rolling through the turns. Slower speeds, if you can call a lap at 180 mph slow, allow for new grooves away from the apron to promote more side-by-side racing.

The trick to getting around Chicagoland is cutting corners, especially the dogleg along the main straightaway. Don't be surprised to see drivers

CHICAGOLAND SPEEDWAY

START/FINISH

Pit Road

TURN 1

TURN 4

TURN 2

TURN 3

Our Ratings	Racing: 🏁 🏁 🏁
	Amenities: 🏁 🏁 🏁 🏁 🏁
	Area Appeal: 🏁 🏁 🏁 🏁 🏁
Track Facts	1.5-mile tri-oval
	Seating capacity: 75,000
	500 Speedway Boulevard
	Joliet, IL 60433
	(815) 727-7223
	www.chicagolandspeedway.com
Annual Events	One 400-mile Nextel Cup race, July
	Companion events: Busch Series, July; ARCA, September
Weather	Average High (F): July 85.0
	Average Low (F): July 63.0
Top Gun	Kevin Harvick, 2 wins
Qualifying Record	Tony Stewart, 184.786 mph

drop on the track apron at the start/finish line to cut a few feet off a lap. And if it gets too rough on the flat apron, don't worry. Kevin Harvick spun out driving on the apron in 2002, but there's so much room in the infield grass between the raceway and pit road that he was able to slide through the grass, get back up to speed, and win the race.

Pit road is long and wide, but the race outcome generally is dictated by the driver who can avoid making pit stops. The 400-mile distance seems to lend itself to fuel mileage strategies, so you can expect a handful of teams, cautions permitting, to try to cover the distance with just three pit stops. Watching all the pit strategies, especially when cars pit out of sequence under green-flag conditions, can be as compelling as the action on the track.

How to Get There

Chicagoland is about 30 miles from downtown Chicago on Speedway Boulevard, which is just south of Joliet and Interstate 80.

From the northwest corridor (Red Line): Take Interstate 55 south to eastbound I–80. Do not take Joliet Road off I–55. Get off at Illinois Highway 53 at exit 132A; the speedway is ahead on the left.

From the northeast corridor (Green Line): Take I–80 westbound to U.S. Highway 30 (exit 137); turn left, go 1 mile to Gouger Road, and turn left again. Go to Laraway Road, and turn right into the speedway.

From the southeast corridor (Blue Line): Take Interstate 57 northbound to Wilmington Road (exit 327), and turn left. Go to U.S. Highway 45, and turn right. Go to U.S. Highway 52, and turn left to Schweitzer Road, then turn left to the speedway.

From the southwest corridor (Yellow Line): Take I–55 northbound to River Road (exit 241), and turn left. Travel to IL 53; turn left to Schweitzer Road, and turn right to the speedway.

Best Seats in the House

Like the other modern tracks built in the last ten years, the grandstands at Chicagoland are raised above the outside wall. That puts even the lowest seat in the house more than seven feet above the racetrack and provides a good view of the entire circuit.

The best seats are in the upper half of the grandstands, but they can be the toughest to buy, especially as part of the Track Pack plan. Be persistent, make sure to get on the waiting list early, and you just may end up with some of the best seats on the entire circuit.

While every seat has a great view of the speedway, keep this in mind: Unless you're in the top twenty rows, there's no shade in the grandstands. Bring plenty of sunscreen, sunglasses, and a hat because the days are long and the sun is bright in early July.

Doing Deluxe

If you know somebody with ties to one of Chicago's biggest corporations, then you just might get a seat in one of the handful of suites. For the most part, however, these are only for a well-connected few.

The seating in the grandstands can be just as well appointed, however. Chicagoland offers stadium-style seats, and if you're lucky enough to get your ticket through Track Packs, you also have the luxury of in-seat concession service and preferred parking.

Tony Stewart on Chicagoland

Like most of the other drivers, Tony Stewart wasn't fond of Chicagoland's one-groove racetrack during the first two years, but it finally won him over when he returned for the third time in 2003. He liked the way his car could run along the apron—and sometimes below it—as well as up against the outside wall.

"The track came right into it," he said after the 2003 race. "You couldn't have asked for a better racetrack today. It got probably four lanes wide with three legitimate racing lines that you could run. You could run three-wide and really not have a problem. For a track that is only in its third season, that's pretty uncommon.

"I think the people in Illinois have a track to be really proud of. This is going to be a place where we're going to put on some really good races in the future. It wasn't a track that you couldn't pass on. I passed a bunch of cars on the high side, and that's not something I thought we would see today. We had a fun race from the standpoint of being able to race guys one on one and to be able to move around there on the racetrack and not have to play follow the leader all day."

And if you're a true race fan like Stewart, you'll be next door at Route 66 Raceway on Friday and Saturday nights to watch the World of Outlaws. The ability to watch stock cars during the day and sprint cars at night is a mix that's hard to beat.

Chicagoland Memories

The speedway's only been open since 2001, so it's not steeped in tradition. But a memory that someday will become lore was **Kevin Harvick's** 2002 victory. That was the year he turned a spin through the infield grass into a win.

After spinning out with sixty-six laps to go, Harvick had to stop for new tires and gas. Nobody thought about it then, but that gave him enough gas to finish the race. As the other lead-lap cars made their scheduled stops later in the race, Harvick moved up the leaderboard until he inherited the lead with twenty-five laps to go. After he got out front, he ran away for the victory, not realizing just how beneficial that spin proved to be.

Make It a Vacation

Let's face it: There's a lot to do in Chicago. Our top choice is to come in a few days early or stay a few days after the race and catch a baseball game on the North Side at historic **Wrigley Field,** home of the National League's Cubs (773–404–2827), or on the South Side at **U.S. Cellular Field (Comiskey Park),** home of the American League's White Sox (312–674–1000). Split the difference and stay downtown—try either the **Chicago Marriott Downtown** (312–836–0100), **Hyatt on Printers Row** (312–986–1234), or **Hilton Chicago** (312–922–4400)—to enjoy the very best shopping, restaurants, and nightlife Chicago has to offer. A trip to Chicago wouldn't be complete without a visit to the top of the John Hancock Building and a slice of Chicago-style pizza. If you go to a Cubs game, don't be afraid to be a bleacher bum and sit in the outfield. But remember, if you catch a home run ball from the opposing team, it's customary to throw the ball back.

Away from the Track

The best part of going to Chicagoland Speedway is that there's still enough to do in the local area if you want to escape the hustle and bustle of Chicago. Here are some quick escapes from the Chicagoland Speedway.

Thrill-seekers and high rollers will love **Harrah's Joliet Casino** (151 North Joliet Street, Joliet; 800–HARRAHS), 5 miles from the track. The casino hosts a block party Friday and Saturday nights of race weekends, and fans of all ages can walk away with a bagful of autographs, posters, cups, hats, and T-shirts from their favorite drivers and car owners. Inside, adults have a selection of hundreds of the favorite casino table games and slot machines.

Although the **Empress Casino** (2300 Empress Drive, Joliet; 888–436–7737) doesn't have the block party, it does have a playground of table games at slot machines.

Challenge Park Xtreme (2903 Schweitzer Road, Joliet; 815–726–2800) and **Haunted Trails Family Amusement** (1425 North Broadway, Joliet; 815–722–7800), both within 5 miles of the speedway, have games for everyone in the family.

For a relaxing break try the **Bird Haven Greenhouse and Conservatory** (225 North Gougar Road, Joliet; 815–741–7278; www.jolietpark.org). Part of the Joliet Park District, Bird Haven has a tropical house, cacti room, and outdoor gardens that have become popular with tourists and locals during the summer.

Where to Eat

Leave your taste for the national chains at home. Chicago has a flavor of its own that can't be duplicated. First and foremost Midwesterners are meat eaters: the bigger and thicker, the better. **Al's Steakhouse** (1990 West Jefferson Street, Joliet; 815–725–2388) serves up big steaks, giant pork chops, and seafood. For authentic Chicago-style pizza, you don't have to go far to find **Aurelio's Pizza** (1630 Essington Road, Joliet; 815–254–2500) or **Giordano's Pizza** (3058 Caton Farm Road, Joliet; 815–254–2700). And no trip to the Chicago area would be complete without trying a local hot dog. Don't expect the mustard, ketchup, and relish routine at **Portillo's Hot Dogs**. Their dogs also include toma- toes, lettuce, pickles, and hot peppers on a poppy- seed roll. The closest location is thirty minutes away from the track (1992 West Jefferson, Naperville; 630–420–7156), but it's worth the drive. And if you're in the mood to drive to downtown Chicago, try **Harry Caray's** (33 West Kinzie Street, Chicago; 312–828–0966). The late and legendary voice of the Chicago Cubs turned one of Al Capone's old hangouts into a restaurant that specializes in steaks, seafood, and Italian food. Legend has it that Capone built a bulletproof vault off the upstairs office to hide from lawmen and fellow gangsters.

Where to Stay

A race crowd hardly makes the hotel radar screen in a town like Chicago, and that's good for fans looking for rooms. The handful of hotels in and around Joliet include the **Best Western Inn and Suites** (4380 Enterprise Drive; 815–730–7500); **Comfort Inn North** (3235 Norman Avenue; 815–436–5141); **Comfort Inn South** (135 South Larkin Avenue; 815–744–1770); and **Fairfield Inn North** (3239 Norman Avenue; 815–436–6577). We suggest looking halfway between Chicago and Joliet to take advantage of better rates. Towns like Downer's Grove, Naperville, Aurora, Bolingbrook, and Wheaton have more than fifty hotels for half the price of one closer to the track. Check with any of the national chains. Chicagoland Speedway also has an on-line reservation service—**Vroomz.com**—that offers fans a variety of locations and price ranges. For further information you can also call Vroomz.com at (877) 326–7666.

Chicagoland Area Restaurants

Al's Steakhouse
1990 West Jefferson
   Street
Joliet, IL
(815) 725–2388

Applebee's
2795 Plainfield Road
Joliet, IL
(815) 254–9070

Aurelio's Pizza
1630 Essington Road
Joliet, IL
(815) 254–2500

Baby Back Blues BBQ
23145 Lincoln Highway
Plainfield, IL
(815) 254–6939

Bob Evans
1776 McDonough Road
Joliet, IL
(815) 725–0160

Bourbon Street Cafe
195 West Remington
   Boulevard
Bolingbrook, IL
(630) 771–1111

Branmor's American Grill
300 South Naperville Road
Bolingbrook, IL
(630) 226–9926

Chicago Street Bar and
   Grill
75 North Chicago Street
Joliet, IL
(815) 727–7171

Chili's
1275 West Broughton
   Road
Bolingbrook, IL
(630) 378–5461

Cracker Barrel
1511 Riverboat Center
   Drive
Joliet, IL
(815) 744–0985

David's Pasta
2006 West Jefferson
   Street
Joliet, IL
(815) 744–5253

Diamond's Family
   Restaurant
3000 Plainfield Road
Joliet, IL
(815) 436–1070

Earl's Cafe
1987 West Jefferson
   Street
Joliet, IL
(815) 729–1971

Empress Restaurant
2300 Empress Drive
Joliet, IL
(815) 744–9400

Friday's
1078 Louis Joliet Mall
Joliet, IL
(815) 254–1882

Giordano's Pizza
3058 Canton Farm Road
Joliet, IL
(815) 254–2700

Harrah's Restaurants
151 North Joliet Street
Joliet, IL
(815) 744–2624

Harrison's Brewing
  Company
15845 LaGrange Road
Orland Park, IL
(708) 226–0100

Harry Caray's
33 West Kinzie Street
Chicago, IL
(312) 828–0966

Heroes and Legends
  Sports Bar and Grill
2400 West Jefferson
  Street
Joliet, IL
(815) 741–9207

Lone Star Steakhouse
2705 Plainfield Road
Joliet, IL
(815) 436–7600

Old Country Buffet
2811 Plainfield Road
Joliet, IL
(815) 254–0045

Old Fashioned Pancake
  House
2022 West Jefferson
  Street
Joliet, IL
(815) 741–4666

Portillo's Hot Dogs
1992 West Jefferson
  Street
Naperville, IL
(630) 420–7156

Red Lobster
2950 Plainfield Road
Joliet, IL
(815) 439–1339

Reel 'Em Inn
704 North Division
Plainfield, IL
(815) 254–5900

Syl's Restaurant
829 Moen Avenue
Rockdale, IL
(815) 725–1977

Texas Roadhouse
3002 Plainfield Road
Joliet, IL
(815) 577–9003

Tuckaway Tavern
2545 Plainfield Road
Joliet, IL
(815) 436–9520

Chicagoland Area Lodging

Baymont Inn and Suites
855 Seventy-ninth Street
Willowbrook, IL
(630) 654–0077

Best Western
4380 Enterprise Drive
Joliet, IL
(815) 730–7500

Best Western
1617 Naperville Road
Naperville, IL
(630) 505–0200

Best Western Inn and
  Suites
1280 West Normantown
  Road
Romeoville, IL
(815) 372–1000

Chicago Marriott
  Downtown
540 North Michigan
  Avenue
Chicago, IL
(312) 836–0100

Comfort Inn
8800 West 159th Street
Orland Park, IL
(708) 403–1100

Comfort Inn North
3235 Norman Avenue
Joliet, IL
(815) 436–5141

Comfort Inn South
135 South Larkin Avenue
Joliet, IL
(815) 744–1770

Country Inn and Suites
1847 West Diehl Road
Naperville, IL
(630) 548–0966

Courtyard
1155 East Diehl Road
Naperville, IL
(630) 505–0550

Exel Inn
1585 Naperville Wheaton
    Road
Naperville, IL
(630) 357–0022

Fairfield Inn
820 West Seventy-ninth
    Street
Willowbrook, IL
(630) 789–6300

Fairfield Inn
1501 Riverboat Center
    Drive
Joliet, IL
(815) 741–3499

Fairfield Inn
1820 Abriter
Naperville, IL
(630) 577–1820

Fairfield Inn North
3239 Norman Avenue
Joliet, IL
(815) 436–6577

Hampton Inn
3555 Mall Loop Drive
Joliet, IL
(815) 439–9500

Hampton Inn
1521 Riverboat Center
    Drive
Joliet, IL
(815) 725–2424

Hampton Inn
1087 Diehl Road
Naperville, IL
(630) 505–1400

Hampton Inn
18501 North Creek Drive
Tinley Park, IL
(708) 633–0602

Hampton Inn
5200 Lincoln Highway
Matteson, IL
(708) 481–3900

Harrah's Joliet Hotel
    Casino
151 North Joliet Street
Joliet, IL
(815) 740–7800

Hawthorn Suites
1843 Diehl Road
Naperville, IL
(630) 548–0881

Hilton
722 South Michigan
    Avenue
Chicago, IL
(312) 922–4400

Holiday Inn
500 Holiday Plaza Drive
Matteson, IL
(708) 747–3500

Holiday Inn
7800 Kingery Road
Willowbrook, IL
(630) 325–6400

Holiday Inn Express
411 South Larkin Avenue
Joliet, IL
(815) 729–2000

Holiday Inn Express
2055 Weisbrook Drive
Oswego, IL
(630) 844–4700

Holiday Inn Hotel and
    Suites
205 Remington Boulevard
Bolingbrook, IL
(630) 679–1600

Holiday Inn Select
1801 North Naperville
   Boulevard
Naperville, IL
(630) 505–4900

Homestead Studios
1827 Centre Point Circle
Naperville, IL
(630) 577–0200

Hyatt on Printers Row
500 South Dearborn
   Street
Chicago, IL
(312) 986–1234

Oakwood Lincoln at the
   Parks
1995 Yellowstone Drive
Naperville, IL
(602) 687–3322

Ramada Limited
520 South Bolingbrook
Bolingbrook, IL
(630) 972–9797

Ramada Limited
1520 Commerce Lane
Joliet, IL
(815) 730–1111

Ramada Limited
3231 Norman Avenue
Joliet, IL
(815) 439–4200

Red Roof Inn
1750 McDonough Street
Joliet, IL
(815) 741–2304

Red Roof Inn
1698 West Diehl Road
Naperville, IL
(630) 369–2500

Sleep Inn
1831 West Diehl Road
Naperville, IL
(630) 778–5900

Springhill Suites
125 Remington Boulevard
Bolingbrook, IL
(630) 759–0529

Super 8 Motel
1521 Riverboat Center
   Drive
Joliet, IL
(815) 439–3838

Wingate Inn
101 McDonald Avenue
Joliet, IL
(815) 741–2100

Wyndham Garden Hotel
1837 Centre Point Circle
Naperville, IL
(630) 505–3353

Chicagoland Area Camping

Leisure Lake
21900 Southwest
   Frontage Road
Joliet, IL
(815) 741–9405

Martin Campgrounds
2303 New Lenox Road
Joliet, IL
(815) 726–3173

Tom Raper RVs Camp-
   ground at Chicagoland
   Speedway
500 Speedway Boulevard
Joliet, IL
(800) 727–3778

No other racetrack on the planet is more recognized—and revered—than the Indianapolis Motor Speedway. NASCAR hasn't been to the Brickyard long enough to build the kind of tradition and lore that the open-wheeled Indy Cars (which have been racing there since 1911) have, but that hasn't lessened the profound impact NASCAR has made on the stock car community.

The series got a glimpse of what was to come when a group of cars arrived to a crowd of 30,000 fans for the first test session in 1994. A few weeks later, a throng of 325,000 fans, many of them drawn by a unique sense of curiosity, watched the first Brickyard 400. It was electrifying that first year to see cars with roofs, fenders, and bumpers rip down the main straightaway to take the green flag for the first time. It was equally compelling to watch the bulky 3,400-pound sedans rumble through the four corners without knocking down the outside wall.

The feeling was mutual. Dale Earnhardt used to tell a story of walking into the empty racetrack for the first time, standing on the famed yard of bricks that still serve as the finish line, and getting goose bumps.

No other speedway in the world has such a prominent schedule. The Indianapolis 500, the marquee event for the IRL IndyCar Series, still is considered the biggest race in the world; the Brickyard 400 is one of the top three races on the NASCAR Nextel Cup Series; and the United States Grand Prix is the only time the Formula One circuit makes an annual stop in the States.

When the NASCAR Nextel Cup Series first arrived at the Indianapolis Motor Speedway, it came as an appreciative benefactor of the speedway's goodwill. Ten years later, Indianapolis has come to realize that it needed NASCAR as much as NASCAR needed it.

"The speedway's always been known for Indy Cars, but we've carved our way with the stock cars over the past few years," driver Bill Elliott says. "I think everybody views Indy a little differently. Of all the tracks we go to, this track has more history than any other. You go back to the early 1900s when racing started; this was the facility they chose. That's kind of a special feeling to me."

To us, too.

INDIANAPOLIS MOTOR SPEEDWAY

TURN 3

TURN 2

Pit Road

TURN 4

TURN 1

START/FINISH

Our Ratings	Racing: 🏁 🏁 🏁
	Amenities: 🏁 🏁 🏁 🏁 🏁
	Area Appeal: 🏁 🏁 🏁 🏁 🏁

Track Facts

2.5-mile oval

Seating capacity: 325,000 seats

4790 West Sixteenth Street

Indianapolis, Indiana 46222

www.brickyard.com

Annual Events

One Nextel Cup Series race, August

Companion events: International Race of Champions, August

Weather

Average High (F):   August 84.0

Average Low (F):   August 63.0

Top Gun

Jeff Gordon, 3 wins

Qualifying Record

Kevin Harvick, 184.343 mph

Let's Go Racing

For all of its tradition and enormity—both in stature and size—the Indianapolis Motor Speedway doesn't lend itself to great racing. The relatively flat 9-degree banking in the corners isn't good for side-by-side racing. The cars are so big and so fast, they need to enter the corners as close to the track apron as possible so that they have enough room to swing wide, within an inch or two of the outside wall exiting the turn.

The only way to make a pass is to win a drag race down either one of the long straightaways or out-brake somebody getting into one of the turns. Since passing is so difficult, teams rely more on taking shortcuts on pit road: stretching gas mileage or skipping the urge to change tires.

The flat banking also means that cars have to hit the brakes four times a lap. Unlike at a high-banked racetrack like the Talladega Superspeedway, if a driver gambles on fuel or tires here and comes up short, the penalty is more severe. A driver can't maintain speed around the track to coast onto pit road like he could on a high-banked track, which adds to the drama of a finish.

How to Get There

The Indianapolis Motor Speedway is a little less than 2 miles inside the Interstate 465 loop and in the middle of a residential neighborhood. But don't worry. Police have been dealing with the crowds since 1911, so they know what they're doing.

I–465 loops around Indianapolis, and the raceway is located on the west side of town. The easiest way into the track is to take I–465 and use exit 16A at Crawfordsville Road. Go east on Crawfordsville Road and work your way left or right off the boulevard into one of the surrounding neighborhoods. Just about every homeowner around the racetrack sells parking spaces in their yards. Another parking option is the huge lot northwest of the speedway. If you come in from I–465 on Crawfordsville Road, as soon as you pass the shopping center on the left, turn left and get over to High School Road. Turn right onto High School Road; there are several huge lots close to the speedway. From the middle of town, take Sixteenth Street west to the speedway. One option from the north is to take I–465 to the western loop, exit at Thirty-eighth Street, and travel east to Georgetown Road. Turn right onto Georgetown Road, and take it to the speedway.

With more than 325,000 fans all converging on a local neighborhood, there's no easy and fast way to arrive unless you come before sunrise. The speedway doesn't open its doors until 7:00 A.M.—a full five hours before the green flag. It's easy to know when the doors are open for business: The speedway shoots off a cannon.

Best Seats in the House

For all its grandeur and historic significance, the view at Indianapolis is lousy. There are grandstands on both sides of the track along the main straightaway, and the infield bleachers block the view along the backstretch. Fans, however, don't seem to mind watching their favorite driver pass in front of them for a few seconds every minute and watching the rest of the lap on one of the giant TV screens.

No other racetrack could get away with such terrible sight lines, but Indianapolis pulls it off because, well, it's Indianapolis. The atmosphere is that intoxicating.

If you have the choice, look for seats in the upper half of the grandstands in the first or fourth turn. That way you can see cars approach from one direction and watch them race through the turn and head away in another direction.

Off-Limits Infield

Although Indianapolis 500 still claims to be the "Greatest Spectacle in Racing," the Brickyard 400 draws considerably higher television ratings. The only thing that differentiates the Indy 500 from the Brickyard 400 is the infield.

Race organizers allow fans to park and watch the race from the infield during the Indianapolis 500, but the infield remains off limits during the Brickyard 400. The big open areas in the infield are nothing more than a big parking lot during the August stock car race as speedway officials try, no matter how artificially, to keep the Indianapolis 500 as the cornerstone of its racing schedule.

Indianapolis Memories

It didn't take long for the Indianapolis Motor Speedway to create a memory that forever will be part of its young stock car history.

Jeff Gordon, who used to live thirty minutes west of the speedway in Pittsboro, won the inaugural race with a stunning performance that was wildly popular with the thousands of fans who watched him grow up in the go-cart, quarter-midget, and midget sprint cars around the Midwest.

After completing the hat dance in Victory Lane—wearing a hat of every race and team sponsor for photos—and finishing all the interviews and shaking hands and signing autographs until dark, Gordon finally retired to his hotel room. He hadn't eaten in nearly ten hours, and he had trouble finding a pizza parlor willing to drive through lingering traffic to make a delivery. He finally talked one into delivering his favorite, a large pizza with ham and pineapple, and rewarded the driver with a $100 tip. Don't worry, though. Gordon still had a little more than $500,000 left over from his winnings that day.

Dale Jarrett, who along with Gordon is the only repeat winner in the first eleven years of Brickyard 400 history, started a tradition after he won his first race at the Brickyard in 1996. Indy Car drivers have their tradition of drinking milk in Victory Lane. The Brickyard now has a tradition started by Jarrett: The winning team kisses the bricks at the finish line.

Tony Stewart
on Indianapolis

As a child growing up a half hour away from the Indianapolis Motor Speedway, Tony Stewart developed a love affair with the Brickyard at an early age. His career started in open-wheeled USAC midgets and progressed to the Indy Cars of the IRL circuit, where he won the series championship in 1997. With that kind of background, the man locals call the Rushville Rocket makes no secret that the Indianapolis 500 always will be the most important race in his life.

When NASCAR announced that it was expanding its schedule to include the Brickyard, Stewart, the Indy Car purist, wasn't happy. Now a stock car driver, it didn't take long for him to change his mind.

"I wasn't extremely excited, just because of the history of the place," Stewart says. "But now, NASCAR has taken it to another level and to another level again. A lot of times, people are scared of change, but as the years have gone on, people have accepted it. They've seen what a good change it's been for Indianapolis and for the community."

Whether it happens in an Indy Car or a stock car, Stewart's obsession with the Indianapolis Motor Speedway will exist until he finally wins a race there. He explains, "There's something in everybody's life that he or she is very passionate about. To me it's winning at the Brickyard. It's just that it only happens once a year. That's the hard part—you only have one chance out of every 365 days to accomplish your goal."

Make It a Vacation

If you have octane in your blood, Indianapolis is your ticket. There's so much to do in this town, and most of it—at least the interesting stuff—has to do with racing.

You can spend a day at the **Indianapolis Motor Speedway Hall of Fame Museum** inside the Indianapolis Motor Speedway (4790 West Sixteenth Street, Indianapolis; 317–492–6784; www.brickyard.com). The facility, a National Historic Landmark, has 30,000 square feet of exhibits, including seventy-five cars. Among the historic race cars on display are the Boyle Maserati that Wilbur Shaw drove to victories in 1939 and 1940; the Blue Crown Spark Plug Special driven by Mauri Rose in his 1947 and 1948 victories; the Fuel Injection Special of Bill Vukovich's 1953 and 1954 wins; the Belond Special that Sam Hanks (1957) and Jimmy Bryan (1958) drove to victories; and the Dave Evans Cummins Diesel Special that won the 1931 race without a pit stop. There are thirty winning cars from the Indianapolis 500. Admission is only $3.00 for adults, $1.00 for children ages six to fifteen, and free for children age five and younger.

Less than twenty minutes to the west of the Brickyard is **Indianapolis Raceway Park** (10267 East Indiana Highway 136, Clermont; 317–291–4090; www.na-motorsports.com), a complex owned by the National Hot Rod Association that includes a drag strip, a 2.5-mile road course, and a 0.686-mile short track. That speedway hosts USAC races for midgets, sprints, and Silver Crown cars on Thursday before the Brickyard 400; a NASCAR Craftsman Truck Series race on Friday; and a Busch Series race on Saturday night.

If you want some recreation with the smell of burning tires, play a round of golf at **Brickyard Crossing Golf Course** (4400 West Sixteenth Street, Indianapolis; 317–484–6570; www.brickyardcrossing.com). Listed as No. 47 among the "100 Greatest Public Courses" by *Golf Digest,* the 7,000-yard layout has four holes inside the Indianapolis Motor Speedway. Golfers use a tunnel under the backstretch to play holes seven through ten in the infield.

Away from the Track

Believe it or not, there is more to Indianapolis than racing. As hard as it is to accept, especially for gearheads, the town also has culture. You could spend the afternoon at **President Benjamin Harrison's Home** (1230 North Delaware Street; 317–631–1888; www.presidentbenjaminharrison.org); the **Thomas Kinkade Gallery** (49 West Maryland Street, Suite G19; 317–955–1224); or the **Indianapolis Museum of Art** (1200 West Thirty-eighth Street; 317–923–1331). One neat spot is the **State Soldiers' and Sailors' Monument Circle,** a 284-foot memorial with an observation tower at the top and a Civil War exhibit (City Circle, corners of Meridian and Michigan Streets).

Where to Eat

If you get into Indianapolis, chances are that you'll catch a few drivers out on the town. The best place to do some star gazing a day or two before the speedway opens for practice is **St. Elmo Steak House** (127 South Illinois; 317–635–0636) or **Shula's Steak House** (50 South Capitol Avenue; 317–231–3900). The steaks at both places are as legendary as A. J. Foyt.

Downtown—especially around the **City Market** area—is a vibrant area with lots of clubs and trendy outdoor restaurants. Parking can be a bit challenging, but it's worth the effort—especially if you have a date. Some of the best restaurants here include the **Old Spaghetti Factory** (210 South Meridian Street; 317–635–6325); **Bertolini's Authentic Trattoria** (49 West Maryland Street, Suite B3; 317–638–1800); **Palomino** (49 West Maryland Street; 317–974–0400); and the **Rock Bottom Brewery** (10 West Washington Street; 317–681–8180).

There are a couple popular hangouts around the speedway, especially for current and retired sprint car drivers. **Kelly's Pub and Wine Bar** (5620 Georgetown Road; 317–297–4404) is an old hangout for Tony Stewart and Kenny Irwin. **Union Jack's Pub** (6225 West Twenty-fifth Street, Speedway; 317–243–3300) also is frequented by the local racing crowd.

Where to Stay

One good thing about this town's hosting the two largest sporting events in the nation—the Indianapolis 500 and the Brickyard 400—is that Indianapolis is prepared for the crush of visitors.

Although there is a handful of hotels within two miles of the speedway, reservations for those rooms generally are automatically renewed each year.

However, there are plenty of other options. I–465, the beltway around the city, has a glut of rooms on the western side of the corridor, including **Country Hearth Inn** (317–297–1848), **Days Inn Northwest** (317–293–6550), **Signature Inn** (317–299–6165), **Hampton Inn** (317–244–1221), **LaQuinta** (317–247–4281), **Days Inn Airport** (317–248–0621), **Budgetel Inn** (317–244–8100), **Adam's Mark** (317–248–2481), **Red Roof Inn** (317–872–3030), **Residence Inn** (317–872–0462), **Courtyard by Marriott** (317–248–0300), **Holiday Inn Airport** (317–244–6861), and **Ramada Inn Airport** (317–244–3361).

Downtown offers the usually array of national full-service hotels such as the **Marriott Hotel, Hilton Garden Inn, Omni Severin Hotel, The Westin Hotel,** and **Hyatt Regency.**

No matter where you stay, make sure you book early. As hotels fill up, the prices go up.

Let's Go RVing

One of the biggest differences between the fans that travel with the Indy Car and stock car series are recreational vehicles. Most Indy Car fans still rely on hotels; stock car fans are more inclined to bring their accommodations with them. The lots along High School Road will be packed with thousands of campers, turning the Brickyard 400 into one of the most popular destinations for fans who bring their rooms with them on the road.

Indianapolis Area Restaurants

Applebee's
2659 East Main Street
Plainfield, IN
(317) 838–0650

Bellacino's Pizza and
　Grinders
2683 East Main Street
Plainfield, IN
(317) 838–7300

Bertolini's Authentic
　Trattoria
49 West Maryland Street
Suite B3
Indianapolis, IN
(317) 638–1800

Boulder Creek Dining Co.
1551 North Green Street
Brownsburg, IN
(317) 858–8100

Brickyard Crossing Golf
　Resort and Inn
4400 West Sixteenth
　Street
Speedway, IN
(317) 241–2500

Cazuelas Mexican
　Restaurant
10224 East U.S.
　Highway 36
Plainfield, IN
(317) 271–7225

Chanteclair
2501 South High School
　Road
Indianapolis, IN
(317) 243–1040

Charbono's
128 State Road 267
Avon, IN
(317) 272–1900

Charlie Brown's Pancake and Steak House
1038 Main Street
Speedway, IN
(317) 243–2502

Daddy Jack's Restaurant and Bar
9419 North Meridian Street
Indianapolis, IN
(317) 843–1609

El Rodeo
2606 North High School Road
Speedway, IN
(317) 328–7953

Iaria's Italian Restaurant
317 South College
Indianapolis, IN
(317) 638–7706

Kelly's Pub and Wine Bar
5620 Georgetown Road
Indianapolis, IN
(317) 297–4404

Kona Jack's Fish Market and Oyster Bar
9413 North Meridian Street
Carmel, IN
(317) 843–2600

La Famiglia
2376 East Main Street
Plainfield, IN
(317) 839–9945

Loon Lake Lodge Restaurant
6880 East Eighty-second Street
Indianapolis, IN
(317) 845–9011

New Orleans House
8845 Township Line Road
Indianapolis, IN
(317) 872–9670

Old Spaghetti Factory
210 South Meridian Street
Indianapolis, IN
(317) 635–6325

On the Border
10299 East US 36
Avon, IN
(317) 271–9160

Palomino
49 West Maryland Street
Indianapolis, IN
(317) 974–0400

Peter's Restaurant and Bar
8505 Keystone Crossing Boulevard
Indianapolis, IN
(317) 465–1155

Rathskeller Restaurant
401 East Michigan Street
Indianapolis, IN
(317) 636–0396

Rick's Café Boatyard
4050 Dandy Trail
Indianapolis, IN
(317) 290–9300

Rock Bottom Brewery
10 West Washington Street
Indianapolis, IN
(317) 681–8180

St. Elmo Steak House
127 South Illinois Street
Indianapolis, IN
(317) 635–0636

Sakura Japanese Restaurant
7201 North Keystone
Indianapolis, IN
(317) 259–4171

Shaffer's
6125 Hillside Avenue
Indianapolis, IN
(317) 253–1404

Shula's Steak House
50 South Capitol Avenue
Indianapolis, IN
(317) 231–3900

Tavola di ToSa
6523 Ferguson Street
Indianapolis, IN
(317) 202–0240

Texas Roadhouse
10340 East US 36
Avon, IN
(317) 209–9352

Tony Roma's
6530 East Eighty-second Street
Indianapolis, IN
(317) 915–1541

Union Jack's Pub
6225 West Twenty-fifth
    Street
Speedway, IN
(317) 243–3300

Wasabi on 82nd Sushi
    and Cuisine
5025 East Eighty-second
    Street
Suite 800
Indianapolis, IN
(317) 594–1188

The Working Man's Friend
234 North Belmont
Indianapolis, IN
(317) 636–2067

Indianapolis Area Lodging

Adam's Mark
2544 Executive Drive
Indianapolis, IN
(317) 248–2481

Adam's Mark
120 West Market Street
Indianapolis, IN
(317) 972–0600

Amerihost Inn
6105 Cambridge Way
Indianapolis, IN
(317) 838–9300

AmeriSuites Airport
5500 Bradbury Avenue
Indianapolis, IN
(317) 227–0950

AmeriSuites Keystone
9104 Keystone Crossing
Indianapolis, IN
(317) 843–0064

BayMont Indianapolis
    Airport
2650 Executive Drive
Indianapolis, IN
(317) 244–8100

BayMont Inn and Suites
2349 Post Drive
Indianapolis, IN
(317) 897–2300

Best Western
410 South Missouri Street
Indianapolis, IN
(317) 822–6400

Best Western Country
    Suites
3871 West Ninety-second
    Street
Indianapolis, IN
(317) 879–1700

Best Western South
4450 Southport Crossings
Indianapolis, IN
(317) 888–5588

Best Western Waterfront
    Plaza
2930 Waterfront Parkway
Indianapolis, IN
(317) 299–8400

Brickyard Crossing Golf
    Resort and Inn
4400 West Sixteenth
    Street
Speedway, IN
(317) 241–2500

Candlewood Suites
8111 Bash Street
Indianapolis, IN
(317) 595–9292

The Canterbury Hotel
123 South Illinois
Indianapolis, IN
(317) 634–3000

Clarion Inn and Suites
7001 Corporate Drive
Indianapolis, IN
(317) 298–3700

Comfort Inn
9760 Crosspoint Boulevard
Indianapolis, IN
(317) 578–1200

Comfort Inn
530 South Capitol Avenue
Indianapolis, IN
(317) 631–9000

Comfort Inn
7015 Western Select
    Drive
Indianapolis, IN
(317) 359–9999

Comfort Inn
3880 West Ninety-second
    Street
Indianapolis, IN
(317) 872–3100

Comfort Inn
6107 Cambridge Way
Plainfield, IN
(317) 839–9600

Comfort Inn
5040 South East Street
Indianapolis, IN
(317) 783–6711

Comfort Inn
5855 Rockville Road
Indianapolis, IN
(317) 487–9800

Country Hearth Inn
3851 Shore Drive
Indianapolis, IN
(317) 297–1848

Country Inn and Suites
4325 Southport Crossings
  Drive
Indianapolis, IN
(317) 859–6666

Courtyard
10290 North Meridian
  Street
Carmel, IN
(317) 571–1110

Courtyard
8670 Allisonville Road
Indianapolis, IN
(317) 576–9559

Courtyard
5525 Fortune Circle West
Indianapolis, IN
(317) 248–0300

Courtyard
320 Senate Drive
Indianapolis, IN
(317) 684–7733

Courtyard
7226 Woodland Drive
Indianapolis, IN
(317) 297–7700

Courtyard
4650 Southport Crossings
Indianapolis, IN
(317) 885–9799

Courtyard
501 West Washington
  Street
Indianapolis, IN
(317) 635–4443

Days Inn
4326 Sellers Street
Indianapolis, IN
(317) 542–1031

Days Inn
7314 East Twenty-first
  Street
Indianapolis, IN
(317) 359–5500

Days Inn
401 East Washington
  Street
Indianapolis, IN
(317) 637–6464

Days Inn
8275 Craig Street
Indianapolis, IN
(317) 841–9700

Days Inn
602 East Thompson
Indianapolis, IN
(317) 788–0331

Days Inn Airport
5860 Fortune Circle West
Indianapolis, IN
(317) 248–0621

Dollar Inn
6231 West Washington
  Street
Indianapolis, IN
(317) 486–1100

Dollar Inn
6331 Crawfordsville Road
Indianapolis, IN
(317) 248–8500

Dollar Inn
4630 Lafayette Road
Indianapolis, IN
(317) 293–9060

Dollar Inn
3401 South Keystone
  Avenue
Indianapolis, IN
(317) 788–0500

Dollar Inn
4033 East Southport
  Road
Indianapolis, IN
(317) 888–0900

Embassy Suites Down-
  town
110 West Washington
  Street
Indianapolis, IN
(317) 236–1800

Fairfield Inn
7110 East Twenty-first
  Street
Indianapolis, IN
(317) 322–0101

Fairfield Inn
8325 Bash Road
Indianapolis, IN
(317) 577–0455

Fairfield Inn
9251 Wesleyan Road
College Park, IN
(317) 879–9100

Fairfield Inn
4504 Southport Crossings
Indianapolis, IN
(317) 888–5535

Fairfield Inn
5905 West Eighty-sixth
  Street
Indianapolis, IN
(317) 228–9082

Fairfield Inn Airport
5220 West Southern
  Avenue
Indianapolis, IN
(317) 244–1600

Hampton Inn
7220 Woodland Drive
Indianapolis, IN
(317) 290–1212

Hampton Inn
5601 Fortune Circle West
Indianapolis, IN
(317) 244–1221

Hampton Inn
105 South Meridian
  Street
Indianapolis, IN
(317) 261–1200

Hampton Inn
I–70 at Shadeland Avenue
Indianapolis, IN
(317) 359–9900

Hampton Inn
6817 East Eighty-second
  Street
Indianapolis, IN
(317) 576–0220

Hampton Inn
7045 McFarland Boulevard
Indianapolis, IN
(317) 889–0722

Holiday Inn North at the
  Pyramids
3850 DePauw Boulevard
Indianapolis, IN
(317) 872–9790

Holiday Inn
5120 Victory Drive
Indianapolis, IN
(317) 783–4409

Holiday Inn
6990 East Twenty-first
  Street
Indianapolis, IN
(317) 359–1949

Holiday Inn
5151 South East Street
Indianapolis, IN
(317) 783–5151

Holiday Inn
2501 South High School
  Road
Indianapolis, IN
(317) 244–6861

Holiday Inn
520 East Thompson Road
Indianapolis, IN
(317) 787–8341

Holiday Inn Express
3514 South Keystone
Indianapolis, IN
(317) 788–3100

Homewood Suites
2501 East Eighty-sixth
  Street
Indianapolis, IN
(317) 253–1919

Howard Johnson Express
6850 East Twenty-first
  Street
Indianapolis, IN
(317) 353–9781

Hyatt Regency
1 South Capitol Avenue
Indianapolis, IN
(317) 632–1234

Intown Suites
3650 West Eighty-sixth
   Street
Indianapolis, IN
(317) 802–9844

Knights Inn
7101 East Twenty-first
   Street
Indianapolis, IN
(317) 353–8484

Knights Inn
4909 Knights Way
Indianapolis, IN
(317) 788–0125

LaQuinta
5316 West Southern
   Avenue
Indianapolis, IN
(317) 247–4281

Marriott Hotel
7202 East Twenty-first
   Street
Indianapolis, IN
(317) 352–1231

Marriott Hotel
350 West Maryland Street
Indianapolis, IN
(317) 822–3500

Motel 6
2851 North Shadeland
   Avenue
Indianapolis, IN
(317) 546–5864

Motel 6
5151 Elmwood
Indianapolis, IN
(317) 783–5555

Motel 6
6330 Debonair Lane
Indianapolis, IN
(317) 293–3220

Motel 6
5241 West Bradbury
   Avenue
Indianapolis, IN
(317) 248–1233

Motel 6
11551 Pendleton Pike
Indianapolis, IN
(317) 823–4415

Omni
8181 Shadeland Avenue
Indianapolis, IN
(317) 849–6668

Omni Severin Hotel Down-
   town
40 West Jackson Place
Indianapolis, IN
(317) 634–6664

Quality Inn
3525 North Shadeland
   Avenue
Indianapolis, IN
(317) 549–2222

Quality Inn
I–465 at US 31
Indianapolis, IN
(317) 788–0811

Quality Inn
9090 Wesleyan Road
Indianapolis, IN
(317) 875–7676

Radisson
2500 South High School
   Road
Indianapolis, IN
(317) 244–3361

Radisson Hotel
   City Centre
31 West Ohio
Indianapolis, IN
(317) 635–2000

Ramada Inn
520 East Thompson
Indianapolis, IN
(317) 787–8341

Ramada Limited
108 North Pennsylvania
   Street
Indianapolis, IN
(317) 614–1400

Red Roof Inn
5221 Victory Drive
Indianapolis, IN
(317) 788–9551

Red Roof Inn
I–465 at Speedway
Indianapolis, IN
(317) 872–3030

Red Roof Inn Airport
2631 South Lynhurst
   Drive
Indianapolis, IN
(317) 381–1000

Suburban Lodge
5820 West Eighty-fifth
   Street
Indianapolis, IN
(317) 871–0809

University Place
850 West Michigan
Indianapolis, IN
(317) 269–9000

The Westin Hotel
50 South Capitol
Indianapolis, IN
(317) 262–8100

Super 8 West
2602 North High School
   Road
Speedway, IN
(317) 291–8800

Indianapolis Area Camping

Indy Lakes
4001 West Southport
   Road
Indianapolis, IN
(317) 888–6006

Jameson Camp
2001 Bridgeport Road
Indianapolis, IN
(317) 241–2661

Kansas Speedway:
Plains, Trains, and Automobiles

The Kansas Speedway was a hit long before the first shovel of dirt was turned. Fans started buying tickets two years before the newest member of the International Speedway Corp. empire was completed. In fact, the suites were sold out two years before the first car turned a lap.

Although it resembles the Chicagoland Speedway—both were built by the same company—there are some subtle differences. The banking isn't as steep as in Illinois, and that makes Kansas a little slower and, drivers feel, a little more under control.

The entire experience in Kansas is breathtaking. The Heartland in fall is special to sports fans, especially when the NFL's Chiefs are playing, Major League Baseball's Royals are wrapping up a play-off push, and college football programs at Missouri, Kansas, and Kansas State are in full stride. This is a town that continually proves it can handle racing, professional and college football, and baseball at the same time.

Hall of Fame player and Kansas City Royals legend George Brett bought the first Preferred Access Speedway Seating (PASS) ticket, and every race has been a sell-out since.

Let's Go Racing

Much like Chicagoland, Kansas hasn't grown into a top-notch facility—yet. But everyone feels it's only a matter of time before the pavement wears down and the cars start to move up the banking in a second racing groove.

Although the grandstands, racing surface, garage area, and other modern amenities make Kansas a gem on the schedule, the quality of racing isn't up to speed just yet. As with any new pavement, the grip is so good that drivers don't have to back that far out of the gas while they're in the turns. Since the fastest way around any speedway is along the bottom groove, races there have been follow-the-leader affairs.

To get around the single-groove game plan, some teams will take greater chances with their engines to give them more power coming off the corners. That also puts more engines at risk and pushes the cars closer to the brink of disaster. In 2002 Sterling Marlin stepped beyond that line and crashed, rocketing off the second turn. He left Kansas with a broken neck that forced him to take the rest of the season off.

KANSAS SPEEDWAY

START/FINISH

Pit Road

TURN 1

TURN 4

TURN 2

TURN 3

Our Ratings	Racing: 🏁 🏁 🏁
	Amenities: 🏁 🏁 🏁 🏁 🏁
	Area Appeal: 🏁 🏁 🏁 🏁 🏁

Track Facts

1.5-mile tri-oval

Seating capacity: 78,000

400 Speedway Boulevard

Kansas City, KS 66111

(913) 328–7223

www.kansasspeedway.com

Annual Events

One Nextel Cup Series race, October

Companion event: Busch Series, October

Weather

Average High (F):   October 69.0

Average Low (F):   October 49.0

Top Gun

Jeff Gordon, 2 wins

Qualifying Record

Jimmie Johnson, 180.373 mph

One man who's had no trouble figuring Kansas out is Jeff Gordon. He won the first two races there, enhancing his reputation as being one of the best at new tracks. In all, Gordon has won inaugural races at Kansas, Indianapolis, and California.

How to Get There

The speedway is smartly located on the corners of Interstates 70 and 435. That makes it easy to get in and out from all directions.

From the airport: Take Interstate 29 north to I–435 south toward Topeka. The speedway is about 25 miles away.

From downtown Kansas City: Take I–70 west to I–435 north.

From Wichita and Topeka: Take the Kansas Turnpike (Interstate 335) north to I–70 east. Get off at I–435.

There's plenty of parking around the speedway, and the traffic patterns help the flow move easily. Getting in and out of the Kansas Speedway makes you wonder why everyone else can't figure out a traffic pattern that works as well as this one.

Jeff Gordon on Kansas

Don't tell Jeff Gordon that Chicagoland and Kansas aren't old enough to be great racetracks. In the first three races at Chicagoland, he posted a second- and a fourth-place finish, and he won the first two races at its sister track at Kansas. "I guess it's good to come to Kansas, because I do like this track," Gordon says. "The track's been good to us, obviously. It's been real good to us."

He says there's something about the way the track is designed that fits perfectly with his driving style and the setup on his Hendrick Motorsports Chevrolet. It's such a match, he's probably the only one who doesn't want Kansas to change with age.

"When they dropped the green flag [in 2002] and I drove by a couple cars, I knew right then it was going to be a good day," Gordon says. "Coming into [the races at Kansas], we just had that feeling. We had that sense we were going to have something strong."

Best Seats in the House

A ticket in the grandstands here already qualifies as one of the best seats in the house. The stands are high enough above the racing surface that even the lower seats have a pretty good view of the backstretch. Of course, the higher you go the better. In fact, if you can get in the upper twenty rows, you can catch some of the shade created by the towering suites late in the race.

The PASS ticket is nothing more than a season ticket. The only way to get one of the premium seats for the NASCAR Nextel Cup Series race is to buy tickets to include Busch, ARCA, and IRL IndyCar Series events as a package deal. While it seems like extortion, it's not a bad deal if you like racing. Besides, you also get a spot in one of the reserved lots. That doesn't leave a lot of seats, if any, for everyone else. Our suggestion is to buy your tickets a year in advance and hope for the best. Like we've already said, there's no bad seat in the house.

The infield is marked off into reserved spots for campers. Although they have a lot more room than at most other infields, their view is limited to action on the backstretch.

Kansas Memories

This brings us right back to **Jeff Gordon.**

Gordon was involved in a compelling points race battle with **Tony Stewart, Ryan Newman,** and **Jimmie Johnson** in 2002. After finishing thirty-seventh due to a chain-reaction crash a week earlier at the Dover International Speedway, he said that if he wasn't able to turn it around at Kansas, his chances in the championship hunt were done.

"I was not real happy after [the race at Dover], and I think everybody knew that," Gordon said. "It wasn't anybody's fault, but you see it get so close and then you see it fall apart. I was pretty upset. When I left, I said right there on TV that if we didn't do something at Kansas, we'd be in trouble. I'm glad I said it now, but at the time I wasn't so sure it was the right thing to say."

The 2002 race also was memorable because it went head to head with a Kansas City Chiefs–Miami Dolphins football game at nearby Arrowhead Stadium. It was a big test for a town not thought to be big enough to support two major events at the same time, which went against an age-old scheduling practice. Hopefully NASCAR and the National Football League can work together in the future. Kansas City, however, proved it was up to the challenge. There were enough hotel rooms for fast cars and football, and both stadiums were filled to capacity.

Make It a Vacation

The Kansas-Missouri state line cuts Kansas City in two. The big-city sprawl is on the Missouri side; the more-open country sprawl is on the Kansas side. Put them together, and Kansas City has a little bit of everything to offer.

There are a lot of reasons to spend a few extra days in Kansas City, especially in October. There's enough culture, history, recreation, and wonderful autumn weather to keep you busy all the way up to—and after—the race. We recommend staying in town. Kansas City is only 15 miles from the track, and it's an easy drive on I–70. If you make downtown your starting point, many attractions are just a few blocks away.

No vacation here, whether it's an hour or a week, would be complete without sampling some Kansas City barbecue or one of the city's thick and juicy steaks. Come hungry—and forget about cholesterol while you're here.

Another must is spending an evening at one of the local blues and jazz clubs. Legends Count Basie, Charlie "Bird" Parker, and Orin "Hot Lips" Page all got their starts in the smoky Kansas City clubs like **The Phoenix Piano Bar and Grill** (302 West Eighth Street, Kansas City, Missouri; 816–472–0001); **Jardine's Restaurant and Jazz Club** (4536 Main Street, Kansas City, Missouri; 816–561–6480); and **Blue Room** (1616 East Eighteenth Street, Kansas City, Missouri; 816–474–2929).

If you're looking for downtown lodging, try the **Doubletree Hotel** (816–474–6664), the **Historic Suites of America** (816–842–6544), **Hotel Phillips** (816–221–7000), **Hyatt Regency Crown Center** (816–421–1234), **Marriott Downtown** (816–421–6800), and **Westin Crown Center** (816–474–4400). But there are at least fifty other places, many of them smaller and more quaint, to stay in the downtown area.

Away from the Track

Kansas City is a rare mix of old and new, so there's a little something for everyone. Baseball fans can visit the **Negro Leagues Baseball Museum** (1616 East Eighteenth Street, Kansas City, Missouri; 816–221–1920) to study the history of minorities in baseball; children can play all day at **Worlds of Fun** (4545 Worlds of Fun Avenue, Kansas City, Missouri;

816–454–4545), an amusement park featuring a tumble-and-spin ride called ThunderHawk guaranteed to make you wish you hadn't eaten a chili dog an hour earlier; and train fanatics will appreciate **Union Station Kansas City** (30 West Pershing Road, Kansas City, Missouri; 816–460–2020), a gathering place for shopping and entertainment built around a remodeled train and station. Union Station is also home to **Science City,** an interactive place to turn your curiosity into knowledge.

The **Harry S. Truman Library** (U.S. Highway 24 and Delaware, Independence, Missouri; 816–833–1225; www.trumanlibrary.org), a museum dedicated to the former president, is just a short drive away. Among the collection are artifacts pertaining directly to Truman's presidency and personal love letters written by his wife, Bess.

The pinnacle of Kansas City's nightlife is **Westport,** through which the California, Oregon, and Sante Fe Trails all passed, making it the gateway to the western frontier. Now it's a collection of modern restaurants, night clubs, and stores, as well as historical sites dedicated to Civil War battles and the West. A great place to start your journey is the **Westport Historical Society** (400 Baltimore, Kansas City, Missouri; 816–561–1821).

Where to Eat

The question isn't where to eat, it's where to eat first. Kansas City is a carnivore's paradise, and local chefs have found some wonderful ways to turn a side of beef into a gastronomic delight.

We start at **Arthur Bryant's BBQ** (1727 Brooklyn Avenue, Kansas City, Missouri; 816–231–1123), where they serve up a mountain of chopped or sliced barbecue on a lunchroom tray; then we move on to **Oklahoma Joe's Barbecue and Catering** (3002 West Forty-seventh Avenue, Kansas City, Kansas; 913–722–3366), which has all the necessary ingredients to be a classic restaurant—gas pumps, liquor store, and the "Best Sauce on the Planet." Next we hit **LC's Bar-B-Q** (5800 Blue Parkway, Kansas City, Missouri; 816–923–4484), where "our grits need no explaining," and wrap it up at **Board Room Bar-B-Q** (9600 Antioch Road, Shawnee Mission, Kansas; 913–642–6273), where sauce is king. Finally there are our favorite spots for a late stop: **Gates Bar-B-Q** (1026 State Avenue, Kansas

City, Kansas; 913–621–1134), where they specialize in both "dry" and "wet" barbecue, and **K.C. Masterpiece BBQ** (4747 Wyandotte Street, Kansas City, Missouri; 816–531–7111), where the slabs of ribs are as big as a Buick.

Now that we've had our fill of barbecue—if there is such a thing—we move to steaks. With all due respect to the American Heart Association, here is a sampling of the best: **Hereford House Restaurant** (2 East Twentieth Street, Kansas City, Missouri; 816–842–1080); **Majestic Steakhouse** (931 Broadway Street, Kansas City, Missouri; 816–471–8484); **Peppercorn Duck Club** (2345 McGee Street, Kansas City, Missouri; 816–435–4199); **J. Gilbert's Wood Fired Steaks** (8901 Metcalf Avenue, Shawnee Mission, Kansas; 913–642–8070, and **Plaza III—The Steakhouse** (4749 Pennsylvania Avenue, Kansas City, Missouri; 816–753–0000).

For a change of pace, there's the **River Market Brewing Co.** (500 Walnut, Kansas City, Missouri; 816–471–6300); **Stanford and Sons Restaurant and Comedy Club** (504 Westport Road, Kansas City, Missouri; 816–561–7454); and **McCormick and Schmick's Seafood Restaurant** (448 West Forty-seventh Street, Kansas City, Missouri; 816–531–6800).

Where to Stay

With only 78,000 seats at the speedway, Kansas City has no problem leaving the hotel light on for you. With talk of expanding speedway capacity to 150,000 seats, hotels may someday become a premium, so once you find a place to stay, ask if you can be placed on an automatic renewal list.

There are three basic areas to find rooms: downtown, by the airport, and south near Overland Park. We've already covered some of the major downtown hotels; here are some smaller ones to consider: **Cherry Street Inn** (921 Cherry Street, Kansas City, Missouri; 816–471–1775); **Fairfield Inn by Marriott at Union Hill** (3001 Main Street, Kansas City, Missouri; 816–931–5700); **Residence Inn by Marriott at Union Hill** (2975 Main Street, Kansas City, Missouri; 816–561–3000); **Harrah's Hotel and Casino** (1 Riverboat Drive, Kansas City, Missouri; 816–472–7777); and **Four Points Barcelo Hotel** (1 East Forty-fifth Street, Kansas City, Missouri; 816–753–7400).

At the airport, there's plenty to pick from, and these locations give you the least-congested route into the speedway. You can pick from **Ramada Inn Airport** (7301 Northwest Tiffany Springs Parkway, Kansas City, Missouri; 816–741–9500); **Embassy Suites Airport** (7640 Northwest Tiffany

Springs Parkway, Kansas City, Missouri; 816–891–7788); **Microtel Inn and Suites Airport** (11831 Northwest Plaza Circle, Kansas City, Missouri; 816–270–1200); **Best Western Country Inn Airport** (11900 Plaza Circle, Kansas City, Missouri; 816–464–2002); **Holiday Inn Express Airport** (11130 Northwest Ambassador Drive, Kansas City, Missouri; 816–891–9111); **Fairfield Inn Airport** (11820 Northwest Plaza Circle, Kansas City, Missouri; 816–464–2424); **Hampton Inn Airport** (11212 North Newark Circle, Kansas City, Missouri; 816–464–5454), **Drury Inn and Suites** (7900 Tiffany Springs Parkway, Kansas City, Missouri; 816–880–9700); **Hilton Hotel Airport** (8801 Northwest 112th Street, Kansas City, Missouri; 816–891–8900); **Marriott Kansas City Airport** (775 Brasilia, Kansas City, Missouri; 816–464–2200); **Courtyard by Marriott Airport** (7901 North Tiffany Springs Parkway, Kansas City, Missouri; 816–891–7500); and **Econo Lodge Airport** (11300 Northwest Prairie View Road, Kansas City, Missouri; 816–464–5082).

To the south near Overland Park, your choices include **Fairfield Inn** (4401 West 107th Street, Overland Park, Kansas; 913–381–5700); **AmeriSuites** (6801 West 112th Street, Overland Park, Kansas; 913–451–2553); **Courtyard by Marriott** (11301 Metcalf Avenue, Overland Park, Kansas; 913–339–9900); **Doubletree Hotel at Corporate Woods** (10100 College Boulevard, Overland Park, Kansas; 913–451–6100); and **Drury Inn and Suites** (10951 Metcalf Avenue, Overland Park, Kansas; 913–345–1500).

Kansas City Area Restaurants

Arthur Bryant's BBQ
1727 Brooklyn Avenue
Kansas City, MO
(816) 231–1123

Blue Room
1616 East Eighteenth
  Street
Kansas City, MO
(816) 474–2929

Board Room Bar-B-Q
9600 Antioch Road
Shawnee Mission, KS
(913) 642–6273

Cheesecake Factory
4701 Wyandotte Street
Kansas City, MO
(816) 960–1919

City Tavern
101 West Twenty-second
  Street
Kansas City, MO
(816) 421–3696

Crown Center
2405 Grand
Suite 200
Kansas City, MO
(816) 274–8374

Fiorella's Jack Stack
  Barbeque
9520 Metcalf Avenue
Shawnee Mission, KS
(913) 385–7427

Fitz's Restaurant
Union Station
30 West Pershing Road
Kansas City, MO
(816) 474–4900

Gates Bar-B-Q
1026 State Avenue
Kansas City, KS
(913) 621–1134

Gates Bar-B-Q
3205 Main Street
Kansas City, MO
(816) 753–0828

Gojo Japanese Steak
House
4163 Broadway Street
Kansas City, MO
(816) 561–2501

Hayward's Pit Bar-B-Que
11051 Antioch Road
Shawnee Mission, KS
(913) 451–8080

Hereford House Restau-
rant
2 East Twentieth Street
Kansas City, MO
(816) 842–1080

Hibachi Japanese Steak
House
4745 Wyandotte Street
Kansas City, MO
(816) 753–0707

J. Gilbert's Wood Fired
Steaks
8901 Metcalf Avenue
Shawnee Mission, KS
(913) 642–8070

JJ's
910 West Forty-eighth
Street
Kansas City, MO
(816) 561–7136

Jardine's Restaurant and
Jazz Club
4536 Main Street
Kansas City, MO
(816) 561–6480

Jess and Jim's Steak
House
517 East 135th Street
Kansas City, MO
(816) 941–9499

Joe's Crab Shack
11965 South Strang Line
Road
Olathe, KS
(913) 393–2929

K.C. Masterpiece BBQ
4747 Wyandotte Street
Kansas City, MO
(816) 531–7111

K.C. Masterpiece BBQ and
Grill Restaurant
10985 Metcalf
Overland Park, KS
(913) 345–1199

Kiki's Bon Ton Maison
1515 Westport Road
Kansas City, MO
(816) 931–9417

LC's Bar-B-Q
5800 Blue Parkway
Kansas City, MO
(816) 923–4484

Majestic Steakhouse
931 Broadway Street
Kansas City, MO
(816) 471–8484

McCormick and Schmick's
Seafood Restaurant
448 West Forty-seventh
Street
Kansas City, MO
(816) 531–6800

Morton's of Chicago
2475 Grand Boulevard
Kansas City, MO
(816) 474–0555

Oklahoma Joe's Barbecue
3002 West Forty-seventh
Street
Kansas City, KS
(913) 772–3366

Pam Pam
200 West Twelfth Street
Kansas City, MO
(816) 421–6800

Peppercorn Duck Club
2345 McGee Street
Kansas City, MO
(816) 435–4199

The Phoenix Piano Bar
and Grill
302 West Eighth Street
Kansas City, MO
(816) 472–0001

Plaza III—The Steakhouse
4749 Pennsylvania
Avenue
Kansas City, MO
(816) 753–0000

River Market Brewing Co.
500 Walnut
Kansas City, MO
(816) 471–6300

Rosedale Barbecue
600 Southwest Boulevard
Kansas City, KS
(913) 262–0343

Ruth's Chris Steak House
700 West Forty-seventh
    Street
Kansas City, MO
(816) 531–4800

Skies
2345 McGee Street
Kansas City, MO
(816) 435–4199

Smokehouse BBQ
6402 North Oak Turfway
Gladestone, MO
(816) 454–4500

Stanford and Sons
    Restaurant and
    Comedy Club
504 Westport Road
Kansas City, MO
(816) 561–7454

Sutera's West Restaurant
140 North 130 Street
Bonner Springs, KS
(913) 721–5549

Tanner's Bar and Grill
7425 Broadway Street
Kansas City, MO
(816) 822–7525

Wyandot Barbeque
8441 State Avenue
Kansas City, KS
(913) 788–7554

Yahooz
4701 Town Center Drive
Leawood, KS
(913) 451–8888

Kansas City Area Lodging

Adam's Mark
9103 East Thirty-ninth
    Street
Kansas City, MO
(816) 737–0200

Ameristar Casino and
    Hotel
3200 North Station Drive
Kansas City, MO
(816) 414–7000

Amerisuites
6801 West 112th Street
Overland Park, KS
(913) 451–2553

Best Western Country
    Inn KCI Airport
11900 Plaza Circle
Kansas City, MO
(816) 464–2002

Cherry Street Inn
921 Cherry Street
Kansas City, MO
(816) 471–1775

Comfort Inn
Seventy-eighth Street at
    I–70
Kansas City, KS
(913) 299–5555

Comfort Inn
7300 Northeast Parvin
    Road
Kansas City, MO
(816) 454–3500

Comfort Suites
11951 Northwest Ambas-
    sador Drive
Kansas City, MO
(816) 464–5500

Comfort Suites
8200 North Church Road
Kansas City, MO
(816) 781–7273

Country Hearth Inn
6901 Northwest Eighty-
    third Street
Kansas City, MO
(816) 587–6262

Country Hearth Inn
199 Macon Street
Kansas City, MO
(816) 781–7273

Courtyard by Marriott
    Airport
7901 North Tiffany
    Springs Parkway
Kansas City, MO
(816) 891–7500

Days Inn
11801 Blue Ridge Boulevard
Kansas City, MO
(816) 765–1888

Days Inn
2232 Taney Street
Kansas City, MO
(816) 461–6000

Days Inn and Suites KCI
11120 Northwest Ambassador Drive
Kansas City, MO
(816) 746–1666

Doubletree Hotel
1301 Wyandotte Street
Kansas City, MO
(816) 474–6664

Drury Hotel
3830 Blue Ridge Cutoff
Kansas City, MO
(816) 923–3000

Drury Inn and Suites
7900 Tiffany Springs Parkway
Kansas City, MO
(816) 880–9700

Econo Lodge KCI Airport
11300 Northwest Prairie View Road
Kansas City, MO
(816) 464–5082

Embassy Suites KCI Airport
7640 Northwest Tiffany Springs Parkway
Kansas City, MO
(816) 891–7788

Fairfield Inn
4401 West 107th Street
Overland Park, KS
(913) 381–5700

Fairfield Inn
8101 North Church Street
Kansas City, MO
(816) 792–4000

Fairfield Inn
2975 Main Street
Kansas City, MO
(816) 561–3000

Fairfield Inn KCI Airport
11820 Northwest Plaza Circle
Kansas City, MO
(816) 464–2424

Four Points Barcelo Hotel
1 East Forty-fifth Street
Kansas City, MO
(816) 753–7400

Grand Crowne
430 State Highway 165
Branson, MO
417–332–8344

Hampton Inn
1051 North Cambridge Street
Kansas City, MO
(816) 483–7900

Hampton Inn
8551 Church Road
Kansas City, MO
(816) 415–9600 .

Hampton Inn
4600 Summitt
Kansas City, MO
(816) 448–4600

Hampton Inn KCI Airport
11212 North Newark Circle
Kansas City, MO
(816) 464–5454

Harrah's Hotel and Casino
1 Riverboat Drive
Kansas City, MO
(816) 472–7777

Hilton Kansas City Airport
8801 Northwest 112th Street
Kansas City, MO
(816) 891–8900

Historic Suites of America
612 Central Street
Kansas City, MO
(816) 842–6544

Holiday Inn
1215 Wyandotte Street
Kansas City, MO
(816) 471–1333

Holiday Inn
801 Westport Road
Kansas City, MO
(816) 931–1000

Holiday Inn Express
I–70 at Kansas Highways 7 and 73
Bonner Springs, KS
(913) 721–5300

Holiday Inn Express Airport
11130 Northwest Ambassador Drive
Kansas City, MO
(816) 891–9111

Holiday Inn KCI Airport
11832 Plaza Circle
Kansas City, MO
(816) 464–2345

Holiday Inn Sports
Complex
4011 Blue Ridge Cutoff
Kansas City, MO
(816) 353–5300

Homestead Village
4535 Main Street
Kansas City, MO
(816) 531–2212

Hotel Phillips
106 West Twelfth Street
Kansas City, MO
(816) 221–7000

Hyatt Regency Crown
Center
2345 McGee Street
Kansas City, MO
(816) 421–1234

Marriott Country Club
Plaza
4445 Main Street
Kansas City, MO
(816) 531–3000

Marriott Downtown
200 West Twelfth Street
Kansas City, MO
(816) 421–6800

Marriott Kansas City
Airport
775 Brasilia
Kansas City, MO
(816) 464–2200

Marriott Overland Park
10800 Metcalf Avenue
Overland Park, KS
(913) 451–8000

Microtel Inn and Suites
KCI Airport
11831 Northwest Plaza
Circle
Kansas City, MO
(816) 270–1200

Radisson
11828 Northwest Plaza
Circle
Kansas City, MO
(816) 464–2423

Ramada Inn Kansas City
Airport
7301 Northwest Tiffany
Springs Road
Kansas City, MO
(816) 741–9500

Red Roof Inn
3636 Randolph Road
Kansas City, MO
(816) 452–8585

Residence Inn
2975 Main Street
Kansas City, MO
(816) 561–3000

Vanity Fair Plaza Suites
700 West Forty-eighth
Street
Kansas City, MO
(816) 561–2900

Westin Crown Center
1 East Pershing Road
Kansas City, MO
(816) 474–4400

Kansas City Area Camping

Camp Mo-Kan
16200 East US 40
Kansas City, MO
(816) 373–4153

Gaea Retreat Center
800 East Armour
Boulevard
Kansas City, MO
(816) 931–4443

Heartland Presbyterian
Camp and Conference
Center
16965 Northwest Mis-
souri Highway 45
Kansas City, MO
(816) 891–1078

Heart Mobile Village
7000 East US 40
Kansas City, MO
(816) 923–7444

Linden Mobile Court
400 Northeast Seventy-
sixth Terrace
Kansas City, MO
(816) 436–0860

Winning in the West

If you want more proof that NASCAR's boundaries now reach far enough to dangle its toes in the warm Pacific surf—and beyond—just head west. These are the raceways of rattlesnake roundups, ten-gallon hats, rolling dice, vineyards, and purple haze. In 1989 there were two races west of the Mississippi River. Now there are six, with the Phoenix International Raceway, Las Vegas Motor Speedway, and Texas Motor Speedway actively campaigning for a second Nextel Cup Series racing date. While the speedways that make up the Wild, Wild West aren't rich in NASCAR history, they add a unique flavor to stock car racing.

Infineon Raceway
Sonoma, California

Las Vegas Motor Speedway
Las Vegas, Nevada

California Speedway
Fontana, California

Phoenix International Raceway
Avondale, Arizona

Texas Motor Speedway
Justin, Texas

Infineon Raceway:
Days of Wine and Road Courses

The best part of watching the cars turn left and right on the twisting road course formerly known as Sears Point Raceway is getting there. Whether you approach from the south and drive over the Golden Gate Bridge, or come from the north through the lush and fertile Sonoma Valley, the views are spectacular.

Track owner O. Bruton Smith pumped $50 million into the speedway three years ago. He got help when he sold the naming rights to European technology company Infineon for $34.6 million, and he invested the money smartly by adding new grandstands and redesigning the course to make it more fan-friendly.

This track now has all the comforts of the newer speedways on the circuit. But unlike the cookie-cutter tracks, Infineon Raceway has a subtle charm that can't be matched.

The vast, rolling hills are home to some of the world's greatest wineries and apricot and cherry orchards. The towns are quaint and look as though they're right out of Norman Rockwell's imagination. The racing's not bad here, but the trip and surrounding area are even better. By the time you leave, the race will be little more than the excuse for coming here— and the excuse you'll use to come back again and again.

Let's Go Racing

Only a handful of drivers seem to have a knack for driving on road courses. Infineon requires a lot more than an ability to make both left- and right-hand turns; it requires a rhythm. Two miles of twists, turns, and hills are a real challenge. Dale Earnhardt Jr. used to hate road-course racing, once saying that he wished he'd just as soon finish last and skip the whole thing. Sterling Marlin still hates them, saying the last lap is like winning a reprieve from the governor before execution.

The truth is, the scenery is three times as good as the racing. There aren't a lot of places to pass, because it's hard to gain inside position when the course turns left and right. If you can get inside another driver in one turn, three seconds later you're on the outside—and at a big disadvantage—when the course turns the other direction.

The best place for passing is the long paperclip-like carousel that sets

INFINEON RACEWAY

Our Ratings

Racing: 🏁🏁 🏁🏁 🏁🏁

Amenities: 🏁🏁 🏁🏁 🏁🏁 🏁🏁

Area Appeal: 🏁🏁 🏁🏁 🏁🏁 🏁🏁 🏁🏁

Track Facts

2.0-mile, 10-turn road course

Seating capacity: 64,000

California Highways 37 and 121

Sonoma, CA 95476

(707) 938–8448

www.infineonraceway.com

Annual Events

One NASCAR Nextel Cup Series race, June

Companion race: NASCAR West Series, June

Weather

Average High (F):   June 86.0

Average Low (F):   June 50.0

Top Gun

Jeff Gordon, 3 wins

Qualifying Record

Jeff Gordon, 93.699 mph

up the short sprint to the finish line. There's a lot of action here, like Ricky Rudd's bump of Davey Allison on the final lap in 1991—a bump that prompted NASCAR to strip Rudd of the victory and award Allison the trophy—and Robby Gordon's pass of Richard Childress Racing teammate Kevin Harvick while racing back to the caution flag in 2003; that pass helped Gordon eventually win the race.

How to Get There

While the roads into Infineon Raceway are picturesque, the traffic can be stifling. The only way into the massive complex is a couple of two-lane highways, so plan to come early and stay late.

From San Francisco: Take U.S. Highway 101 north and turn right onto California Highway 37. Then make a left onto California Highway 121 to the speedway.

From Oakland: Take Interstate 80 north to CA 37. Go north to CA 121, and make a left to the speedway.

From Sacramento: Take I–80 west to CA 37. Make a right onto CA 121, and turn left toward the speedway.

Jeff Gordon
on Infineon

During a three-year stretch that started in 1998, nobody could touch Jeff Gordon at the Infineon Raceway. He was born a half hour away in Vallejo, and he immediately displayed a knack for the intricacies of slinging a 3,400-pound Chevrolet around a circuit designed for lighter, more nimble sports cars.

Part of his success was the carousel turn, where he wasn't afraid to use his front bumper to knock slower cars out of the way. "It is a battle out there," he said following his victory in 2000. "It is so hard to pass, and you have only one area to pass in. Guys were bumping and banging. I got into a couple guys. It's such hard racing; you're going for it every corner. You really have to work for it."

Best Seats in the House

By design, a road course doesn't offer many good seats. The new grandstand at the start/finish line allows fans to see cars race into the first turn and around the final left-hand turn past the carousel.

Watching a road-course race takes a different mindset than oval racing. Cars pass about every seventy-seven seconds, then they disappear over a hill or around one of the turns. To best capture the experience, we suggest roughing it. There are spots out near Turns 5, 6, and 7 where you can spread a blanket on one of the hillsides and watch the action. And if you want to act like a local, bring a bottle of wine.

Infineon Memories

To this day, **Ricky Rudd** still doesn't like talking about the 1991 victory that was taken away by NASCAR. And **Jerry Nadeau** still grimaces every time he thinks back to his near-win in 2002.

Rudd gave **Davey Allison** a bump on the final lap coming through the carousel, sending Allison skidding and Rudd to Victory Lane. Moments later, NASCAR declared Allison the winner and dropped Rudd to the tail end of the lead lap in the final rundown.

Dale Earnhardt made a career out of the bump-and-run move, and none of his victories were challenged. Rudd still insists that wasn't the case that afternoon. He said Allison slowed down on purpose to get Rudd out of his rhythm, and that's what prompted the crash. What compounded the problem was that **Dick Beaty,** NASCAR's competition director, missed that race, leaving **Les Richter,** a former NFL football player, in charge of imposing the penalty. Most believe that if Beaty had been there, Rudd would have kept the win.

In 2002 it wasn't politics that cost Nadeau a chance to win. Hired to drive one of the Dodges for Petty Enterprises, he led by more than a football field when the rear-end gear broke with less than three laps to go. Nadeau was reduced to tears when his car finally rolled to a stop in the middle of the course. The driver who benefited from Nadeau's misfortune that day was none other than Ricky Rudd.

Make It a Vacation

There are few places in America where you can wear a winter jacket at night and get sunburned in the daytime. That's what makes the Bay area so unique.

San Francisco is a spectacular city to visit; and a day trip through the **Napa Valley** is so soothing. In San Francisco you can easily spend the day down at **Fisherman's Wharf** (The Embarcadero and Taylor Street) and **Pier**

39 (the Embarcadero and Powell Street) walking through all the shops, watching all the local sleight-of-hand street performers and sea lions, and making the short ferry trip over to **Alcatraz Island** to see the old prison. No trip to San Francisco would be complete without seeing, then driving over, the **Golden Gate Bridge** or standing atop the **Twin Peaks** (Twin Peaks Boulevard) for the breathtaking view of the whole city.

While San Francisco is a city rich in culture, diversity, and great restaurants, it's not a city for the budget-minded visitor. It's very expensive—you could spend a day's pay just parking downtown. However, there are a handful of high-quality hotels available for a reasonable price compared with the average room rates for the area. The **Phoenix Hotel** (601 Eddy Street; 415–776–1380); **Hotel Del Sol** (3100 Webster Street; 415–921–5520); **Alisa Hotel** (447 Bush Street; 866–786–8763); and **The Mosser Victorian** (54 Fourth Street; 415–986–4400) are some pretty smart options.

The prices in San Francisco are why we suggest staying across the San Francisco Bay in Oakland or down the road a bit in San Jose. A couple of good tips in Oakland are the **Executive Inn and Suites** (1755 Embarcadero; 510–536–6633) and the **Waterfront Plaza** (10 Washington Street; 800–729–3638). They're still in the $110–$170 a night range, but for the area that's about as good as it gets. And while you're in Oakland, you can spend the afternoon at the **Oakland Zoo** (9777 Golf Links Road; 510–632–9525).

Away from the Track

It's hard to believe that the Napa and Sonoma Valleys are just thirty minutes from the high-rise hustle and bustle of San Francisco and Oakland. Out here, nothing moves fast. There are no twenty-four-hour "superstores" or twenty-four-screen multiplexes. The only things this area has to offer are wine, art, and a lifestyle that, for most of us, is surreal.

There are plenty of art galleries in downtown Sonoma, and it's easy to lose an afternoon walking around the town square doing nothing more than window-shopping. Out in the valley there are more than forty wineries, and most of them allow visitors.

Stopping at the better known wineries like **Robert Mondavi Winery** (California Highway 29, Oakville; 888–766–6328); **E. and J. Gallo Winery**

(3387 Dry Creek Road, Healdsburg; 707–431–5500); and **Benziger Family Winery** (1883 London Ranch Road, Sonoma; 888–490–2739) are smart moves. We recommend one of the area's great little secrets—the **Sebastiani Vineyards** (389 Fourth Street, Sonoma; 707–938–5532).

The **Changing Seasons Gallery and Gifts** (103 West Napa Street, Sonoma; 707–935–8646) has artwork, glasswork, oils, prints, watercolors, and pottery for every budget. The **di Rosa Preserve** (5200 Carneros Highway, Sonoma; 707–226–5991) has thousands of Bay-area art pieces that can be viewed by appointment only.

Where to Eat

As you can imagine, just about every area restaurant features locally grown produce and, of course, wine. If you're not used to the aristocratic protocol of drinking wine, be prepared to watch people spit $50 bottles of wine into buckets on the middle of the table. (Some wine connoisseurs feel that it's more proper to sip a wine, swish it around in your mouth, then spit it out.) Another local tradition is for a group to meet at a restaurant, with everyone bringing his or her own bottle of wine to enjoy. They not only share sips of different bouquets, they share the same spit bucket.

The area is just as famous for its produce, and that makes for some unforgettable dishes. **The Deuce** (691 Broadway, Sonoma; 707–933–3823) uses locally grown fruits, vegetables, and beef, and the menu changes to reflect which crops are in season. **The General's Daughter** (400 West Spain Street, Sonoma; 707–938–4004) has more than one hundred different wines; **Follini and Eichenbaum** (19100 Arnold Drive, Sonoma; 707–996–3287) boasts the best pastrami and corned beef in northern California.

For burgers try **Pearl's Diner** (561 Fifth Street West, Sonoma; 707–996–1783); for a lighter cuisine go to **Maya Restaurant** (101 East Napa Street, Sonoma; 707–935–3500); and for a cup of coffee and a morning pastry with the locals, stop in at **Basque Boulangerie** (460 First Street East, Sonoma; 707–935–7687).

Where to Stay

Although we still suggest staying about a half hour away from Sonoma in Santa Rosa, San Rafael, Vallejo, or Novato to avoid the very high costs that come with such a quaint and chic area, there are more than seventy-five places in the Sonoma Valley alone to stay. Most of them are smaller inns and bed-and-breakfasts, and the experience is likely to be unforgettable. But it will come with a high price, especially during race weekend.

If you want to soak up the entire experience—and we believe you should do it at least once—here are a few places to consider: **Alexandria's Plaza Suite** (440 Second Street East, Sonoma; 707–938–8381); **Casita Carneros** (21235 Hyde Road, Sonoma; 707–996–0996); and **Sonoma Hotel** (110 West Spain Street, Sonoma; 707–996–2996). There's a complete listing of all the places to stay in the area at www.sonomavalley.com.

If you want to venture away from the valley, we suggest that you check into the **Embassy Suites** (101 McInnis Parkway, San Rafael; 415–499–9222); **Comfort Inn** (1185 Admiral Callaghan Lane, Vallejo; 707–648–1400 and 2632 North Cleveland Avenue, Santa Rosa; 707–542–5544); **Regency Inn** (4326 Sonoma Boulevard, Vallejo; 707–643–4150); **Best Western Marine World** (1596 Fairgrounds Drive, Vallejo; 707–554–9655); and **Courtyard by Marriott** (1400 North Hamilton Parkway, Novato; 415–883–8950).

Infineon Raceway Area Restaurants

Adobe Net Cafe
135 West Napa Street
Sonoma, CA
(707) 935–0390

Amigos Grill and Cantina
19315 Sonoma Highway
Sonoma, CA
(707) 939–0743

Basque Boulangerie
460 First Street East
Sonoma, CA
(707) 935–7687

Bella Santina's
8 Spain Street
Sonoma, CA
(707) 996–6866

The Breakaway Cafe
19101 Sonoma Highway
Sonoma, CA
(707) 996–5949

Cafe Andalusia
165 West Napa Street
Sonoma, CA
(707) 996–5556

Cafe La Haye
140 East Napa Street
Sonoma, CA
(707) 935–5994

Coffee Garden Cafe
415 First Street West
Sonoma, CA
(707) 996–6645

Cucina Viansa
400 First Street East
Sonoma, CA
(707) 935–5656

Della Santinas Trattoria
133 East Napa Street
Sonoma, CA
(707) 935–0576

The Depot Hotel
241 First Street West
Sonoma, CA
(707) 938–2980

The Deuce
691 Broadway
Sonoma, CA
(707) 933–3823

Fior d'Italia
601 Union Street
San Francisco, CA
(415) 986–1886

Follini and Eichenbaum
19100 Arnold Drive
Sonoma, CA
(707) 996–3287

Garden Court Cafe and
  Bakery
18252 Comstock Avenue
Sonoma, CA
(770) 935–1565

The General's Daughter
400 West Spain Street
Sonoma, CA
(707) 938–4004

Girl and the Fig
110 West Spain Street
Sonoma, CA
(707) 938–3634

The Hilltop Cafe
850 Lamont Avenue
Novato, CA
(415) 892–2222

La Casa Restaurant
121 East Spain Street
Sonoma, CA
(707) 996–3406

LaSalette
18625 Sonoma Highway
Sonoma, CA
(707) 938–1927

Mary's Pizza Shack
452 First Street
Sonoma, CA
(707) 938–8300

Maya Restaurant
101 East Napa Street
Sonoma, CA
(707) 935–3500

Moylan's Brewery and
    Restaurant
15 Rowland Way
Novato, CA
(415) 898–4677

Murphy's Irish Pub
464 First Street
Sonoma, CA
(707) 935–0660

Pearl's Diner
561 Fifth Street West
Sonoma, CA
(707) 996–1783

Piatti Restaurant and Bar
405 First Street West
Sonoma, CA
(707) 996–2351

Pizzeria Capri
1266 Broadway
Sonoma, CA
(707) 935–6805

The Plaza Bistro
420 First Street East
Sonoma, CA
(707) 996–4466

The Red Grape
529 First Street West
Sonoma, CA
(707) 996–4103

Restaurant Mirepoix
275 Windsor River Road
Windsor, CA
(707) 838–0162

Rin's Thai Restaurant
139 East Napa Street
Sonoma, CA
(707) 938–1462

Ristorante Orsi
340 Ignacio Boulevard
Novato, CA
(415) 883–0960

Rob's Rib Shack
18709 Arnold Drive
Sonoma, CA
(707) 938–8520

Saddles Steakhouse
29 East MacArthur
Sonoma, CA
(707) 933–3191

Schellville Grill
22900 Broadway
Sonoma, CA
(707) 996–5151

Sonoma Meritage Restau-
    rant and Wine Bar
522 Broadway
Sonoma, CA
(707) 938–9430

Taste of the Himalayas
464 First Street East
Sonoma, CA
(707) 996–1161

Uncle Patty's
13 Boyes Boulevard
Sonoma, CA
(707) 996–7979

Vaquero Restaurant and
    Bar
144 West Napa Street
Sonoma, CA
(707) 996–1440

The Winemaker
875 West Napa Street
Sonoma, CA
(707) 938–8489

Infineon Raceway Area Lodging

Alexandria's Plaza Suite
440 Second Street East
Sonoma, CA
(707) 938–8381

Alisa Hotel
447 Bush Street
San Francisco, CA
(866) 786–8763

Best Western Marine
World
1596 Fairgrounds Drive
Vallejo, CA
(707) 554–9655

Best Western Novato
Oaks Inn
215 Alameda de Prado
Novato, CA
(415) 883–4400

Best Western Petaluma Inn
200 South McDowell
Highway
Petaluma, CA
(707) 763–0994

Casita Carneros
21235 Hyde Road
Sonoma, CA
(707) 996–0996

Comfort Inn
1185 Admiral Callaghan
Lane
Vallejo, CA
(707) 648–1400

Comfort Inn
2632 North Cleveland
Avenue
Santa Rosa, CA
(707) 542–5544

The Continental Inn
26985 Highway One
Tomales, CA
(707) 878–2396

Cottages of Old Sonoma
1190 East Napa Street
Sonoma, CA
(800) 273–4714

Courtyard by Marriott
1400 North Hamilton
Parkway
Novato, CA
(415) 883–8950

Days Inn
300 Fairgrounds Drive
Vallejo, CA
(707) 554–8000

Doubletree Hotel
1 Doubletree Drive
Rohnert Park, CA
(707) 584–5466

El Dorado Hotel
405 First Street
Sonoma, CA
(707) 996–3030

El Pueblo Inn
896 West Napa Street
Sonoma, CA
(707) 996–3651

Embassy Suites
101 McInnis Parkway
San Rafael, CA
(415) 499–9222

Executive Inn and Suites
1755 Embarcadero
San Francisco, CA
(510) 536–6633

Four Points Sheraton
1010 Northgate Drive
San Rafael, CA
(415) 479–8800

Hidden Oak Inn
214 East Napa Street
Sonoma, CA
(707) 996–9863

Hotel Del Sol
3100 Webster Street
San Francisco, CA
(415) 921–5520

Inn at Sonoma
630 Broadway
Sonoma, CA
(888) 568–9818

Inn Marin
250 Entrada
Novato, CA
(415) 883–5952

The Lodge at Sonoma
1325 Broadway
Sonoma, CA
(707) 935–6600

MacArthur Place Inn and
Spa
29 East MacArthur Street
Sonoma, CA
(707) 938–2929

Marin Suites Hotel
45 Tamal Vista Boulevard
Corte Madera, CA
(415) 924–3608

The Mosser Victorian
54 Fourth Street
San Francisco, CA
(415) 986–4400

Napa Valley Marriott
3425 Solano Avenue
Napa, CA
(707) 253–7433

Novato Days Inn
8141 Redwood Boulevard
Novato, CA
(415) 897–7111

Novato Travelodge
7600 Redwood Boulevard
Novato, CA
(415) 892–7500

Phoenix Hotel
601 Eddy Street
San Francisco, CA
(415) 776–1380

Quality Inn
5100 Montero Way
Petaluma, CA
(800) 221–2222

Quality Inn
44 Admiral Callaghan Lane
Vallejo, CA
(707) 643–1061

Regency Inn
4326 Sonoma Boulevard
Vallejo, CA
(707) 643–4150

Skylark Motel
275 Alameda de Prado
Novato, CA
(415) 883–2406

Sonoma Creek Inn
239 Boyes Boulevard
Sonoma, CA
(707) 939–9463

Sonoma Hotel
110 West Spain Street
Sonoma, CA
(707) 996–2996

Sonoma Valley Inn
550 Second Street West
Sonoma, CA
(707) 938–9200

Swiss Hotel
18 West Spain Street
Sonoma, CA
(707) 938–2884

Thistle Dew Inn
171 West Spain Street
Sonoma, CA
(707) 938–2909

Trojan Horse Inn
19455 Sonoma Highway
Sonoma, CA
(707) 996–2430

Victorian Garden Inn
316 East Napa Street
Sonoma, CA
(800) 543–5339

Vineyard Inn Hotel
23000 Arnold Drive
Sonoma, CA
(707) 938–2350

Waterfront Plaza
10 Washington Street
San Francisco, CA
(800) 729–3638

Infineon Raceway Area Camping

KOA Campgrounds
20 Rainsville Road
Petaluma, CA
(707) 763–1492

U.S. Army Corps of
    Engineers Lake Sonoma
3333 Skaggs Springs Road
Geyserville, CA
(707) 433–9483

California Speedway:
America's Ultimate Race Place

Smartly and quietly hidden among the industrial wasteland and the cross-roads of humming power lines is the oasis that is the California Speedway. The old Kaiser Steel Mill was used to shoot the final scenes of the first *Terminator* movie, then it was razed to build a raceway that closely resembles the Michigan International Speedway. California is a racetrack of lush green grass, palm trees, and a spectacular view of the San Gabriel Mountains built amid the blight of an industrial park and all its decay.

Located a little more than an hour from downtown Los Angeles and close enough to hear the ghostly echoes of the old Riverside International Raceway, California Speedway has become a jewel of the NASCAR schedule. It's important because it gives the Nextel Cup Series a presence in the second-largest media market in the country—a market that is without professional football during the September race.

California was able to combine the best aspects of Michigan—its wide racing surface with variable-degree banking that promotes side-by-side racing—with the modern comforts now being demanded by race fans. The result is one of the best facilities in the business.

The vacuum created by a town without the National Football League was too much for NASCAR to ignore. The sanctioning body made a bold, if not controversial, decision midway into the 2003 season to strip the famed Darlington Raceway of its traditional Southern 500 on Labor Day weekend and move it to California. That makes California the only speedway in the west to host two annual events since 1987.

Let's Go Racing

The banking here is 4 degrees less than at Michigan, so it requires a little more driver's skill to work through the corners. It's wide and smooth, and that generally leads to some pretty compelling racing.

Jeff Gordon dominated the speedway during its infancy by winning two of the first three races. Since then, it's been wide open. Four different drivers—Jeremy Mayfield, Rusty Wallace, Jimmie Johnson, and Kurt Busch—have won since 2000, and all used a variety of strategies, ranging from fuel mileage to pit strategy to simply having the fastest car.

CALIFORNIA SPEEDWAY

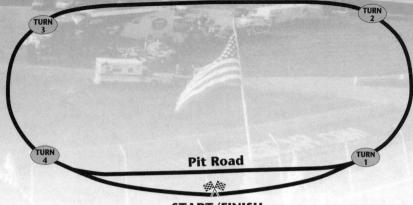

Pit Road

🏁🏁

START/FINISH

Our Ratings	Racing: 🏁🏁🏁🏁
	Amenities: 🏁🏁🏁🏁🏁
	Area Appeal: 🏁🏁🏁🏁
Track Facts	2.0-mile, D-shaped oval
	Seating capacity: 92,000
	9330 Cherry Avenue
	Fontana, CA 92335
	(800) 944–RACE
	www.californiaspeedway.com
Annual Events	Two NASCAR Nextel Cup Series races, May and September
	Companion races: Busch Series, May and September
Weather	Average High (F): May 80.0 September 91.0
	Average Low (F): May 53.0 September 62.0
Top Gun	Jeff Gordon, 2 wins
Qualifying Record	Ryan Newman, 187.432 mph

That's what makes California so compelling: There are a lot of ways to win and lose a race there. And that's why it's so popular with fans—even those from Southern California, who view the world through rose-colored glasses.

How to Get There

The speedway is close to a pair of important Southern California freeways, and that makes it easy to find from any direction.

From Los Angeles: Take Interstate 10 east.

From all points east of Fontana: Take I–10 west. Exit at Cherry Avenue and go north. The speedway is less than a mile away on the left.

From San Diego to the south and Las Vegas to the north: Take Interstate 15 to Fourth Street and go east to Cherry Avenue. Turn left at Cherry Avenue; the speedway's on the left.

Best Seats in the House

We like any seat that's above Row 25. The grandstands were built to provide a great view of the entire track, so there really isn't a bad seat in the place. If you get a chance to pick, look for seats at the beginning or end of pit road. You will get a great look at the exit of Turn 4 if you're at the beginning of pit road, or the entrance to Turn 1 if you're at the end of pit road.

The suites are built behind pit road, so they can block the view of the backstretch if you're in one of the lower seats. The suites are for people with connections to one of the major corporations—those who can buy the opportunity to rub elbows with some of the sport's biggest stars.

For most of us the suites are off-limits, but this is one place where status doesn't matter. While the people in the suites have clout, we can find comfort knowing that we have better seats. Given the choice of a buffet and air-conditioning over a great view of the race, take the view.

Rusty Wallace
on California

Rusty Wallace won the last two races at the Riverside International Raceway, which has since been leveled and replaced with houses, so his 2001 return to Victory Lane at California Speedway was special. At the time Wallace had no way of knowing it would be the start of the longest losing streak in his career. After his California win he went more than two years without another win.

"The last time I won out here was at the last two Riverside races before they shut it down," he says. "To win here at California Speedway is something I can be proud of."

Wallace led Jeff Gordon by 40 car lengths late in the race, before Gordon made a charge in the closing laps. "He made a gallant effort," Wallace says. "But you can't let your guard down. If I had gone into the corner and screwed up a little bit, he probably would have gotten me."

Compounding the importance of Wallace's victory was the fact that his car owner, Roger Penske, started the California project. It eventually was bought by International Speedway Corp. and remains one of that company's most prized possessions.

California Memories

When **Jimmie Johnson** made his debut here as a rookie in 2002, the first thing on his mind was getting a care package from home. He moved away from his home in El Cajon about 90 miles south of here to start his stock car career on the American Speed Association and Busch Series circuits, so he was starved—literally—for some home cooking.

"What I miss most is a burrito," he says. "You can't find burritos like we have back home anywhere else."

With so many friends and family making the short trip north on Interstate 15, Johnson got his fill of burritos prepared less than 10 miles from the Mexican border. And just for fun, he won the race.

"I am just blown away," Johnson says. "To be this competitive in (Nextel) Cup racing has been a dream of mine. You always think you have the ability to come out here and be competitive, but you just don't know until the right situation presents itself."

Johnson was so happy about winning his first Nextel Cup Series race that he blew up the Hendrick Motorsports engine and broke the transmission doing a victory burnout in his home state.

"When you get in this situation, you'd like to have something to say but you have nothing," Johnson said. "You're just soaked (with champagne)."

And full of burritos.

Make It a Vacation

The Los Angeles area is a great way to tie in a vacation with a race. The beaches of **Santa Monica, Venice,** and **Zuma** are world famous, as is a day trip to **Catalina Island,** and a tour of Hollywood allows you to do some stargazing. The **Los Angeles Dodgers** of the National League and the **Anaheim Angels** of the American League will be playing in May and September, and the **Los Angeles Lakers** are certain to be in the National Basketball Association play-offs during the May stop.

There's **Disneyland, Six Flags Mountain, Aquarium of the Pacific,** and **Universal Studios** to visit. And when you want a change of pace, just head south for a couple days in **San Diego.** The **Old Towne** section is full of trendy restaurants and nightclubs. You can spend a day across the border in **Tijuana** or visit the world famous **Sea World San Diego.**

The Fontana area is close enough to make it your home base during vacation. You won't be more than ninety minutes in any direction from the coast, the mountains, or the Los Angeles valley.

Away from the Track

For a break from the racing routine, there are some fun things to do within 10 miles of the speedway. You can take a tour of the **Graber Olive House** (315 East Fourth Street, Ontario; 909–983–1761) to see how olives are harvested and cured, or you can spend the day—and most of the night—at

Ontario Mills. Built on the corners of Fourth Street and I–15, Ontario Mills is more than a shopping center. It has an abundance of nightclubs and restaurants, as well as an amusement park. If you're only in town for a few days to see the race, it's impossible to see everything Ontario Mills has to offer.

Baseball fans who don't want to deal with Major League Baseball traffic or prices can spend the evening watching the **Rancho Cucamonga Quakes** (8408 Rochester Avenue, Rancho Cucamonga; 909–481–5000), a Class A minor league team from the Anaheim Angels system.

Thrill-seekers will like the **Castle Amusement Park** (3500 Polk Street, Riverside; 909–785–3000) and its three-story video arcade.

If you're looking for something a little more tranquil, visit the **Jurupa Mountains Cultural Center** (7621 Granite Hills, Riverside; 909–685–5818), the earth science museum that features a huge dinosaur exhibit; or the **University of California–Riverside Museum of Photography** (3824 Main Street, Riverside; 909–784–3686) may fill the bill.

Where to Eat

One of the best restaurants of the entire series is just minutes away from the speedway. You'll find drivers every night at **Rosa's** (425 North Vineyard Avenue, Ontario; 909–937–1220), a quiet place that specializes in ambience and Italian food. Driver-turned-television commentator Darrell Waltrip has eaten here for more than twenty-five years. You'll be hooked, too.

Steak eaters will like **Stuart Anderson's Black Angus** (3640 Porsche Way, Ontario; 909–944–6882). If you have a sweet tooth, **Millie's Kitchen and Bakery** is a must (17039 Valley Boulevard, Fontana; 909–829–1404).

Other top-notch places include the **Riverside Brewing Company** (3397 Mission Inn Avenue, Riverside; 909–784–2739); **Cafe Calato** (9640 Center Avenue, Suite 150, Rancho Cucamonga; 909–948–3671); **Siquio's** (1395 Washington Street, Colton; 909–825–8106); and **Claim Jumper** (12499 Foothill Boulevard, Rancho Cucamonga; 909–899–8022).

Where to Stay

Despite a crowd of nearly 100,000 fans, you shouldn't have any trouble finding rooms around the California Speedway. Each has its own advantage, but we recommend staying in Ontario or Riverside. Both cities give you a variety of hotels to fit any budget, and they put you less than twenty minutes from the speedway.

La Quinta Inn (909–476–1112), **Country Suites by Ayres** (800–248–4661), **Ontario Airport Marriott** (909–975–5000), **Ontario Airport Hilton** (909–980–0400), **Ontario Doubletree** (909–983–0909), and **Best Western Ontario** (800–983–9600) are just a few of the hotels near the Ontario International Airport. **Mission Inn** (800–843–7755), **Dynasty Suites** (909–369–8200), and **Hampton Inn** (800–426–7866) are good places to start in Riverside.

You can find bargains about a half hour from the speedway in towns like San Bernardino, Redlands, Loma Linda, and Corona.

California Speedway Area Restaurants

Applebee's
3820 Mulberry Street
Riverside, CA
(909) 369–7447

Benihanas
3760 East Inland Empire
   Boulevard
Ontario, CA
(909) 483–0937

Cafe Calato
9640 Center Avenue
Suite 150
Rancho Cucamonga, CA
(909) 948–3671

Cask 'N Cleaver
8689 Ninth Avenue
Rancho Cucamonga, CA
(909) 982–7108

Chili's
10598 Foothill Boulevard
Rancho Cucamonga, CA
(909) 948–5955

Claim Jumper
12499 Foothill Boulevard
Rancho Cucamonga, CA
(909) 899–8022

Cucina Cucina
960 North Ontario Mills
   Drive
Ontario, CA
(909) 476–2350

Dave and Busters
4821 Ontario Mills Circle
Ontario, CA
(909) 987–1557

DiCenso Italian Restaurant
1651 West Foothill
   Boulevard
Upland, CA
(909) 920–3303

El Charro
16602 Foothill Boulevard
Fontana, CA
(909) 357–9578

El Torito
3680 East Inland Empire
   Boulevard
Ontario, CA
(909) 944–9102

Market Broiler
4553 East Mills Circle
Ontario, CA
(909) 581–0866

Millie's Kitchen and Bakery
17039 Valley Boulevard
Fontana, CA
(909) 829–1404

Olive Garden
4403 East Mills Circle
Ontario, CA
(909) 481–7676

Outback Steakhouse
620 East Hospitality Lane
San Bernardino, CA
(909) 890–0061

Pancho Villas Restaurant
and Cantina
10210 Juniper Avenue
Fontana, CA
(909) 356–0906

Panda Inn
3223 Centrelake Drive
Ontario, CA
(909) 390–2888

Pinnacle Peak Steakhouse
2533 South La Cadena
Colton, CA
(909) 783–2543

Pomona Valley Mining
Company
1777 Gillette Road
Pomona, CA
(909) 623–3515

Red Lobster
195 East Hospitality Lane
San Bernardino, CA
(909) 888–2288

Riverside Brewing Company
3397 Mission Inn Avenue
Riverside, CA
(909) 784–2739

Romano's Macaroni Grill
10742 Foothill Boulevard
Rancho Cucamonga, CA
(909) 484–3200

Rosa's
425 North Vineyard
Avenue
Ontario, CA
(909) 937–1220

Siquio's
1395 Washington Street
Colton, CA
(909) 825–8106

Stuart Anderson's Black
Angus
3640 Porsche Way
Ontario, CA
(909) 944–6882

TGI Friday's
3351 East Centrelake
Drive
Ontario, CA
(909) 390–0050

Vince's Spaghetti
8241 Foothill Boulevard
Rancho Cucamonga, CA
(909) 981–1003

Wolfgang Puck's
1 Ontario Mills Circle
Ontario, CA
(909) 987–2299

California Speedway Area Lodging

AmeriHost Inn and Suites
13500 Baseline Avenue
Fontana, CA
(909) 463–5900

AmeriSuites Hotel
4760 Mills Circle
Ontario, CA
(909) 980–2200

Best Western
294 East Hospitality Lane
San Bernardino, CA
(909) 381–1681

Best Western Country Inn
2359 South Grove Avenue
Ontario, CA
(909) 923–1887

Best Western Heritage Inn
8179 Spruce Avenue
Rancho Cucamonga, CA
(800) 682–7829

California Inn
1150 North Grove Avenue
Ontario, CA
(909) 467–3788

Comfort Inn
1909 South Business
Center Drive
San Bernardino, CA
(909) 889–0090

Comfort Inn Ontario Airport
514 North Vineyard Avenue
Ontario, CA
(909) 937–2999

Country Side Suites
204 North Vineyard Avenue
Ontario, CA
(909) 937–9700

Country Suites by Ayres
1945 East Holt Boulevard
Ontario, CA
(800) 248–4661

Country Suites by Carlson
231 North Vineyard Avenue
Ontario, CA
(909) 937–6000

Country Suites Mills Mall
4370 Mills Circle
Ontario, CA
(909) 481–0703

Days Inn
1405 East Fourth Street
Ontario, CA
(909) 983–7411

Days Inn
1386 East Highland
    Avenue
San Bernardino, CA
(909) 881–1702

Desert Inn
607 West Fifth Street
San Bernardino, CA
(909) 889–9763

Doubletree
222 North Vineyard Avenue
Ontario, CA
(800) 733–5466

Doubletree Club Hotel
429 North Vineyard
    Avenue
Ontario, CA
(800) 582–2946

Dynasty Suites
3735 Iowa Avenue
Riverside, CA
(909) 369–8200

Econo Inn and Suites
777 West Sixth Street
San Bernardino, CA
(909) 889–3561

Econo Lodge
606 North H Street
San Bernardino, CA
(909) 383–1188

Econo Lodge
2301 South Euclid Avenue
Ontario, CA
(909) 986–3556

Econo Lodge
17133 Valley Boulevard
Fontana, CA
(909) 822–5411

Extended StayAmerica
3990 East Inland Empire
    Boulevard
Ontario, CA
(909) 944–8900

Fairfield Inn
710 West Kimberly
    Avenue
Placentia, CA
(714) 996–4410

Fairfield Inn
3201 Centrelake Drive
Ontario, CA
(909) 390–9855

Guesthouse Inn
16780 Valley Boulevard
Fontana, CA
(909) 822–3350

Guesthouse Inn
1120 East Holt Boulevard
Ontario, CA
(909) 984–9655

Guesthouse Inn
1280 South E Street
San Bernardino, CA
(909) 888–0271

Hilton
285 East Hospitality Drive
San Bernardino, CA
(909) 889–0133

Holiday Inn Airport
3400 Shelby Street
Ontario, CA
(800) 642–2617

La Quinta Inn
205 East Hospitality Lane
San Bernardino, CA
(909) 888–7571

La Quinta Inn and Suites
3555 Inland Empire
    Boulevard
Ontario, CA
(909) 476–1112

La Villa Del Lago
38898 Big Bear Boulevard
Big Bear Lake, CA
(310) 666–6020

Loma Linda Lodge
1235 East Rosewood
    Drive
San Bernardino, CA
(909) 796–2536

Mission Inn
3640 Mission Inn Avenue
Riverside, CA
(800) 843–7755

Motel 6
10195 Sierra Avenue
Fontana, CA
(909) 823–8686

Motel 6
1960 Ostrems Way
San Bernardino, CA
(909) 887–8191

Motel 7
1363 North E Street
San Bernardino, CA
(909) 884–5559

New Kansan
9300 Foothill Boulevard
Rancho Cucamonga, CA
(909) 944–0221

Ontario Airport Hilton
700 North Haven
Ontario, CA
(909) 980–0400

Ontario Airport Marriott
2200 East Holt Boulevard
Ontario, CA
(909) 975–5000

Quality Inn
1655 East Fourth Street
Ontario, CA
(909) 986–8898

Quality Inn
2000 Ostrems Way
San Bernardino, CA
(909) 880–8425

Ramada Limited
1841 East G Street
Ontario, CA
(909) 988–0602

Rancho Motel
1440 West Mission Inn
    Boulevard
Ontario, CA
(909) 986–4021

Radisson Hotel and
    Convention Center
295 North E Street
San Bernardino, CA
(909) 381–6181

Red Roof Inn
1818 East Holt Boulevard
Ontario, CA
(909) 988–8466

Relax Inn
1790 East Highland
    Avenue
San Bernardino, CA
(909) 883–8777

Residence Inn
2025 East Convention
    Center Way
Ontario, CA
(909) 937–6788

Sheraton Ontario Airport
429 North Vineyard
    Avenue
Ontario, CA
(909) 937–8000

Super 8 Motel
2441 South Euclid Avenue
Ontario, CA
(909) 983–7721

Travelodge
225 East Hospitality Lane
San Bernardino, CA
(909) 888–6777

Valley Motel
16762 Valley Boulevard
Fontana, CA
(909) 829–8874

Western Inn
661 West Holt Boulevard
Ontario, CA
(909) 983–4118

California Speedway Area Camping

Arrowhead Ranger District
28104 California High-
way 18
Skyforest, CA
(909) 337–2444

Big Bear Ranger District
North Shore Drive
Fawnskin, CA
(909) 866–3437

Cajon Ranger District
1209 Lytle Creek Road
Lytle Creek, CA
(909) 887–2576

Fairplex RV Park
2200 North White Avenue
Pomona, CA
(909) 593–8915

Frank G. Bonelli Regional
Park
120 East Via Verde Street
San Dimas, CA
(909) 599–8411

Glen Helen Regional Park
2555 Glen Helen Parkway
San Bernardino, CA
(909) 880–2522

Lake Elsinore Recreation
Area
32040 Riverside Drive
Lake Elsinore, CA
(909) 471–1212

Lake Perris State Recre-
ation Area
17801 Lake Perris Drive
Perris, CA
(909) 657–0676

Lake Skinner Park
37701 Warren Road
Winchester, CA
(909) 926–1541

Prado Regional Park
16700 Euclid Avenue
Chino, CA
(909) 597–4260

Rancho Jurupa Park
4800 Crestmore Road
Riverside, CA
(909) 684–7032

San Gorgonio Ranger
District
34701 Mill Creek Road
Mentone, CA
(909) 794–1123

San Jacinto Ranger
District
54270 Pinecrest
Idyllwild, CA
(909) 659–2117

Yucaipa Regional Park
33900 Oak Glen Road
Yucaipa, CA
(909) 790–3127

Las Vegas Motor Speedway:
The Desert Jewel

The neon lights of town make a glow over the first and second turn walls late in the afternoon at the Las Vegas Motor Speedway, a reminder that once the racing is done for the day, the fun is just getting started.

Las Vegas is a town known for its excesses, and the speedway is no exception. It's a masterpiece with wide, sweeping turns that stir up as much excitement as a high roller on a binge. This place has a 1.5-mile quad-oval, a drag strip, a dirt track, a road course, and an off-road racing course. Add a few go-cart tracks, and it might be the most-complete racing facility in the country.

Unlike any other speedway in the Nextel Cup Series, the Las Vegas experience goes around the clock. You can see Dale Jarrett race during the afternoon, watch white tigers disappear at night, and play blackjack until dawn. All that's left to make the experience complete is the $1.99 steak-and-eggs breakfast. Then it's time to start all over again.

For everything the city and the racetrack have to offer, this is one of our favorite trips.

Let's Go Racing

This racetrack was built for speed and close-quarter racing. When it opened it was the first superspeedway built in the United States in more than twenty years, and that allowed designers to take the best ideas of existing tracks and discard the ideas that didn't work. The result: a modern raceway that became the standard for the new tracks that followed.

Car owner Jack Roush was on a roll the first three times the Nextel Series came to this jewel in the desert. Mark Martin gave Roush a victory in the inaugural race, and that was followed by a pair of wins by Jeff Burton. Matt Kenseth gave Roush his fourth win in six races at Las Vegas with another win in 2003.

This speedway requires the total package. Not only must the engine be strong and fast but the car must be perfectly balanced to negotiate the 12-degree banking. A driver has to be willing to run two-wide in the turns and five-wide down the straightaway, and the pit crew must calculate fuel mileage to the last drop.

Putting it all together is as difficult as drawing a 5 with 16 in a hand of blackjack. But just like the card games that never stop a couple miles

LAS VEGAS MOTOR SPEEDWAY

START/FINISH

Pit Road

TURN 1

TURN 4

TURN 2

TURN 3

Our Ratings	Racing: 🏁 🏁 🏁 🏁
	Amenities: 🏁 🏁 🏁 🏁 🏁
	Area Appeal: 🏁 🏁 🏁 🏁 🏁

Track Facts	1.5-mile, quad-oval
	Seating capacity: 126,000
	7000 Las Vegas Boulevard
	Las Vegas, NV 89115
	www.lvms.com

Annual Events	One NASCAR Nextel Cup Series race, March
	Companion races: Busch Series, March

Weather	Average High (F):	March 73.0
	Average Low (F):	March 39.0

Top Gun	Jeff Burton, 2 wins

Qualifying Record	Bobby Labonte, 173.016 mph

over the first and second turn wall, the pay-off when everything falls into place is worth it.

How to Get There

This probably is the easiest track to find in all of racing. From the Strip or Los Angeles: Take Interstate 15 east to Speedway Boulevard (exit 54). The track also is accessible from Las Vegas Boulevard, but the traffic doesn't flow nearly as well as from the interstate.

Best Seats in the House

The grandstands were built to provide a good view all the way around the track. Like at any other speedway, a seat in the upper half will provide the best view.

For those who have motor homes, the speedway allows people to park on Motorhome Hill along the backstretch. Not only does that provide an excellent view, but all the comforts of home are within arm's reach.

Doing Deluxe

At the majority of tracks, the only way to get into most suites is to know a corporate president. Not at Las Vegas. The general public can buy tickets for the Club and Suite Levels, and each ticket comes with a buffet lunch and a private bar. It's a little pricey, but it's one of the few times a fan gets the chance to see how the other half lives. Our feeling: If the price doesn't scare you—or if you haven't lost all your money at the craps table—it's a great way to live like a high roller.

Las Vegas Memories

There are lots of ways to win a race, but counting on rain in the desert proved to be the strangest for **Jeff Burton** in 2000.

Burton took the lead thirteen laps before rain swept through the normally arid area and that prompted NASCAR to pull the plug on the 400-mile race 178 miles short of the scheduled finish. For Burton it marked the third consecutive time he had won a rain-shortened main event, earning him the nickname "Rain Man."

"We'll take bizarre finishes as long as we keep coming out on top," Burton says. "The key is putting yourself in position."

He passed **Mark Martin,** his Roush Racing teammate, just before the rain hit. Martin said he didn't know bad weather was coming. "No one told me that it was fixing to rain," Martin says. "The thought never crossed my mind that the race was fixing to be over."

A year earlier, Jeff Burton won a dramatic late-race duel with his older brother, **Ward Burton.** Apparently, strange finishes have become common with Jeff Burton. "The rain certainly made it easier for us, but it would have been hard to beat us regardless; we made the right decisions and keep making the car better."

Kurt Busch
on Las Vegas

Before he started driving trucks and stock cars for Jack Roush, Kurt Busch used to read water meters in Las Vegas. He won his job with Roush in a tryout with three other drivers at Las Vegas, a competition now laughingly known as "The Gong Show."

Now that he's a winner on the Nextel Cup Series, Las Vegas remains a very special, if not obsessive, place for Busch. "It's gorgeous; it's a lot of fun," Busch says. "You can drive five-wide down the front straightaway and then funnel down to two-wide going into the corners with no stress whatsoever. The asphalt has matured well enough to where you can do a lot of things—run low, run the middle, and the high groove is coming in as well. You can race side by side for quite a long time around there. You can pin somebody low or keep somebody up high, and you've got a whole different feel there than you do at the other places that are shaped just like it."

Because it's close to home, Busch mentions Las Vegas in the same breath as Daytona and Indianapolis. "Winning here probably would be the biggest thing for me in terms of winning a single race," he said. "The Daytona 500 and the Brickyard 400 at Indianapolis are right up there, but I can't imagine anything being any bigger than winning in Vegas."

Make It a Vacation

Even without the $200 million speedway, Las Vegas is a premier vacation destination.

There are casinos on every corner, slot machines in grocery stores, video poker at gas stations. Every casino offers a different ambience, and

the key is to find a place where you can have fun whether you're winning or losing. If you like to make big bets, every place is town will give you action. If you're a smaller player, there are places to fit your budget as well. Remember, the key to any vacation is to have fun.

There are more than 100,000 hotel rooms on the Strip alone. In fact, the corners of Tropicana Avenue and Las Vegas Boulevard have more rooms with the **MGM Grand, Excalibur, Tropicana,** and **New York–New York** hotels than all the rooms combined in Atlantic City.

With so many places to pick from, it's easy to shop for a deal. Every major casino has its own Web site, so shop around. For even better rates think about staying off the Strip. There are plenty of hotels over on Boulder Highway or on the north side of I–15. If you want to move even farther away from the Strip, consider Boulder City. A little homework can save you a lot of money.

Away from the Track

It's nearly impossible to spend any significant time in Las Vegas and not gamble. But for those who need a break from the clanging slot machines and runs of bad luck, there are some surprisingly interesting things to do around town that have nothing to do with making a bet.

A day trip to wondrous **Hoover Dam** (702–293–8367) is well worth it.

Don't make the hour drive yourself; buy a ticket for one of the many tours that bus you to the Nevada-Arizona border.

If you're the outdoors type, there are seven state parks, including Hoover Dam, around Las Vegas. Pick from **Floyd Lamb State Park** (702–486–5413), **Mt. Charleston** (702–872–7098), **Lee Canyon** (702–872–5453), **Red Rock Canyon** (702–515–5350), **Spring Mountain Ranch State Park** (702–875–4141), and **Valley of Fire State Park** (702–397–2088).

With so much attention being paid and money being spent south of town along Las Vegas Boulevard, casinos in the old downtown area are working hard to attract people. The **Fremont Street Experience** is alive with outdoor vendors and the old casinos that once were the backbone of Las Vegas's success. A 2-block area of Fremont Street has been covered with more than a million lights, and there's a free show on the hour every night. And while you're downtown, stop in at **Binion's Horseshoe Hotel and Casino** (128 East Fremont Street; 702–382–1600), where you can still find games that remind you of the Old West. It's also home of the World Series of Poker, and former champions are enshrined on their Wall of Fame.

The best bargain in town is the extravagant **Bellagio Fountains** (3600 South Las Vegas Boulevard). Music and shooting water are choreographed in the massive fountain in front of one of the most elaborate hotels in the world. The show attracts thousands of people, who are awestruck by the beauty and precision of dancing waters. The best part is it's free.

Finally Las Vegas is home to some of the best golf courses in the country. **Badlands Golf Club** (9119 Alta Drive; 800–468–7918); **Las Vegas National Golf Club** (1911 East Desert Inn Road; 800–864–9587); or **TPC at the Canyons** (9851 Canyon Run Drive; 866–447–4653) are three of the most popular, and all three allow you to call well in advance for tee times.

Where to Eat

Las Vegas is known for its all-night buffets and $1.99 steak-and-eggs breakfast. We strongly urge you to treat your taste buds to something a little better. The buffets at any of the major casinos are outstanding, but our favorites are at the **Rio All-Suite Hotel and Casino** (3700 West Flamingo Road; 702–777–7777), where you can find the **Village Seafood Buffet** and the **Carnival World Buffet.** The Village Seafood Buffet has even been designated a four-star restaurant.

If you want a sandwich, you can't go wrong with **Capriotti's Sandwich Shop** (324 West Sahara Avenue; 702–474–0229); the **Stage Deli** (3500

South Las Vegas Boulevard; 702–893–4045); or **In-N-Out Burger** (4888 Industrial Road; 800–786–1000).

For a more elegant meal we like **Lawry's The Prime Rib** (4043 Howard Hughes Parkway; 702–893–2223); **Austin's Steakhouse** (2101 Texas Star Lane; 702–631–1033); and **Rosemary's Restaurant** (8125 West Sahara Avenue; 702–869–2251).

Where to Stay

The big casinos on Las Vegas Boulevard include **MGM Grand** (702–891–1111), **Monte Carlo Resort** (702–730–7777), **Aladdin Resort** (702–785–5555), **Bellagio** (702–693–7111), **Excalibur** (702–597–7777), **Imperial Palace Hotel and Casino** (702–731–3311), **Luxor Hotel and Casino** (702–262–4444), **Mandalay Bay Resort and Casino** (877–632–7800), **Mirage Resort** (702–791–7111), **New York–New York** (702–740–6050), **Paris** (702–946–7000), **Sahara Hotel and Casino** (702–737–2111), **Caesar's Palace** (702–731–7110), **Treasure Island** (800–288–7206), **Tropicana Resort and Casino** (702–739–2222), **Harrah's Casino and Hotel** (702–369–5000), **Bally's** (888–742–9248), **Stardust** (800–824–6033), and **Venetian** (702–414–1000).

Off the strip you can pick from **Rio All-Suite Hotel and Casino** (702–252–7777), the **Orleans** (702–365–7111), **Hard Rock Hotel** (702–693–5000), **Las Vegas Hilton** (702–732–5111), **Sam's Town Hotel and Gambling Hall** (800–634–6371), **Palms Casino Resort** (702–942–7777), and **Texas Station** (702–631–8344).

Las Vegas Area Restaurants

Alan Alberts	Battista's Hole in the Wall	Bradley Ogden
3763 Las Vegas Boulevard	4041 Audrie Street	3570 Las Vegas Boulevard
Las Vegas, NV	Las Vegas, NV	Las Vegas, NV
(702) 795–4006	(702) 732–1424	(702) 731–7731
Aqua	Bellagio Buffet	Buca Di Beppo
3600 Las Vegas Boulevard	3600 Las Vegas Boulevard	412 Flamingo Road
Las Vegas, NV	Las Vegas, NV	Las Vegas, NV
(702) 693–7223	(702) 693–7111	(702) 866–2867
Austin's Steakhouse	Bertolini's	Buccaneer Bay Club
2101 Texas Star Lane	3500 Las Vegas Boulevard	3300 Las Vegas Boulevard
Las Vegas, NV	Las Vegas, NV	Las Vegas, NV
(702) 631–1033	(702) 735–4663	(702) 894–7111

Capriotti's Sandwich Shop
324 West Sahara Avenue
Las Vegas, NV
(702) 474–0229

Carnival World Buffet
3700 West Flamingo Road
(702) 777–7777

Circo
3600 Las Vegas Boulevard
Las Vegas, NV
(702) 693–7223

Craftsteak at MGM Grand
3799 Las Vegas Boulevard
Las Vegas, NV
(877) 880–0880

Commander's Palace
3663 Las Vegas Boulevard
Las Vegas, NV
(702) 892–8272

Cozymel's Coastal Mexi-
   can Grille
355 Hughes Center
Las Vegas, NV
(702) 732–4833

Del Frisco's
3925 Paradise Road
Las Vegas, NV
(702) 796–0063

Delmonico's Steakhouse
   at the Venetian
3355 Las Vegas Boulevard
Las Vegas, NV
(702) 414–3737

Drai's
3595 Las Vegas Boulevard
Las Vegas, NV
(702) 737–0555

Eiffel Tower Restaurant
3655 Las Vegas Boulevard
Las Vegas, NV
(702) 948–6937

808
3570 Las Vegas Boulevard
Las Vegas, NV
(702) 731–7731

Elements Steakhouse
3667 Las Vegas Boulevard
Las Vegas, NV
(702) 785–9000

Emeril's
3799 Las Vegas Boulevard
Las Vegas, NV
(702) 891–7374

Ferraro's
5900 West Flamingo Road
Las Vegas, NV
(702) 364–5300

Francesco's
3300 Las Vegas Boulevard
Las Vegas, NV
(702) 894–7223

Gilley's Saloon
3120 Las Vegas Boulevard
Las Vegas, NV
(702) 794–8200

Gorden Biersch Brewery
3987 Paradise Road
Las Vegas, NV
(702) 312–5247

Grand Lux Cafe
3355 Las Vegas Boulevard
Las Vegas, NV
(702) 414–1000

Hard Rock Cafe
4775 Paradise Road
Las Vegas, NV
(702) 733–7625

Harley-Davidson Cafe
3725 Las Vegas Boulevard
Las Vegas, NV
(702) 740–4555

Il Fornaio
3790 Las Vegas Boulevard
Las Vegas, NV
(702) 650–6500

In–N–Out Burger
4888 Industrial Road
Las Vegas, NV
(800) 786–1000

Lawry's The Prime Rib
4043 Howard Hughes
   Parkway
Las Vegas, NV
(702) 893–2223

Le Village Buffet at Paris
3665 Las Vegas Boulevard
Las Vegas, NV
(702) 946–7000

Lobster House
3763 Las Vegas Boulevard
Las Vegas, NV
(702) 740–4430

Lutece
3355 Las Vegas Boulevard
Las Vegas, NV
(702) 414–2220

Marrakech Restaurant
3900 Paradise Road
Las Vegas, NV
(702) 737–5611

McCormick and Schmicks
Flamingo and Paradise
   Roads
Las Vegas, NV
(702) 836–9000

Michael's
3595 Las Vegas Boulevard
Las Vegas, NV
(702) 737–7111

Morton's of Chicago
400 East Flamingo Road
Las Vegas, NV
(702) 893–0703

Olives
3600 Las Vegas Boulevard
Las Vegas, NV
(702) 693–7223

P.F. Changs China Bistro
4165 Paradise Road
Las Vegas, NV
(702) 792–2207

Picasso
3600 Las Vegas Boulevard
Las Vegas, NV
(702) 693–7223

Postrio
3355 Las Vegas Boulevard
Las Vegas, NV
(702) 796–1110

Prime
3600 Las Vegas Boulevard
Las Vegas, NV
(702) 693–7223

Red Square
3950 Las Vegas Boulevard
Las Vegas, NV
(702) 632–7407

Rio Carnival World Buffet
3700 West Flamingo Road
Las Vegas, NV
(702) 252–7777

Rosemary's Restaurant
8125 West Sahara Avenue
Las Vegas, NV
(702) 869–2251

Rosewood Grill
3339 Las Vegas Boulevard
Las Vegas, NV
(702) 792–9099

Ruth's Chris Steak House
3900 Paradise Road
Las Vegas, NV
(702) 791–7011

Smokey Joe's Cafe
Sam's Town Gambling Hall
5111 Boulder Highway
Las Vegas, NV
(702) 456–7777

Spago
3500 Las Vegas Boulevard
Las Vegas, NV
(702) 369–6300

Stage Deli
3500 South Las Vegas
   Boulevard
Las Vegas, NV
(702) 893–4045

Sterling Brunch
3645 Las Vegas Boulevard
Las Vegas, NV
(702) 967–7999

Tommy Rocker's Cantina
   and Grill
4275 Industrial Boulevard
Las Vegas, NV
(702) 261–6688

Triple Brew Pub
Main Street Station
200 North Main Street
Las Vegas, NV
(702) 387–1896

Valentino Restaurant
3355 Las Vegas Boulevard
Las Vegas, NV
(702) 414–3000

Village Seafood Buffet
3700 West Flamingo Road
Las Vegas, NV
(702) 252–7777

VooDoo Cafe
3700 West Flamingo Road
Las Vegas, NV
(702) 252–7777

Z Tejas Grill
3824 Paradise Road
Las Vegas, NV
(702) 732–1660

Las Vegas Area Lodging

Aladdin Resort and Casino
3667 Las Vegas Boulevard
Las Vegas, NV
(702) 785–5555

Algiers Hotel
2845 Las Vegas Boulevard
Las Vegas, NV
(702) 735–3311

Ambassador Inn
4350 Paradise Road
Las Vegas, NV
(702) 938–2000

AmeriSuites
4520 Paradise Road
Las Vegas, NV
(702) 369–3366

Arizona Charlies Casino
4575 Boulder Highway
Las Vegas, NV
(702) 951–5800

Arizona Charlies Casino
740 South Decatur
  Boulevard
Las Vegas, NV
(702) 258–5200

Bally's
3645 Las Vegas Boulevard
Las Vegas, NV
(888) 742–9248

Barbary Coast
3595 Las Vegas Boulevard
Las Vegas, NV
(702) 737–7111

Bellagio
3600 Las Vegas Boulevard
Las Vegas, NV
(702) 693–7111

Best Western
905 Las Vegas Boulevard
Las Vegas, NV
(720) 385–1213

Best Western
1000 North Main Street
Las Vegas, NV
(702) 382–3455

Best Western
4970 Paradise Road
Las Vegas, NV
(702) 798–5530

Best Western Mardi Gras
3500 Paradise Road
Las Vegas, NV
(702) 731–2020

Best Western Nellis
5330 East Craig Road
Las Vegas, NV
(702) 643–6111

Binion's Horseshoe Hotel
128 Freemont Street
Las Vegas, NV
(702) 382–1600

Boulder Palms Luxury
  Suites
4350 Boulder Highway
Las Vegas, NV
(702) 434–9900

Boulder Station Hotel
4111 Boulder Highway
Las Vegas, NV
(720) 432–7777

Bourbon Street
120 East Flamingo Road
Las Vegas, NV
(702) 737–7200

Budget Suites of America
1500 Stardust Road
Las Vegas, NV
(702) 732–1500

Budget Suites of America
2219 North Rancho Drive
Las Vegas, NV
(702) 638–1800

Budget Suites of America
3684 Paradise Road
Las Vegas, NV
(702) 699–7000

Budget Suites of America
4625 Boulder Highway
Las Vegas, NV
(702) 454–4625

Budget Suites of America
4855 Boulder Highway
Las Vegas, NV
(702) 433–7985

Budget Suites of America
4205 West Tropicana
   Avenue
Las Vegas, NV
(702) 889–1700

Caesars Palace Hotel
3570 Las Vegas Boulevard
Las Vegas, NV
(702) 731–7110

California Hotel
12 Ogden Avenue
Las Vegas, NV
(702) 385–1222

Candlewood Suites
4034 South Paradise
   Road
Las Vegas, NV
(702) 836–3660

Canyon Ranch Spa
3377 Las Vegas Boulevard
Las Vegas, NV
(702) 414–3600

Carriage House Deluxe
   Suites Hotel
105 East Harmon Avenue
Las Vegas, NV
(702) 798–1020

Casino Royale and Hotel
3419 Las Vegas Boulevard
Las Vegas, NV
(702) 737–3500

Castaways Hotel
2800 Fremont Street
Las Vegas, NV
(702) 385–9123

Circus Circus
2880 Las Vegas Boule-
   vard
Las Vegas, NV
(702) 734–0410

Clarion Hotel and Suites
325 East Flamingo Road
Las Vegas, NV
(702) 732–9100

Comfort Inn
4350 Paradise Road
Las Vegas, NV
(702) 938–2000

Courtyard
1901 North Rainbow
   Boulevard
Las Vegas, NV
(702) 646–4400

Days Inn
707 East Fremont Street
Las Vegas, NV
(702) 388–1400

Days Inn
4155 Koval Lane
Las Vegas, NV
(702) 731–2111

Desert Inn Resort
3145 Las Vegas Boulevard
Las Vegas, NV
(702) 733–4444

Doubletree Club Hotel
7250 Pollock Drive
Las Vegas, NV
(702) 948–4000

Econo Lodge
211 East Flamingo Road
Las Vegas, NV
(702) 733–7800

Embassy Suites
4315 Swenson Street
Las Vegas, NV
(702) 795–2800

Embassy Suites
3600 Paradise Road
Las Vegas, NV
(702) 893–8000

Emerald Suites Nellis
4555 Las Vegas Boulevard
Las Vegas, NV
(702) 946–9999

Emerald Suites Tropicana
3890 Graphic Center
   Drive
Las Vegas, NV
(702) 507–9999

Excalibur
3850 Las Vegas Boulevard
Las Vegas, NV
(702) 597–7777

Fairfield Inn
265 East Harmon Avenue
Las Vegas, NV
(702) 691–2600

Fairfield Inn
3850 Paradise Road
Las Vegas, NV
(702) 791–0899

Fitzgeralds Casino Hotel
301 Fremont Street
Las Vegas, NV
(702) 388–2400

Flamingo Hilton Hotel
3555 Las Vegas Boulevard
Las Vegas, NV
(702) 733–3111

Four Queens
202 East Fremont Street
Las Vegas, NV
(702) 385–4011

Four Seasons
3960 Las Vegas Boulevard
Las Vegas, NV
(702) 632–5000

Fremont Hotel
200 East Fremont Street
Las Vegas, NV
(702) 385–3232

French Quarter Suites
4777 Cameron Street
Las Vegas, NV
(702) 365–5500

Gold Coast
4000 West Flamingo Road
Las Vegas, NV
(702) 367–7111

Golden Gate Hotel
1 Fremont Street
Las Vegas, NV
(702) 385–1906

Golden Nugget
129 East Fremont Street
Las Vegas, NV
(702) 385–7111

Hampton Inn
7100 Cascade Valley
    Court
Las Vegas, NV
(702) 360–5700

Hampton Inn
4975 Industrial Road
Las Vegas, NV
(702) 948–8100

Hampton Inn Nellis
4035 North Nellis Boule-
    vard
Las Vegas, NV
(702) 644–5700

Hard Rock Hotel
4455 Paradise Road
Las Vegas, NV
(702) 693–5000

Harrah's Las Vegas
3475 Las Vegas Boulevard
Las Vegas, NV
(702) 369–5000

Hawthorn Suites
5051 Duke Ellington Way
Las Vegas, NV
(702) 739–7000

Holiday Inn Boardwalk
3750 Las Vegas Boulevard
Las Vegas, NV
(702) 735–2400

Holiday Inn Express
8669 West Sahara
    Avenue
Las Vegas, NV
(702) 256–3766

Holiday Royale
4505 Paradise Road
Las Vegas, NV
(702) 733–7676

Howard Johnson
5100 Paradise Road
Las Vegas, NV
(702) 798–2777

Howard Johnson
1401 Las Vegas Boulevard
Las Vegas, NV
(702) 388–0301

Howard Johnson
3111 West Tropicana
    Avenue
Las Vegas, NV
(702) 798–1111

Imperial Palace
3535 Las Vegas Boulevard
Las Vegas, NV
(702) 731–3311

Inn by Marriott
2190 Olympic Avenue
Las Vegas, NV
(702) 434–2700

Inn by Marriott
370 Hughes Center Drive
Las Vegas, NV
(702) 650–0040

J.W. Marriott
221 North Rampart
   Boulevard
Las Vegas, NV
(702) 869–7777

Jockey Club
3700 Las Vegas Boulevard
Las Vegas, NV
(702) 739–8686

Key Largo Hotel
377 East Flamingo Road
Las Vegas, NV
(702) 733–7777

La Quinta Convention
   Center
3970 Paradise Road
Las Vegas, NV
(702) 796–9000

La Quinta Inn
4975 South Valley View
   Boulevard
Las Vegas, NV
(702) 798–7736

La Quinta Inn
7101 Cascade Valley
   Court
Las Vegas, NV
(702) 360–1200

La Quinta Motor Inn
3970 Paradise Road
Las Vegas, NV
(702) 796–9000

La Quinta Nellis
4288 North Nellis
   Boulevard
Las Vegas, NV
(702) 632–0229

La Quinta Suites
9570 West Sahara
   Avenue
Las Vegas, NV
(702) 243–0356

Lady Luck Hotel
725 Rancho Circle
Las Vegas, NV
(702) 477–3000

Las Vegas Hilton
3000 Paradise Road
Las Vegas, NV
(702) 732–5111

Luxor Hotel
3900 Las Vegas Boulevard
Las Vegas, NV
(702) 262–4444

Main Street Station
200 North Main Street
Las Vegas, NV
(800) 713–8933

Mandalay Bay
3950 Las Vegas Boulevard
Las Vegas, NV
(877) 632–7800

Marriott Suites
325 Convention Center
   Drive
Las Vegas, NV
(702) 650–2000

Maxim Hotel
160 East Flamingo Road
Las Vegas, NV
(702) 731–4300

MGM Grand Hotel
3799 Las Vegas Boulevard
Las Vegas, NV
(702) 891–7777

Mirage Resort
3400 Las Vegas Boulevard
Las Vegas, NV
(702) 791–7111

Monte Carlo Resort
3770 Las Vegas Boulevard
Las Vegas, NV
(702) 730–7777

Motel 6
197 East Tropicana Avenue
Las Vegas, NV
(702) 798–0728

Motel 6
4125 Boulder Highway
Las Vegas, NV
(702) 457–8051

Motel 6
5085 Industrial Road
Las Vegas, NV
(702) 739–6747

Nevada Palace
5255 Boulder Highway
Las Vegas, NV
(702) 458–8810

New Frontier
3120 Las Vegas Boulevard
Las Vegas, NV
(702) 794–8200

New York–New York Hotel
3790 Las Vegas Boulevard
Las Vegas, NV
(702) 740–6050

Orleans
4500 West Tropicana
   Avenue
Las Vegas, NV
(702) 365–7111

Palace Station
2411 West Sahara
   Avenue
Las Vegas, NV
(702) 367–2411

Palms Casino Resort
4321 West Flamingo Road
Las Vegas, NV
(702) 942–7777

Paris
3655 Las Vegas Boulevard
Las Vegas, NV
(702) 946–7000

Ramada Inn Suites
3625 Boulder Highway
Las Vegas, NV
(702) 431–7121

Residence Inn
370 Hughes Center Drive
Las Vegas, NV
(702) 650–0040

Residence Inn
3225 Paradise Road
Las Vegas, NV
(702) 796–9300

Rio All-Suite Hotel
3700 West Flamingo Road
Las Vegas, NV
(702) 252–7777

Riviera Hotel
2901 Las Vegas Boulevard
Las Vegas, NV
(702) 734–5110

Rodeway Inn and Suites
167 East Tropicana
   Avenue
Las Vegas, NV
(702) 795–3311

Sahara Hotel
2535 Las Vegas Boulevard
Las Vegas, NV
(702) 737–2111

Sam's Town Hotel
5111 Boulder Highway
Las Vegas, NV
(800) 634–6371

San Remo
115 East Tropicana
   Avenue
Las Vegas, NV
(702) 739–9000

Sante Fe Hotel
4949 North Rancho Drive
Las Vegas, NV
(702) 658–4900

Somerset House Motel
294 Convention Center
   Drive
Las Vegas, NV
(702) 735–4411

Stardust
3000 Las Vegas Boulevard
Las Vegas, NV
(800) 824–6033

Stratosphere
2000 Las Vegas
   Boulevard
Las Vegas, NV
(800) 998–6937

Sun Coast Resorts
9090 Alta Drive
Las Vegas, NV
(702) 636–7111

Super 8
5288 Boulder Highway
Las Vegas, NV
(702) 435–8888

Super 8
4250 Koval Lane
Las Vegas, NV
(702) 794–0888

Texas Station
2101 Texas Star Lane
Las Vegas, NV
(702) 631–8344

Thunderbird Hotel
1213 Las Vegas Boulevard
Las Vegas, NV
(702) 383–3100

Travelodge
3735 Las Vegas Boulevard
Las Vegas, NV
(702) 736–3443

Travelodge
5075 Koval Lane
Las Vegas, NV
(702) 736–3600

Travelodge
2830 Las Vegas Boulevard
Las Vegas, NV
(702) 735–4222

Travelodge
2028 East Fremont Street
Las Vegas, NV
(702) 384–7540

Travelodge
1501 West Sahara Drive
Las Vegas, NV
(702) 733–0001

Treasure Island
3300 Las Vegas Boulevard
Las Vegas, NV
(800) 288–7206

Tropicana Resort
3801 Las Vegas Boulevard
Las Vegas, NV
(702) 739–2222

Vagabond Inn
3265 Las Vegas Boulevard
Las Vegas, NV
(702) 735–5102

Venetian Resort
3355 Las Vegas Boulevard
Las Vegas, NV
(702) 414–1000

Westward-Ho Hotel
2900 Las Vegas Boulevard
Las Vegas, NV
(702) 731–2900

Wild, Wild West
3330 West Tropicana
 Avenue
Las Vegas, NV
(702) 740–0000

Las Vegas Area Camping

American Campground
 and RV Park
3440 Las Vegas Boulevard
Las Vegas, NV
(702) 643–1222

Arizona Charlies East
4445 Boulder Highway
Las Vegas, NV
(702) 951–5911

Boomtown RV Park
3333 Blue Diamond Road
Las Vegas, NV
(702) 263–7777

Boulder Lakes
6201 Boulder Highway
Las Vegas, NV
(702) 435–1157

Boulder Oaks RV Resort
1010 Industrial Road
Boulder City, NV
(702) 294–4425

California RV Park
100 East Stewart Avenue
Las Vegas, NV
(702) 388–2602

Canyon Trail RV Park
1200 Industrial Road
Boulder City, NV
(702) 293–1200

Circusland RV Park
500 Circus Circus Drive
Las Vegas, NV
(702) 794–3757

Cottonwood Cove Resort
1000 Cottonwood Road
Searchlight, NV
(702) 297–1464

Desert Sands RV Park
1940 North Boulder
 Highway
Henderson, NV
(702) 565–1945

Destiny's Oasis Las Vegas
 RV Resort
2711 Windmill Road
Las Vegas, NV
(702) 260–2020

Hitchin' Post RV Park
3640 Las Vegas Boulevard
Las Vegas, NV
(702) 644–1043

Holiday Travel Park
3890 South Nellis Boule-
 vard
Las Vegas, NV
(702) 451–8005

King's Row Trailer Park
3660 Boulder Highway
Las Vegas, NV
(702) 457–3606

KOA Las Vegas
4315 Boulder Highway
Las Vegas, NV
(702) 451–5527

Lakeshore Trailer Village
268 Lakeshore Road
Boulder City, NV
(702) 293–2540

Las Vegas International
 RV Resort
6900 East Russell Road
Las Vegas, NV
(702) 433–1592

Mahoney's Silver Nugget
    RV Park
2236 Las Vegas Boulevard
Las Vegas, NV
(702) 649–7439

Nevada Palace VIP Travel
    Trailer Park
5325 Boulder Highway
Las Vegas, NV
(702) 451–0232

Riviera Travel Trailer Park
2200 Palm
Las Vegas, NV
(702) 457–8700

Roadrunner
4711 Boulder Highway
Las Vegas, NV
(702) 456–4711

Robbin's Nest
479 South Moapa Valley
    Road
Overton, NV
(702) 397–2364

Sam's Town Boulder RV
    Park
5225 Boulder Highway
Las Vegas, NV
(702) 456–7777

Sam's Town Nellis RV Park
4040 Nellis Boulevard
Las Vegas, NV
(702) 456–7777

Showboat RV Park
2805 Fremont Street
Las Vegas, NV
(702) 385–9123

Phoenix International Raceway:
Valley of the Sun

No other raceway offers as much atmosphere as Phoenix International. The valley that spans behind the main grandstands is full of desert hardpan, cacti, and river washes; the backstretch touches the Estrella Mountains. The area behind Turns 3 and 4 is part of the Gila River Indian Reservation, and hearty fans buy tickets from the tribe to crowd the mountainside with blankets and coolers—much like the fans sitting on rooftops across the street from baseball's Wrigley Field—for the most unique seat in all of motorsports.

In the days leading up to the race, the Gila River Indians and Phoenix International Raceway staff have to prepare the surrounding grounds for the crush of 100,000 race fans with an old-fashioned rattlesnake roundup that reportedly bags hundreds of the hissing reptiles.

The restrictions created by the mountains and protected Indian land resulted in an odd-shaped tri-oval. The first and second turns are considerably narrower than Turns 3 and 4. A wall that juts into the outside racing groove exiting the second turn separates the racing surface and the crossover into the infield, and it seems to reach out and grab a driver when he least expects it.

Let's Go Racing

Phoenix is a hard place to figure out. If a car's good at one end of the raceway, it's usually not good at the other. Races last 312 laps—500 kilometers—so it's not nearly as long as the 400- and 500-mile races on the circuit. That seems to eliminate the tendency drivers have to ride along for 100 miles in the middle of the race to save their equipment for the end of the race.

The sand from the desert and the summer sun strips away a little more of the raceway's grip each year and that only makes the racing better. Turns with different degrees of banking—Turns 1 and 2 are angled at 11 degrees; Turns 3 and 4 are banked 9 degrees—and wildly different turning radiuses make it nearly impossible to master. In the first fourteen Nextel Cup Series races at Phoenix, nobody has won the pole position and the main event, and there have been twelve different winners.

How to Get There

From Phoenix: Take Interstate 10 west to the Cotton Lane exit. Turn left, and go to Buckeye Road. Turn left again onto Estrella Mountain Parkway. Make

PHOENIX INTERNATIONAL RACEWAY

START/FINISH

Pit Road

TURN 1

TURN 2

TURN 3

TURN 4

Our Ratings

Racing: 🏁 🏁 🏁 🏁

Amenities: 🏁 🏁 🏁 🏁 🏁

Area Appeal: 🏁 🏁 🏁 🏁 🏁

Track Facts

1.0-mile tri-oval

Seating capacity: 76,812

7602 South 115th Avenue

Avondale, AZ 85323

(602) 252–2227

www.phoenixintlraceway.com

Annual Events

One Nextel Cup Series event, November

Companion events: Craftsman Truck and Busch Series, November

Weather

Average High (F):   November 73.0

Average Low (F):   November 50.0

Top Gun

Davey Allison and Jeff Burton, 2 wins

Qualifying Record

Rusty Wallace, 134.178 mph

a right onto Vineyard Road. Turn left, and follow signs to the speedway.

From Flagstaff: Take Interstate 17 south to I–10. Go west to the Cotton Lane exit. Turn left, and go to Buckeye Road; turn left again onto Estrella Mountain Parkway. Make a right onto Vineyard Road. Turn left, and follow signs to the speedway.

From Chandler, Mesa, and Tempe: Take I–10 west to Riggs Road. Go west on Beltline Road to Fifty-first Avenue. Go north on Fifty-first Avenue to Buckeye Road. Turn left onto Bullard Avenue. Turn left onto Vineyard Road, and follow the signs to the track.

Best Seats in the House

The grandstands in the first and second turns offer the best view of the action. You can look ahead and see cars coming down the main straight-away, and you can see them try to negotiate the tricky first and second turns. The upper half of the frontstretch grandstands allows you to see most of the racetrack, but the heavy infield crowd and motorhomes make it tough to see the backstretch.

For those with recreational vehicles, the speedway sells reserved spots at the **Cruise America Corner,** a reserved lot limited to fifty-five campers between the third and fourth turns.

Thousands of fans climb the mountain above the third and fourth turns to watch the race from the Gila River Indian Reservation, but the view really isn't that spectacular.

Jeff Burton on Phoenix

It took Jeff Burton a while to figure out this racetrack, and once he did, his fortunes—and appreciation for the speedway—changed for good. He won the race here in 2000 and came back a year later to win again.

"I do like the racetrack," he says. "We didn't used to run very well here, and then a couple years ago I changed the way I drove the track. Once I found that, it really helped us a lot."

Despite his success, Burton knows things are constantly changing on the Nextel Cup Series. What worked four years ago probably won't make sense this year. "We've got to look at it and say we have to be willing to change," he says. "Actually, the setups we ran from the first win to the second were quite different. You have to adjust to the track."

Phoenix Memories

Ricky Rudd's first season with Robert Yates Racing in 2000 brought a fifth-place finish in the points championship, but the team failed to win a race. The closest he came was at Phoenix; Rudd had a 70-yard lead over **Jeff Burton** with six laps to go, only to see it change in a heartbeat when **Rick Mast** and **Mike Bliss** crashed in front of him along the backstretch.

Mast abruptly fell off the pace with a flat tire, and Bliss plowed into him. Bliss's car careened across the track—directly in front of Rudd, who couldn't react quickly enough to avoid the crash. He hit Bliss in the door, bending the nose of his Ford and ending his chance to end a winless streak that was more than two years in the making.

"I was trying to get whoaed down, and I had my hand up," Mast says. "Everybody was going by me, but I guess somebody didn't see me."

That was little consolation to Rudd. "Everything was going to be cool," he says. "I don't know if (Bliss's) spotter didn't see it, or he didn't see it, or what happened, but all of a sudden at the last minute (Bliss) saw it and just ran right into the back of (Mast). The next thing I know, he runs right in front of me. There's not a whole lot you can do about it."

Make It a Vacation

Phoenix, Scottsdale, and Tempe make up a vacation paradise. All three are steeped in the history of the Old West. At the same time, all three are thoroughly modern.

The best way to enjoy the Valley of the Sun is at one of the area's many resorts and spas. Most resorts offer golf, tennis, and a health club as well as an impressive selection of fine dining options. The **Camelback Inn Resort** (5402 East Lincoln Drive, Scottsdale; 480–948–1700) is where movie stars hang out. **The Boulders Resort** (34631 North Tom Darlington Drive, Carefree; 480–488–9009), **Arizona Biltmore Resort and Spa** (2400 East Missouri Avenue, Phoenix; 602–955–6600), and **The Phoenician Resort** (6000 East Camelback Road, Scottsdale; 800–888–8234) are some of the area's most luxurious.

Away from the Track

If you come to Phoenix, bring your golf clubs. Ranked by *Golf Digest* as one of the top-five golf destinations in the world, the hardest decision you'll have is picking a course. The best part: There are enough courses to keep the most avid player busy for nearly a year.

TPC of Scottsdale (17020 North Hayden Road, Scottsdale; 480–585–3600) plays host to the PGA Tour's Phoenix Open. The **Papago Golf Course** (5595 East Moreland Street, Phoenix; 602–275–8428) is both posh and affordable. **Raptor Course** at **Grayhawk Golf Club** (8620 East Thompson Peak Parkway, Scottsdale; 480–502–1800) is carved among the mountain foothills.

For a little more relaxed afternoon, visit the **Desert Botanical Garden** (1201 North Galvin Parkway, Phoenix; 480–941–1225) or the **Heard Museum** (2301 North Central Avenue, Phoenix; 602–252–8840).

Perhaps the greatest day trip in all of racing is a ride to the red-rock canyons of **Sedona,** Arizona. The scenery is breathtaking, and there are abandoned silver mines, antiques stores, and an Old West town to explore.

Where to Eat

The two cuisines done extremely well in Phoenix are steaks and Mexican food, so it's no surprise that our favorite menus include T-bones and tacos.

It's hard to beat the atmosphere and view at **T-Bone Steak House** (10037 South Nineteenth Avenue, Phoenix; 602–276–0945), where the steaks are cooked outside by the parking lot and the hostess wears a six-shooter. The restaurant overlooks the entire valley for a memorable dining experience.

In nearby Scottsdale, the **Carlsbad Tavern** (3313 North Hayden Road; 480–970–8164) is known for its red chili pancakes and apple chutney. The **Salt Cellar Restaurant** (550 North Hayden Road; 480–947–1963) has the freshest seafood in the desert. The **Coyote Grill** (7077 East Bell Road; 480–922–8424) is famous for its Southwestern menu.

When it comes to Mexican food, we suggest heading back into Phoenix to one of the following: **La Tolteca Mexican Foods** (1205 East Van Buren Street, 602–253–1511); **Los Compadres Mexican Food** (4414 North Seventh Avenue, 602–265–1162); or **Popo's Fiesta Del Sol** (6542 West Indian School Road, 623–846–2636).

Other places that get high marks are the **5 & Diner** (5270 North Sixteenth Street, Phoenix; 602–264–5220); **Coronado Cafe** (2201 North Seventh Street, Phoenix; 602–258–5149); and **Mastro's** (8852 East Pinnacle Peak Road, Scottsdale; 480–585–9500).

Where to Stay

There is no shortage of hotel rooms in the valley. **Marriott Hotels,** for example, has thirty-one properties in Phoenix, Scottsdale, and Tempe alone. We like staying near the Sky Harbor International Airport or just west of the airport along the I–10 corridor. That puts you thirty minutes or less from the speedway and within minutes of all the great restaurants and sites in town.

If you need a little help finding a room, start with the **Embassy Suites Airport** (602–244–8800), **Radisson Hotel Airport** (602–437–8400), **Comfort Inn I–10** (602–415–1623), or the **Budget Suites of America** (866–877–2000).

For thousands of fans, the place to stay is in a motorhome. Phoenix draws an unusually large RV camping crowd because it has plenty of room, especially behind the speedway, to accommodate them. Call **Cruise America** at (800) 327-7799 for rental information.

Phoenix Area Restaurants

Applebee's
13832 West McDowell
    Road
Goodyear, AZ
(623) 536–8440

Barmouche
3131 East Camelback
    Road
Phoenix, AZ
(602) 956–6900

Bennett's Bar-B-Que
1480 North Litchfield Road
Goodyear, AZ
(623) 536–8000

Blue Adobe Grill
144 North Country Club
    Drive
Mesa, AZ
(480) 962–1000

Carlsbad Tavern
3313 North Hayden Road
Scottsdale, AZ
(480) 970–8164

Chili's
1371 North Litchfield Road
Goodyear, AZ
(623) 535–4222

Compass Atop Hyatt
    Regency
122 North Second Street
Phoenix, AZ
(602) 440–3166

Coronado Cafe
2201 North Seventh Street
Phoenix, AZ
(602) 258–5149

The Coyote Grill
7077 East Bell Road
Scottsdale, AZ
(480) 922–8424

Cracker Barrel
1209 North Litchfield
Goodyear, AZ
(623) 856–5161

Different Pointe of View
11111 North Seventh
    Street
Phoenix, AZ
(602) 863–0912

Don and Charlie's American
    Rib and Chop House
7501 East Camelback
    Road
Scottsdale, AZ
(480) 990–0900

Drivers Sports Grill
14175 West Indian
    School Road
Goodyear, AZ
(623) 536–8571

Durant's
2611 North Central
    Avenue
Phoenix, AZ
(602) 264–5967

El Chorro Lodge
5550 East Lincoln Drive
Paradise Valley, AZ
(480) 948–5170

5 & Diner
5270 North Sixteenth
    Street
Phoenix, AZ
(602) 264–5220

Fleming's Prime Steak-
    house and Wine Bar
6333 North Scottsdale
    Road
Scottsdale, AZ
(480) 596–8265

Garcia's Mexican
    Restaurant
2212 North Thirty-fifth
    Avenue
Phoenix, AZ
(602) 272–5584

Harris' Restaurant
3101 East Camelback
    Road
Phoenix, AZ
(602) 508–8888

Hooters
Arizona Center
455 North Third Street
Phoenix, AZ
(602) 495–1234

Hooters
2834 West Bell Road
Phoenix, AZ
(602) 375–0000

La Tolteca Mexican Foods
1205 East Van Buren
    Street
Phoenix, AZ
(602) 253–1511

Leccabaffi
9719 North Hayden Road
Scottsdale, AZ
(480) 609–0429

Los Compadres Mexican
 Food
4414 North Seventh
 Avenue
Phoenix, AZ
(602) 265–1162

Mary Elaine's
6000 East Camelback
 Road
Scottsdale, AZ
(480) 423–2530

Mastro's
8852 East Pinnacle Peak
 Road
Scottsdale, AZ
(480) 585–9500

Morton's of Chicago
2501 East Camelback
 Road
Scottsdale, AZ
(602) 955–9577

Mrs. White's Golden Rule
 Cafe
808 East Jefferson Street
Phoenix, AZ
(602) 262–9256

On the Border
1507 North Litchfield Road
Goodyear, AZ
(623) 536–2300

Pinnacle Peak Patio
10426 East Jomax Road
Scottsdale, AZ
(480) 585–1599

Pico Pica Tacos
3945 East Camelback
 Road
Phoenix, AZ
(602) 912–0048

Popo's Fiesta Del Sol
6542 West Indian School
 Road
Phoenix, AZ
(623) 846–2636

Rancho Pinot Grill
6208 North Scottsdale
 Road
Scottsdale, AZ
(480) 367–8030

Raul and Therese's
 Restaurant
519 West Main Street
Avondale, AZ
(623) 932–1120

Richardson's
1582 East Bethany Home
 Road
Phoenix, AZ
(602) 265–5886

Roaring Fork
7242 East Camelback
 Road
Scottsdale, AZ
(480) 947–0795

Roman's County Line
10540 West Indian
 School Road
Phoenix, AZ
(623) 877–8191

Rustler's Rooste
7777 South Pointe
 Parkway West
Phoenix, AZ
(602) 431–6474

Ruth's Chris Steak House
2201 East Camelback
 Road
Phoenix, AZ
(602) 957–9600

Salt Cellar Restaurant
550 North Hayden Road
Scottsdale, AZ
(480) 947–1963

Sam's Cafe
455 North Third Street
Suite 114
Phoenix, AZ
(602) 252–3545

Shogun Restaurant
12615 North Tatum
 Boulevard
Phoenix, AZ
(602) 996–4483

T-Bone Steak House
10037 South Nineteenth
 Avenue
Phoenix, AZ
(602) 276–0945

T Cook's at the Royal
 Palms
5200 East Camelback
 Road
Phoenix, AZ
(602) 808–0766

Tarbell's
3213 East Camelback
    Road
Phoenix, AZ
(602) 955–8100

Texaz Grill
6003 North Sixteenth
    Street
Phoenix, AZ
(602) 248–7827

Z Tejas Grill
10625 North Tatum
    Boulevard
Phoenix, AZ
(480) 948–9010

Phoenix Area Lodging

AmeriSuites
10838 North Twenty-fifth
    Avenue
Phoenix, AZ
(602) 997–8800

Budget Suites of America
2722 North Seventh
    Street
Phoenix, AZ
(866) 877–2000

Comfort Suites
10210 North Twenty-sixth
    Drive
Phoenix, AZ
(602) 861–3900

AmeriSuites Phoenix Airport
1413 Rio Salado Parkway
Tempe, AZ
(480) 804–9544

Camelback Inn Resort
5402 East Lincoln Drive
Scottsdale, AZ
(480) 948–1700

Country Inn Suites
20221 North Twenty-ninth
    Avenue
Phoenix, AZ
(623) 879–9000

Arizona Biltmore Resort
    and Spa
2400 East Missouri
    Avenue
Phoenix, AZ
(602) 955–6600

Candlewood Suites
11411 North Black
Canyon Highway
Phoenix, AZ
(602) 861–4900

Crossroads Comfort Inn
1770 North Dysart Road
Goodyear, AZ
(623) 932–9191

Best Western
1100 North Central
    Avenue
Phoenix, AZ
(602) 252–2100

Comfort Inn
5050 North Black Canyon
    Highway
Phoenix, AZ
(602) 242–8011

Crowne Plaza
2532 West Peoria Avenue
Phoenix, AZ
(602) 943–2341

Best Western
1615 East Northern
    Avenue
Phoenix, AZ
(602) 997–6285

Comfort Inn
1344 North Twenty-
    seventh Avenue
Phoenix, AZ
(602) 415–1623

Days Inn
3333 East Van Buren
Phoenix, AZ
(602) 244–8244

The Boulders Resort
34631 T. Tom Darlington
    Drive
Carefree, AZ
(480) 488–9009

Comfort Suites
42415 Forty-first Drive
Phoenix, AZ
(623) 465–7979

Days Inn
1550 North Fifty-second
    Drive
Phoenix, AZ
(602) 484–9257

Doubletree
320 North Forty-fourth
    Street
Phoenix, AZ
(602) 225–0500

Embassy Suites
2630 East Camelback
    Road
Phoenix, AZ
(602) 955–3992

Embassy Suites
2577 West Greenway
    Road
Phoenix, AZ
(602) 375–1777

Embassy Suites
2333 East Thomas Road
Phoenix, AZ
(602) 957–1910

Embassy Suites Airport
1515 North Forty-fourth
    Street
Phoenix, AZ
(602) 244–8800

Fairfield Inn
4702 East University Drive
Phoenix, AZ
(480) 829–0700

Gold Spur Ranch
3808 South Vermeersch
    Road
Avondale, AZ
(623) 932–9307

Hampton Inn
4234 South Forty-eighth
    Street
Phoenix, AZ
(602) 438–8688

Hampton Inn
5152 West Latham
Phoenix, AZ
(602) 484–7000

Hampton Inn
8101 North Black Canyon
    Highway
Phoenix, AZ
(602) 864–6233

Hampton Inn
160 West Catalina Drive
Phoenix, AZ
(602) 200–0990

Hampton Inn
2000 North Litchfield
    Road
Goodyear, AZ
(623) 536–1313

Hawthorn Suites
2990 West Thunderbird
    Road
Phoenix, AZ
(602) 564–8000

Hilton Airport
2435 South Forty-seventh
    Street
Phoenix, AZ
(480) 894–1600

Hilton Suites Downtown
10 East Thomas Road
Phoenix, AZ
(602) 222–1111

Holiday Inn
4321 North Central
    Avenue
Phoenix, AZ
(602) 200–8888

Holiday Inn Express
1313 North Litchfield
    Road
Goodyear, AZ
(623) 535–1313

Holiday Inn Express
15221 South Fiftieth
    Street
Phoenix, AZ
(480) 785–8500

Holiday Inn Express
620 North Sixth Street
Phoenix, AZ
(602) 452–2020

Holiday Inn Express
3401 East University Drive
Phoenix, AZ
(602) 453–9900

Holiday Inn Select
4300 East Washington
Phoenix, AZ
(602) 273–7778

Holiday Inn West
Fifty-First Avenue at
    Interstate 10
Phoenix, AZ
(602) 484–9009

Homewood Suites
2536 West Beryl Avenue
Phoenix, AZ
(602) 674–8900

Howard Johnson
124 South Twenty-fourth
    Street
Phoenix, AZ
(602) 220–0044

Hyatt Regency
122 North Second Street
Phoenix, AZ
(602) 252–1234

La Quinta
2725 North Black Canyon
    Highway
Phoenix, AZ
(602) 258–6271

Marriott Desert Ridge Spa
5350 East Marriott Drive
Phoenix, AZ
(480) 905–0004

Oakwood Paradise Lakes
16220 North Seventh
    Street
Phoenix, AZ
(602) 687–3322

The Phoenician Resort
6000 East Camelback
    Road
Phoenix, AZ
(800) 888–8234

Pointe Hilton Resorts
11111 North Seventh
    Street
Phoenix, AZ
(602) 866–7500

Pointe Hilton Squaw Peak
7677 North Sixteenth
    Street
Phoenix, AZ
(602) 997–2626

Quality Hotel and Resort
3600 North Second
    Avenue
Phoenix, AZ
(602) 248–0222

Radisson Hotel Airport
3333 East University
Phoenix, AZ
(602) 437–8400

Radisson Hotel Midtown
401 West Clarendon
Phoenix, AZ
(602) 234–2464

Ramada Inn
401 First Street
Phoenix, AZ
(602) 258–3411

Ramada Limited Airport
4120 East Van Buren
Phoenix, AZ
(602) 275–5746

Red Roof Inn
17222 North Black
    Canyon Freeway
Phoenix, AZ
(602) 866–1049

Red Roof Inn
5215 West Willetta
Phoenix, AZ
(602) 233–8004

Red Roof Camelback
502 West Camelback
Phoenix, AZ
(602) 264–9290

Sheraton Wild Horse Pass
5594 West Wild Horse
    Pass Boulevard
Phoenix, AZ
(602) 225–0100

Sleep Inn
18235 North Twenty-
    seventh Avenue
Phoenix, AZ
(602) 504–1200

Sleep Inn
2621 South Forty-seventh
    Place
Phoenix, AZ
(480) 967–7100

Super 8 Motel
1710 North Dysart Road
Goodyear, AZ
(623) 932–9622

Travelers Inn
5102 West Latham Street
Phoenix, AZ
(602) 233–1988

Travelodge
1624 North Black Canyon
  Highway
Phoenix, AZ
(602) 269–6281

Travelodge
1424 North Fiftieth
  Avenue
Phoenix, AZ
(602) 455–3700

Wellesley Inn
5035 East Chandler
  Boulevard
Phoenix, AZ
(480) 753–6700

The Wigwam Resort
West Indian School Road
Litchfield Park, AZ
(623) 935–3811

Wyndham Garden Airport
427 North Forty-fourth
  Street
Phoenix, AZ
(602) 220–4400

Wyndham Garden
2641 West Union Hills
  Drive
Phoenix, AZ
(602) 978–2222

Phoenix Area Camping

Apache Palms RV Park
1836 East Apache
  Boulevard
Tempe, AZ
(480) 966–7399

Cotton Lane RV Resort
17506 West Van Buren
  Street
Goodyear, AZ
(623) 853–4000

Covered Wagon RV Park
6540 North Black Canyon
  Highway
Phoenix, AZ
(602) 242–2500

Desert Aire RV Park
12959 West Grand
  Avenue
Surprise, AZ
(623) 972–4518

Desert Edge RV Park
22623 North Black
  Canyon Highway
Phoenix, AZ
(623) 587–0940

Desert Shadows Travel
  Trailer
19203 North Twenty-ninth
  Avenue
Phoenix, AZ
(623) 869–8178

Destiny Phoenix West
416 North Citrus Road
Goodyear, AZ
(623) 853–0537

Green Acres RV Parks
2052 West Main Street
Mesa, AZ
(480) 964–5058

Leaf Verde RV Resort
1500 South Apache Road
Buckeye, AZ
(623) 386–3132

Leon's Park West
12939 West Elm Street
Surprise, AZ
(623) 583–9504

Micasa MHP1
16050 North Church Street
Surprise, AZ
(623) 583–3266

Michigan RV and Mobile
  Home Park
3140 West Osborn Road
Phoenix, AZ
(602) 269–0122

Mountain Shadows
2801 West Foothill Drive
Phoenix, AZ
(623) 516–2800

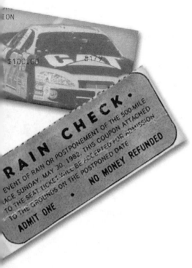

Mountain View Trailer Park
10461 North Eighty-
seventh Avenue
Peoria, AZ
(623) 979–3120

North Phoenix Campground
2550 West Louise Drive
Phoenix, AZ
(623) 581–3969

Paradise RV Resort
10950 West Union Hills
Drive
Sun City, AZ
(623) 977–0344

Parkside Travel Trailer Park
850 East Monroe Avenue
Buckeye, AZ
(623) 386–4819

Phoenix RV
22036 North Black
Canyon Highway
Phoenix, AZ
(623) 582–1479

Pioneer Travel Trailer Park
36408 North Black
Canyon Highway
Phoenix, AZ
(623) 465–7465

Pleasant Harbor RV Resort
8708 West Harbor Boule-
vard
Peoria, AZ
(602) 269–0077

Roles Inn of America
1068 North Cotton Lane
Goodyear, AZ
(623) 853–0140

Roles Inn Pioneer RV Park
36408 North Black
Canyon Highway
Phoenix, AZ
(623) 465–8000

Rose Terrace Trailer Park
4630 Northwest Grand
Avenue
Glendale, AZ
(623) 931–2155

Saddle Mountain RV Park
3607 North 411th Avenue
Tonopah, AZ
(623) 386–3892

Sunflower RV Resort
61501 North El Mirage
Road
Surprise, AZ
(623) 583–0100

Tempe Travel Trailer Villa
1831 East Apache Boule-
vard
Tempe, AZ
(480) 968–1411

Turf Paradise Travel Trailer
1656 West Tierra Buena
Lane
Phoenix, AZ
(602) 942–4500

Welcome Home RV Park
2501 West Missouri
Avenue
Phoenix, AZ
(602) 249–9854

Texas Motor Speedway:
The Bigger, The Better

They do things in a big away in Texas, and the Texas Motor Speedway is a shining example. Here are a couple of the startling statistics about the largest sporting complex west of the Mississippi River: There are 1,633 rest room stalls just for women at the track and enough seats to fill Texas Stadium, home of the Dallas Cowboys, nearly two-and-a-half times.

This place is located between Dallas and Fort Worth, and it's had its share of problems. But to its credit, the speedway has reacted quickly to criticism with solutions, not excuses. When drivers said the transition from the fourth turn to the front straightaway was too severe, they dug it up and rebuilt it. A year later, when water seeped under the pavement in the second turn, they installed a new drainage system. And while the track's only been open for business since 1997, the asphalt's already been replaced.

Every seat here has been sold out for every Nextel Cup Series race—all more than six months in advance. The sport is wildly popular in Texas—so much so that two local fans filed a lawsuit in 2002 to force NASCAR to bring a second racing date to the Texas Motor Speedway.

Jeff Burton won the inaugural race in 1997, but no winning driver has been able to repeat in the speedway's first seven years.

Let's Go Racing

While it closely resembles the other tracks in the Speedway Motorsports Inc. portfolio in size and shape, Texas is distinctly different. The design and banking are identical to its sister track, the Lowe's Motor Speedway near Charlotte, North Carolina, but the new transition sections along the front straightaway makes Texas nearly 8 mph faster.

It takes about twenty-eight seconds to make a qualifying lap around this place, and most drivers say that's about as long as they can hold their breath. The best way to get around here is to keep the gas pedal on the floorboard all the way around the track. It's tempting to touch the brakes, but any hesitation, even for a fraction of a second, scrubs away speed. This track takes more than a driver's skill and a mechanic's aptitude to succeed. It takes guts.

How to Get There

Unfortunately the grand scale that comes with everything Texas includes traffic. This racetrack is famous for monstrous backups, especially from Dallas.

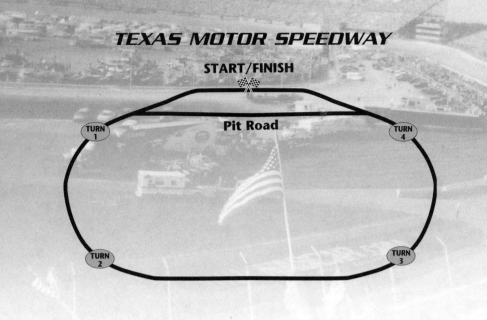

TEXAS MOTOR SPEEDWAY

START/FINISH

TURN 1

TURN 4

Pit Road

TURN 2

TURN 3

Our Ratings	Racing: 🏁 🏁 🏁
	Amenities: 🏁 🏁 🏁 🏁 🏁
	Area Appeal: 🏁 🏁 🏁 🏁
Track Facts	1.5-mile, quad-oval
	Seating capacity: 154,861 seats
	3601 Texas Highway 114
	Justin, TX 76247
	www.texasmotorspeedway.com
Annual Events	One NASCAR Nextel Cup Series race, April
	Companion race: Busch Series, April
Weather	Average High (F): April 76.0
	Average Low (F): April 52.0
Top Gun	Jeff Burton, Mark Martin, Dale Earnhardt Jr., Kurt Busch, Terry Labonte, Matt Kenseth, Dale Jarrett, 1 win
Qualifying Record	Bill Elliott, 194.224 mph

Officially, the direction from Dallas is to take TX 114 to the speedway. Unofficially, you can drive south through the Dallas–Fort Worth International Airport on Texas Highway 97 to Texas Highway 183 west. It blends into Texas Highway 121, and that eventually hooks up with Interstate 820 north. At Interstate 35W, go north to the speedway exit.

From Fort Worth: Take I–35W north to the speedway exit.

Best Seats in the House

If you didn't buy your tickets more than six months in advance, the only seat you'll have is on a milk crate in the infield. Most of the seats in the massive grandstands are part of a season ticket package that includes a Busch Series race, a couple NASCAR Craftsman Truck Series races, and two IRL IndyCar Series events.

The view from the top—from one of the 194 skyboxes—can't be beat. Each skybox comes with a private rest room, lunch, and a cushy seat in air-conditioned comfort.

Doing Deluxe

The towering building in the second turn is the main office for the speedway as well as a luxury condominium and speedway club. For about $900 you can buy a seat in the Victory Lane Club. To sweeten the deal, for every four seats you buy to the club, you get one parking pass for free. Fans there dine in a private restaurant and have access to the other plush amenities usually reserved for a members-only clientele.

Terry Labonte
on Texas Motor Speedway

Terry Labonte grew up in Texas. Although he's lived in North Carolina for the past twenty-five years, he remains keenly fond of his home state. That's why his victory here in 1999 remains one of the greatest moments in a career that includes a pair of NASCAR championships.

Labonte, who still drives with a decal of Texas on the hood of his Chevrolet, set the track record for a 500-mile stock car race with an average speed of 144.276 mph. "To me, this is the biggest race I've ever won," Labonte says. "To come here and win in my home state, this was a great day for us."

The honorary starter for that race was George W. Bush, who was only a governor then. Bush met Labonte before the race and reminded him that the last time a Bush went to a stock car race, Labonte also won. The other Bush was his father, George H. Bush, who was running for vice president when he visited the Darlington Raceway in 1980.

"I know when I come down to Texas that [brother] Bobby and I have a lot of fans," Labonte says. "We sat down before the year, and this one was at the top of my list as far as races if you had a choice to win. We put a lot of effort into coming here and running well."

Texas Memories

Texans loved to see one of their own win with **Terry Labonte,** but the biggest moment came when a third-generation rookie named Earnhardt won his first Nextel Cup Series race here. **Dale Earnhardt Jr.** won in just his twelfth career start, finishing six football fields ahead of **Jeff Burton** in 2000 to trigger a celebration that included a hug from his famous father and car owner, seven-time NASCAR champion **Dale Earnhardt.**

"Guys race and race and race for years and years and years and don't win races," Earnhardt Jr. said after his win. "This here is awesome, man, just incredible."

His father, who died ten months later in a final lap crash at the Daytona 500, was overwhelmed by his son's sudden and profound success.

"I tell you, he's something else," Earnhardt Sr. said. "We knew the kid could do it. The boy drove a good race."

Earnhardt Sr. also gave his son some important advice before he climbed out of his Chevrolet to start the party in Victory Lane. "He just told me he loved me, and he wanted to make sure I took the time to enjoy this. You can get so swept up with what's going on around you that you don't really enjoy yourself personally. He wanted me to celebrate how *I* wanted to celebrate."

Make It a Vacation

Bring your clubs and turn a racing weekend into a weeklong golf getaway. Stay near the airport and you won't be more than an hour from any of the following courses: **Colonial Country Club** (3735 Country Club Circle, Fort Worth; 817–927–4200); **TPC Four Seasons Resort Las Colinas** and **Cottonwood Valley Golf Club** (4150 North MacArthur Boulevard, Las Colinas; 972–717–0700 or 972–717–6138); **Texas Star Golf Course** (1400 Texas Star Parkway, Euless; 817–685–7888); **Tierra Verde Golf Club** (7005 Golf Club Drive, Arlington; 817–478–8500); **Tangle Ridge Golf Club** (818 Tangle Ridge Drive, Grand Prairie; 972–299–6837); **Tenison Highlands and Glen** (3501 Samuel Boulevard, Dallas; 214–670–1402); and **Pecan Valley River Course** (6400 Pecan Drive, Fort Worth; 817–249–1845).

Away from the Track

The **Fort Worth Stockyards** (121 East Exchange Avenue, Fort Worth; 817–626–7921) is not only a National Historical District but it's also a hub of restaurants, nightclubs, shopping, and exhibits that shouldn't be missed. The **Texas Cowboy Hall of Fame** is there, along with the **Stockyards Station.**

Animal lovers will appreciate the **Fort Worth Zoo** (1989 Colonial Parkway, Fort Worth; 817–759–7555).

You can catch a **Dallas Mavericks** basketball game at the American Airlines Center (777 Sports Street, Dallas; 214–747–6287); or you can ride the roller coaster at **Six Flags Over Texas** (2201 Road to Six Flags, Arlington; 817–640–8900).

Conspiracy freaks will be amazed by the exhibits dedicated to the

assassination of President John F. Kennedy at the **Sixth Floor Museum** (411 Elm Street, Suite 120, Dallas; 214–747–6660) and the **Conspiracy Museum** (110 South Market Street, Dallas; 214–741–3040).

Where to Eat

The steaks at the **Cattlemen's Steakhouse** (2458 North Main, Fort Worth; 817–624–3945) are as popular with the drivers as they are with racing fans. Just down the block you can do the boot-scoot boogie at **Billy Bob's Texas** (2520 Rodeo Plaza, Fort Worth; 817–624–7117). For Texas-style barbecue—which here means beef, not pork—try **Riscky's Barbecue** (300 Main Street, Fort Worth; 817–877–3306), and for the best-tasting Mexican food, head to **Abuelo's Mexican Food Embassy** (1041 Interstate 20 West, Arlington; 817–468–2622).

Other places worth consideration are **Bodacious Bar-B-Q** (1206 East Division Street, Arlington; 817–860–4248); **Beto's Mexican Restaurant** (1225 West Airport Freeway, Irving; 972–607–2556); **Nick and Sam's Steak and Fish** (3008 Maple Avenue, Dallas; 214–871–7444); **Arlington Steak House** (1724 West Division Street, Arlington; 817–275–7881); **Colter's Bar-B-Q** (8600 Airport Freeway, Hurst; 817–595–4230); and **Arnold Firewood Company** (201 North Beltline Road, Irving; 972–986–6339).

Where to Stay

The best way to avoid the traffic jam from Dallas is to stay in Fort Worth. For that reason, we recommend starting with hotels like **Best Western Inn and Suites** (817–847–8484), **Candlewood** (817–838–8355), **Comfort Inn** (877–424–6423), **Marriott Hotels** (800–228–9290), **Crosslands Economy Suites** (817–838–3500), **Hampton Inn** (800–439–0400), **Harvey Hotel** (972–929–4500), **Hilton Hotels** (800–774–1500), **Holiday Inn** (800–465–4329), **Homewood Suites** (817–834–3700), **La Quinta Inn** (817–222–2888), **Super 8 Hotel** (817–222–0892), **The Westin Hotel** (817–961–0800), and **Renaissance Worthington** (817–870–1000).

If you'd rather stay closer to the airport, just remember to avoid TX 114, cut through the airport, and take the northern route into the track.

Texas Motor Speedway Area Restaurants

Abuelo's Mexican Food
Embassy
1041 I–20 west
Arlington, TX
(817) 468–2622

Adams Barbeque
1506 Miller Avenue
Fort Worth, TX
(817) 536–2781

Angelo's Barbecue
2533 White Settlement
Road
Fort Worth, TX
(817) 332–0357

Arlington Steak House
1724 West Division Street
Arlington, TX
(817) 275–7881

Arnold Firewood Company
201 North Beltline Road
Irving, TX
(972) 986–6339

Bennigan's
3840 Northeast Loop 820
Fort Worth, TX
(817) 838–2356

Beto's Mexican Restaurant
1225 West Airport Freeway
Irving, TX
(972) 607–2556

Big Daddy's Pizza
TX 114 at Roanoke Center
Roanoke, TX
(817) 491–1245

Big Tom's Bar-B-Q
6500 Denton Highway
Watauga, TX
(817) 656–4433

Billy Bob's Texas
2520 Rodeo Plaza
Fort Worth, TX
(817) 624–7117

Bob's Steak and Chop
House
4300 Lemmon Avenue
Dallas, TX
(214) 528–9446

Bodacious Bar-B-Q
1206 East Division Street
Arlington, TX
(817) 860–4248

Cactus Flower
2401 Westport Parkway at
I–35W
Alliance Airport, TX
(817) 491–9524

Cattlemen's Steakhouse
2458 North Main Street
Fort Worth, TX
(817) 624–3945

Chili's Bar and Grill
6350 North Freeway
Fort Worth, TX
(817) 232–5515

Chili's Bar and Grill
800 West TX 114
Grapevine, TX
(817) 329–1030

Classic Cafe
504 North Oak
Roanoke, TX
(817) 430–8185

Colter's Bar-B-Q
3904 West Camp Wisdom
Road
Dallas, TX
(972) 298–3335

Como Bar-B-Q
5837 Humbert Avenue
Fort Worth, TX
(817) 737–9031

Cotton Patch Cafe
4020 William D. Tate
Grapevine, TX
(817) 545–5511

Cousins Bar-B-Q
5125 Bryant Irvin Road
Fort Worth, TX
(817) 346–3999

Del Frisco's
812 Main Street
Fort Worth, TX
(817) 877–3999

Denny's
1505 William D. Tate
Avenue
Grapevine, TX
(817) 251–1993

Dickey's Barbecue Pit
1989 Colonial Parkway
Fort Worth, TX
(817) 759–7420

Don Pablo's Restaurant
1709 Cross Road Drive
Grapevine, TX
(817) 421–2981

Dove Creek Cafe
204 South Texas High-
way 377
Roanoke, TX
(817) 491–4973

El Fenix Mexican
Restaurant
401 TX 114
Grapevine, TX
(817) 421–1151

Grady's American Grill
650 West TX 114
Grapevine, TX
(817) 329–1198

Hearth House
3200 South Cooper Street
Suite 108
Arlington, TX
(817) 467–4848

Hickory Stick Bar-B-Q
900 East Enon Avenue
Fort Worth, TX
(817) 478–9997

Hong Kong Deli
1816 East Pioneer
Parkway
Arlington, TX
(817) 277–0089

J. Christen's
6480 North Freeway
Fort Worth, TX
(817) 847–9802

Joe's Crab Shack
201 West TX 114
Grapevine, TX
(817) 251–1515

La Madeleine French
Bakery and Cafe
900 West TX 114
Grapevine, TX
(817) 251–0255

Los Vaqueros
2609 North Main Street
Fort Worth, TX
(817) 624–1511

Meats and Treats
5700 Bonnell Avenue
Fort Worth, TX
(817) 737–8150

Nick and Sam's Steak
and Fish
3008 Maple Avenue
Dallas, TX
(214) 871–7444

Panda Bar-B-Que
4104 West Airport
Freeway
Irving, TX
(972) 790–9999

The Rib Factory
4708 East Rosedale Street
Fort Worth, TX
(817) 535–8557

Riscky's Barbeque
8100 Grapevine Highway
North Richland Hills, TX
(817) 581–7696

Riscky's Barbeque
300 Main Street
Fort Worth, TX
(817) 877–3306

Robinson Bar-B-Q
1028 East Berry Street
Fort Worth, TX
(817) 924–1009

Romano's Macaroni Grill
6300 North Freeway
Fort Worth, TX
(817) 306–9722

Saltgrass Steakhouse
5845 Sandshell Drive
Fort Worth, TX
(817) 306–7900

Sammy's Bar-B-Q
3801 East Belknap Street
Fort Worth, TX
(817) 831–6081

The Smoke Pit BBQ
2401 East Belknap Street
Fort Worth, TX
(817) 222–0455

Smokey's Ribs
5300 East Lancaster
Avenue
Fort Worth, TX
(817) 451–5639

Sonny Bryan's Smokehouse
2421 Westport Parkway
Alliance Airport, TX
(817) 224–9191

Sonny Bryan's Smokehouse
2202 Inwood Road
Dallas, TX
(214) 357–7120

Spring Creek Barbeque
3608 South Cooper Street
Arlington, TX
(817) 465–0553

Stooges Barbecue
407 West Abram Street
Arlington, TX
(817) 265–2205

Swinford's Pit Bar-B-Que
   and Grill
1101 Terminal Road
Fort Worth, TX
(817) 624–8781

Taisia's BarBQ
3701 Esters Road
Suite 106
Irving, TX
(972) 252–2566

Taqueria Tres Coronas
2657 East Vickery
   Boulevard
Fort Worth, TX
(817) 535–3662

Tony Roma's
415 West TX 114
Grapevine, TX
(817) 424–3477

Trail Dust Steak House
21717 Lyndon B. Johnson
   Freeway
Mesquite, TX
(972) 289–5457

Williams Steak House
5532 Jacksboro Highway
Fort Worth, TX
(817) 624–1272

Texas Motor Speedway Area Lodging

AmeriSuites City View
5900 Cityview Boulevard
Fort Worth, TX
(817) 361–9797

Best Western
7301 West Freeway
Fort Worth, TX
(817) 244–7444

Best Western
125 Northeast Loop 820
Fort Worth, TX
(817) 590–0628

Best Western Executive
   Inn
2000 Beach Street
Fort Worth, TX
(817) 534–4801

Best Western Inn and
   Suites
6700 Fossil Bluff Drive
Fort Worth, TX
(817) 847–8484

Candlewood
5201 Endicott Avenue
Fort Worth, TX
(817) 838–8355

Clarion Hotel
600 Commerce Street
Fort Worth, TX
(817) 332–6900

Comfort Inn
4850 North Freeway
Fort Worth, TX
(817) 834–8001

Comfort Inn
8345 West Freeway
Fort Worth, TX
(817) 244–9446

Comfort Inn
2050 Beach Street
Fort Worth, TX
(817) 535–2591

Comfort Inn
6504 South Freeway
Fort Worth, TX
(817) 568–9500

Comfort Inn and Suites
801 West TX 114
Roanoke, TX
(817) 490–1455

Comfort Suites Fossil
  Creek
3751 Tanacross Drive
Fort Worth, TX
(817) 222–2333

Country Inn and Suites
2200 Mercado Drive
Fort Worth, TX
(817) 831–9200

Country Inn and Suites
5151 Thaxton Parkway
Fort Worth, TX
(817) 268–6879

Courtyard
3150 Riverfront Drive
Fort Worth, TX
(817) 335–1300

Courtyard
2280 Valley View Lane
Irving, TX
(972) 790–8990

Courtyard Fossil Creek
3751 Northeast Loop 820
Fort Worth, TX
(817) 847–0044

Crosslands Economy Suites
3804 Tanacross Drive
Fort Worth, TX
(817) 838–3500

Days Inn
42131 West S Freeway
Fort Worth, TX
(817) 923–1987

Days Inn
8500 Interstate 30 and
  Las Vegas Trail
Fort Worth, TX
(817) 246–4961

Fairfield Inn
1505 University Drive
Fort Worth, TX
(817) 335–2000

Fairfield Inn
3701 Northeast Loop 820
Fort Worth, TX
(817) 232–5700

Hampton Inn
13600 North Freeway
Fort Worth, TX
(817) 439–0400

Hampton Inn
South Cherry Lane
Fort Worth, TX
(817) 560–4180

Hampton Inn
4681 Gemini Place
Fort Worth, TX
(817) 625–5327

Harvey Hotel
4545 West John Carpen-
  ter Freeway
Irving, TX
(972) 929–4500

Harvey Hotel
4550 West John Carpen-
  ter Freeway
Irving, TX
(972) 929–4499

Hawthorn Suites
13400 North Freeway
Fort Worth, TX
(817) 750–7000

Hilton Conference Center
1800 Texas Highway 26E
Grapevine, TX
(817) 481–8444

Hilton Garden Inn
4400 North Freeway
Fort Worth, TX
(817) 222–0222

Holiday Inn
100 Alta Mesa Boulevard
Fort Worth, TX
(817) 293–3088

Holiday Inn Express
4609 City Lake Boulevard
Fort Worth, TX
(817) 292–4900

Holiday Inn North
  Conference
2540 Meacham Boulevard
Fort Worth, TX
(817) 625–9911

Holiday Inn Select
4441 West John Carpenter
  Freeway
Irving, TX
(972) 929–8181

Homewood Suites
3701 Tanacross Drive
Fort Worth, TX
(817) 834–3700

Hyatt Regency Hotel
20 International Parkway
Fort Worth, TX
(972) 453–1234

La Quinta Inn
4700 North Freeway
Fort Worth, TX
(817) 222–2888

La Quinta Inn
4900 Bryant Irvin Road
Fort Worth, TX
(817) 370–2700

La Quinta Inn
7888 I–30W
Fort Worth, TX
(817) 246–5511

La Quinta Inn
7920 Bedford Euless
    Road
Fort Worth, TX
(817) 485–2750

Marriott DFW
8440 Freeport Parkway
Irving, TX
(972) 929–8800

Marriott Solana
5 Village Circle
Westlake, TX
(817) 430–3848

Motel 6
8701 I–30W
Fort Worth, TX
(817) 244–9740

Motel 6
1236 Oaklawn Boulevard
Fort Worth, TX
(817) 834–7361

Radisson Eagle Point
2211 I–35E
Denton, TX
(940) 565–8499

Radisson Hotel
4600 West Airport
    Freeway
Irving, TX
(972) 513–0800

Radisson Plaza
815 Main Street
Fort Worth, TX
(817) 870–2100

Ramada Inn
1401 University Drive
Fort Worth, TX
(817) 336–9311

Ramada Inn
1701 Commerce Street
Fort Worth, TX
(817) 335–7000

Regency Inn
4201 South Freeway
Fort Worth, TX
(817) 923–8281

Renaissance Worthington
    Hotel
200 Main Street
Fort Worth, TX
(817) 870–1000

Residence Inn
5801 Sandshell
Fort Worth, TX
(817) 439–1300

Residence Inn
1701 University Drive
Fort Worth, TX
(817) 870–1011

StudioPLUS Deluxe Suites
3261 Northeast Loop 820
Fort Worth, TX
(817) 232–1622

Super 8 Hotel
5225 North Beach Street
Fort Worth, TX
(817) 222–0892

Sheraton Grand
4440 West John Carpenter
    Freeway
Irving, TX
(972) 929–8400

TownePlace Suites
4200 International Plaza
Fort Worth, TX
(817) 732–2224

The Westin Beechwood
    Hotel
3300 Championship
    Parkway
Fort Worth, TX
(817) 961–0800

Texas Motor Speedway Area Camping

Fort Worth Midtown RV
Park
2906 West Sixth Street
Fort Worth, TX
(817) 335–9330

Fowler's RV Park
12465 Business High-
way 267
North Fort Worth, TX
(817) 439–3898

Heritage RV Park
105 Beaver Creek Drive
Azle, TX
(817) 444–3760

Hilltop Mobile Home Park
7800 Jacksboro Highway
Fort Worth, TX
(817) 237–9973

Mockingbird Hill Mobile
Home and RV Park
1990 South Burleson
Boulevard
Burleson, TX
(817) 295–3011

Pat's Court
2817 Elinor Street
Fort Worth, TX
(817) 222–9201

Pat's Court
3749 Northeast Twenty-
eighth Street
Fort Worth, TX
(817) 834–9459

Rollahome Park
216 South Grants Lane
Fort Worth, TX
(817) 246–4025

Sunset RV Park
5017 White Settlement
Road
Fort Worth, TX
(817) 738–0567

Twin Points Resort and
Beach
10200 Ten Mile Bridge
Fort Worth, TX
(817) 237–3141

White Settlement Travel
Trailer Park
410 North Cherry Lane
Fort Worth, TX
(817) 246–7008